SUCCESSFUL PEOPLE ARE TALKING

about *Speaking to Groups: Eyeball to Eyeball*

"Speaking to Groups: Eyeball to Eyeball is a winner!"

-- Charles Garfield, Ph.D., author *Peak Performers:*
The New Heroes of American Business

"If your business (or your paycheck) depends on how
well you can speak to people, **you owe it to yourself to
immediately buy and read** *Speaking to Groups:
Eyeball to Eyeball.*"

-- George A. Snyder, Vice President
Prudential-Bache Securities Inc.

"For any teacher, consultant, or trainer who helps
people learn to speak more effectively, **this wonderful
book is an incredibly helpful teaching tool for the
classroom or used one-to-one.** It gives solid
approaches that the teacher can adapt to help individual
students relate to their own needs."

-- Jeanne B. Pasquariello, M.A., Director
Potomac Training Associates

"Jim Anderson's system really works! **It taught me
immediately how to face tough, new speaking
situations, on-the-job, and to succeed.** The secrets in
this book should help any speaker do better, especially
when talking to a difficult audience under pressure."

-- John Norman (USMC, ret.), systems auditor
Office of the Comptroller, Department of Navy

"If you read just one self-help book, this is the one. **Buy this book; it will help you succeed with confidence and competence in everything you do in life.** The principles and procedures outlined focus on public speaking, but they can be applied with great benefit to many other important areas of each of our lives."

-- Leopold O. Walder, Ph.D., psychologist
President, BSC, Inc.

"This is a thorough, professional book, obviously based on years of practical knowledge and real-world experience. In addition, *Speaking to Groups* **is great fun. Start reading it and you can't put it down.** It's an excellent reference for anyone who wishes to become an extraordinary speaker in any situation."

-- Brenda Bowman, training consultant
Washington, D.C.

"*Speaking to Groups* is a complete study of the subject, especially good on how to add impact to your words. **This book covers everything you need to consider before you stand up to face a tough audience.**"

-- Dan Poynter, author
The Expert Witness Handbook

Dedicated with love and appreciation to:

My wife, *Catherine Abbott Anderson*

and

My mother, *Florence Wade Anderson*

Without your loving patience, kind help, and generous encouragement, this book would never have existed.

SPEAKING TO GROUPS

Eyeball to Eyeball

James B. Anderson, Ph.D.

WYNDMOOR PRESS
Vienna, Virginia
1989

Publisher: WYNDMOOR PRESS, P.O. Box 2105, Vienna, VA 22183 USA

Disclaimer: This publication is designed to provide accurate and authoritative information in regard to the subject matter covered. It is sold with the understanding that the publisher is not engaged in rendering legal, accounting, or other professional services. If legal advice or other expert assistance is required, the services of a competent professional person should be sought. FROM A DECLARATION OF PRINCIPLES JOINTLY ADOPTED BY A COMMITTEE OF THE AMERICAN BAR ASSOCIATION AND A COMMITTEE OF PUBLISHERS.

FIRST EDITION

Printed by Thomson-Shore, Inc.
Cover Design by Tim Girvin Design, Inc.

Library of Congress Cataloging-in-Publication Data

Anderson, James B., 1942-
    Speaking to groups : eyeball to eyeball / James B. Anderson.
-- 1st ed.
        p.   cm.
    Bibliography: p.
    Includes index.
    ISBN 0-922749-05-1 : $29.95. -- ISBN 0-922749-06-X (pbk.) :
$19.95
    1. Business communication. 2. Oral communication. 3. Public
speaking. I. Title.
HF5718.A7426 1989
001.54'2--dc19   88-38510
                                                                         CIP

Manufactured in the United States of America

Contents

Acknowledgments

Many people helped make this the best book possible, and to all of them my professional debt and personal gratitude are immense.

In particular, I must acknowledge those extraordinary people whom I have gladly served for over 15 years behind-the-scenes as consultant, workshop leader, or coach.

As you faced tough, real-world situations--often speaking well in front of difficult audiences despite fear, discomfort, or risk--you showed a courage and determination that proves we can *all* potentially become peak performers in our everyday lives.

Each of you, in special ways, has challenged, taught, and inspired me. You will recognize yourself--in spirit though not by name--many times throughout the pages of this book.

In addition, I offer thanks to all past organizational clients of the Anderson Management Group, Inc., whose professional assignments provided the opportunity to explore and refine the techniques captured in *Speaking to Groups: Eyeball to Eyeball*.

Special thanks for providing opportunities for professional growth while welcoming innovative ideas must go to Rose Mary Byrne, Chuck Bush, Steve Wills, Jack Brooks, Jo Ann Devaux, Norm Riggins, and Noreen Rice.

My sincere personal thanks are also due to:

Barbara Richardson - whose first, friendly proddings of encouragement nudged the writing of *Speaking to Groups* to begin seven years ago.

Dr. Charles Garfield (The Garfield Group) - whose challenging work in Peak Performance provided the inspiration, tools, and action plan for converting what was once a hopeful dream into what is now a living reality.

Dr. Leo Walder (BSC, Inc.) - for special insights on the treatment of fear and speaking to groups from the standpoint of behavioral science and psychology.

Dr. Vince Vaccaro (U.S. Department of Defense) - for his careful, thoughtful reading of the early manuscript and for his rigorous demand that it sustain logical consistency and precision of expression throughout.

Doris Anne Martin (International Director, Toastmasters International) - for specific suggestions on my coverage of Platform Skills and for gracious encouragement of this project in general.

Dr. Kent J. Wilson (Department of Speech and Hearing Sciences, University of Arizona) - for his comments on my treatment of the topic of Voice to help me keep my terminology and overall approach professionally correct.

Dan Poynter (Para Press) - for his generosity of spirit and enthusiastic encouragement, and for sharing the practical knowledge needed to enable this book to be published.

John Norman (Office of the Comptroller, U.S. Department of Navy) - for practical suggestions on improving the book, and for proving there are no barriers to speaking success for a hard-working person with intelligence, motivation, and integrity.

I am grateful, in addition, for the kind encouragement and useful suggestions of those readers of the book in early manuscript who helped improve it in many ways, especially: Bill Butler (Crestar Bank); Jeanne B. Pasquariello (Potomac Training Associates); George A. Snyder (Prudential-Bache Securities); and Brenda Bowman.

For technical guidance and assistance during production, thanks to Jim Edwards, Joe Anderson, Wade Spray, Carlos Acosta, Doug Rhoades, Chuck Schiller, and Bill Thomas. For excellent editorial assistance, thanks to Pat Lengi, Florence Anderson, Pat Garnier, and Raissa Modrak. Special recognition is deserved for Nina Deuel, whose daily help and friendly competence were often outstanding beyond the call of duty.

Above all, thanks to my wife, Catherine Anderson, whose contributions to this book, both tangible and intangible, can be acknowledged but never fully measured. Her help--in solid editorial judgments and in cheerful availability as a constant sounding board--were invaluable. For her help, I am grateful and for our loving teamwork, I am proud.

Many others also made important contributions to the development of this book. Some gave what may have seemed to them at the time to be only a small favor or suggestion, yet it was often the vital thing needed at a critical moment. To all who helped, I am most appreciative.

Any mistakes or inconsistencies in this book are my full responsibility. Comments by readers and suggestions for future editions are welcomed (see page 367 for follow-up addresses).

James B. Anderson, Ph.D.
Vienna, Virginia 1/10/89

Chapter 1

THE MOMENT OF TRUTH

"The mind is a wonderful thing. It starts
working the minute you're born and never stops
until you get up to speak in public."
-- Jacob M. Braude

MOMENT OF TRUTH

You want action and you need it NOW . . . what's your best way to get results instantly?

Few busy managers, needing a quick decision, would answer: "Go draft a letter or send a memo." No, they'd say to go *talk* directly to the right person face-to-face.

Are you a trial lawyer? . . . you can't sit alone in your office writing long, incisive briefs: you must stand, face a jury, and speak. Or you're a manager? . . . you must motivate people and explain your decisions. You are a football coach? . . . you rally the team at halftime by "talking things up." A business person? . . . you must sell proposals. A scholar? . . . you must defend your papers. A Presidential candidate? . . . you must debate opponents.

For everyone--preachers or teachers, salesmen and Senators--the right tool for success is often the spoken word.

Sooner or later, like it or not, for *you* to win big, you'll have to stand on your feet, too, and speak to a group. To reach others--to lead--you can't keep your mouth shut; you must speak up and speak well.

However . . . if you're like most people, you face such encounters with anxious dread and sweaty palms. It's the human reaction ("Oh-My-God") when someone gets asked to speak to a group: your inner "butterflies" start to flutter.

One surprising survey of 3,000 Americans found, in fact, that of all our possible fears (snakes, heights, bridges, and such), the thing people dread most--worse even than death!-- is . . . speaking before a group.[1]

So, if speaking to groups makes you nervous, you are definitely not alone: you're like most people.

THE FEAR OF SPEAKING

Sadly, too, the fear of speaking can inhibit and defeat you before you start.

Many people, while talking to a group, undergo the same body changes as someone in a life-or-death struggle: their adrenaline pumps, mouth gets dry, heart beats faster, blood pressure jumps, digestion shuts down, sweat flows, and more. It's the classic "fight-or-flight" reaction to high-tension stress.

However, you are *least* likely to do your best when gripped by the choking, internal tension of being under pressure.

To do your best in any human activity--whether you're an Olympic skier in the downhill finals or a mid-level manager briefing the boss--you are *most* likely to operate at Peak Performance (doing your personal best) in an inner state of "relaxed alertness."[2]

If you get uptight beforehand, worrying that you'll mess up completely, you're more likely to do badly--just as suspected. Your strong expectations (negative or positive) are self-fulfilling. Usually, your thinking makes it so: you perform about as well as you *expect* to perform.

----

[1]David Wallechinsky, Irving Wallace, and Amy Wallace, *The Book of Lists* (New York: Bantam Books, 1978), pp. 469-470, citing a survey in the London *Sunday Times* (October 7, 1973). The top-ranked fears were: speaking before a group (41%); heights (32%); insects and bugs, financial problems, deep water (22% each). [Death was tied in fourth place at 19%.]

[2]For more on Peak Performance, see the works of Charles Garfield. A good introduction is his audiocassette program, *Peak Performance* (Chicago: Nightingale-Conant, 1983). Also see the book, *Mentally Tough*, by James L. Loehr and Peter McLaughlin (New York: M. Evans, 1986). Highly recommended is Charles Garfield, *Peak Performance: The New Heroes of American Business* (New York: William Morrow, 1986).

Plus, you'll often be speaking to your group at a crux point where some make-or-break decision is being debated. Clearly, your ability to speak well, with comfort, can be critical.

Isn't it a shame, then, if you deliver your best ideas in a form (like the stand-up briefing) that you fear the most and perform the worst?[3]

TRIAL BY FIRE

On the job, some nervous managers even suspect their bosses of using intimidation to exploit the natural vulnerabilities of speakers. A tough boss can easily unsettle employees with harsh, unexpected questions--supposedly just to keep them "on their toes," but really (it's felt) to knock them off-balance.

In the early 1960's, one notorious trial by fire and embarrassment was regularly orchestrated by Harold S. Geneen, president of International Telephone and Telegraph Corporation (ITT).

Once a month, each division manager within ITT had to face Geneen for a stand-up oral report inside a large enclosed conference room in front of over a hundred people arrayed in swiveling chairs around a table as long as a city block.

For most people, this high-pressure atmosphere alone (calculated or not) could easily cause "butterflies" as they were led in to speak. In addition, however, Geneen possessed a razor-sharp memory and unfailing nose for

---

[3]The realization that attitudes have power to be self-fulfilling is at the core of the "positive thinking" movement, seen in the works of Norman Vincent Peale, Napoleon Hill, W. Clement Stone, Earl Nightingale, Maxwell Maltz, Robert Schuller, Denis Waitley, and many others.

In addition, behavioral scientists (most notably, Robert Rosenthal) have used experimental testing to show the impact of "expectations" in human psychology. See, for example, Rosenthal's article, "The Pygmalion Effect Lives," in *Psychology Today*, September 1973, pp. 56-63.

For insights on how the expectations of leaders affect the performance of their followers, see: J. Sterling Livingston, "Pygmalion in Management," *Harvard Business Review*, July-August 1969; and Warren Bennis and Burt Nanus, *Leaders* (New York: Harper & Row, 1985).

weakness or uncertainty. Every speaker suffered an intense, unyielding cross-examination by everyone else in the room, in search of what Geneen himself called "the unshakable facts" (justified, it was asserted, by his need to have "no surprises").

Not surprisingly, these meetings reportedly provoked more than one senior manager to faint, cry, or get blind drunk for two days afterwards.[4]

EYEBALL TO EYEBALL

Nevertheless, in modern organizations today, to get your ideas across and get things done, you often have to speak--to individuals and groups, in public and private--eyeball to eyeball.

Lee Iacocca, for instance, in his autobiography recalls engineers with "terrific ideas" who were unable to explain them to anyone else. To Iacocca, "It's always a shame when a guy with great talent can't tell the board or a committee what's in his head."[5]

In their landmark study, *In Search of Excellence*, Thomas Peters and Robert Waterman suggest that a vital reason for success in the best-run American companies is an "intensity of communications." The best companies (IBM, Walt Disney, McDonald's, 3M, and others) keep a bias against detached bureaucracy in favor of person-to-person contact. (At Hewlett-Packard, this attitude was captured by the phrase, "MBWA"--"management by walking around.")

Excellent managers are not isolated: they are accessible; they stroll around and *talk* to people in daily situations, openly and often.[6]

---

[4]Terrence E. Deal and Allen A. Kennedy, *Corporate Cultures* (Reading Mass.: Addison-Wesley, 1982, pp. 41-43); and Anthony Sampson, *The Sovereign State of ITT* (New York: Stein and Day, 1973). See also: Robert J. Schoenberg, *Geneen* (New York: W.W. Norton, 1985). For Geneen's view of management, see: Harold Geneen, with Alvin Moscow, *Managing* (Garden City, N.Y.: Doubleday & Co., 1984).
[5]Lee Iacocca, with William Novak, *Iacocca: An Autobiography* (New York: Bantam Books, 1984), p. 54.
[6]Thomas J. Peters and Robert H. Waterman, Jr., *In Search of Excellence* (New York: Harper & Row, 1982); see especially Chapter 5: "A Bias for

Still, too many adults today feel awkward, fearful, and inarticulate when called upon to speak to others. But why?

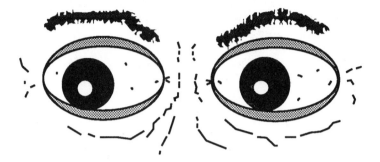

WHY DO WE FEAR SPEAKING TO GROUPS?

The sources of human fear are complex and varied, but the everyday fear of speaking has at least six root causes:

1. YOU FEEL NAKED AND EXPOSED.

In an oral presentation, your natural shyness or fear of failure is magnified because you're the center of attention. By being more in the spotlight, you feel more on-the-spot. All your mistakes are more obvious, under scrutiny, and very public.

2. YOU KNOW MISTAKES ARE LIKELY.

The fear of speaking also springs from a justifiable belief that, sooner or later, something *will* go wrong (Murphy's Law)! Human beings do make mistakes so, in self-defense, you procrastinate or evade speaking opportunities (and thus avoid mistakes) altogether.

Action" (pp. 119-155). The works of Peters and Waterman form an essential body of work that any thinking manager must read. See: Tom Peters and Nancy Austin, *A Passion for Excellence* (New York: Random House, 1985); Robert H. Waterman, Jr., *The Renewal Factor* (Toronto: Bantam Books, 1987); Tom Peters, *Thriving on Chaos* (New York: Alfred A. Knopf, 1987).

3. YOU LACK GOOD EXPERIENCE.

If you intentionally make your fear familiar--through experience--you can demystify it. One proven way to conquer a fear is to bravely do the thing you fear. Unfortunately, most people who fear speaking to groups shun it at all costs and thus stay inexperienced (and intensely fearful).

4. YOU ARE UNTRAINED.

Few people get professional training in speaking. Typically in school, classes in English Composition are mandatory; classes in Speech are elective. Most tests are written; few are oral. So, most adult speech-makers "learned it by doing it" and thus developed bad habits (including the *habit* of fear).

5. YOU HAVE NO SYSTEMATIC APPROACH.

Even experienced speakers dread making a speech if they lack a systematic approach. If you needlessly reinvent the wheel for each new talk--not knowing how to get started again or what to do next--you'll stay inefficient and more susceptible to nervous stress.

6. YOU FACE THE GHOST OF SPEECHES PAST

Most of us carry the memory of some traumatic catastrophe where, speaking to a group, we "blew it" and performed badly. We felt foolish, got embarrassed, were even ridiculed. It hurt and we never forgot. Whether that past disaster happened in school, on-the-job, or elsewhere, the damage went deep. You probably walked away swearing you'd never, ever stand up and speak to a group again.

No wonder so many of us fear public speaking.

In this world, though, that's unfortunate because it's not only what you *know* or *think* that counts . . . it's how well you get it across.

YOUR PERSONAL QUEST

Good ideas--if presented poorly--can fail to win acceptance while bad ideas sometimes get sold by persuasive communicators who use the right angle.

So, what can *you* do about it now?

First, recognize three basic truths about the process of speaking to groups:

1. Good speakers are made, not born. In other words, speaking to groups is a learnable skill.

2. By focusing on the right things, anyone (including *you*) can learn to speak to groups successfully.

3. The more you do it--with proper guidance and the right tools--the better (and easier) it gets.

Your own "moment of truth" is waiting. Will you still walk away from such encounters, murmuring to yourself, "I was *right*, blast it! I *know* I was right! . . . if only I'd spoken up . . . if only I'd *said* it another way"?

No, instead, you're soon going to face all new speaking situations with self-confidence and positive anticipation. Soon as a speaker you'll be a relaxed winner.

There is a proven, step-by-step, SYSTEMATIC APPROACH you can use to prepare your future talks and this book will give it to you.

And as you accomplish your objectives, fulfilling your personal quest, you'll realize these skills are not only invaluable but also (the best news) learnable and easy to apply. All *you* need is to find the desire and to make the effort.

So let's relax and start the quest . . .

Chapter 2

THE HIT-OR-MISS SPEAKER

"All managers, like it or not, are
in the business of words."

-- Robert Heller

DO YOU RECOGNIZE YOURSELF?

Let's imagine for a moment that your organization faces a sink-or-swim decision (on Project SLAMDUNK), whose success depends on approval by a group of powerful outsiders (for example, a subcommittee of the U.S. Congress).

But don't worry. Mary Allworthy--that dynamic, crackerjack of a speaker--will carry the ball for your team in the next session, until . . . surprise! . . . Mary was just rushed to the hospital for an emergency appendectomy and *you* are now "volunteered" to pinch-hit for her today.

Your boss tried, but failed, to delay or reschedule the session. So you are suddenly expected--within the hour--to make a critical oral presentation to important strangers (who have a bad reputation for acting impatient and being tough).

You're thoroughly familiar with the subject, so you are Mary's natural backup. But, you wonder . . . will what you know get lost because of the way you may present it?

Imagine, in a word, your honest reaction right now? What emotion would you probably be feeling?:

(1) FEAR?: *"No way! I'm no speaker--send somebody else! It's stupid! Forget it! I'm not doing it!"*

(2) ANXIETY?: *"Why me? What if those scoundrels take potshots at me? I'll get so nervous I'll probably mess it up."*

(3) WILLINGNESS?: *"I guess I could try. It might be okay. Under the circumstances, I could probably find the right words."*

(4) ENTHUSIASM?: *"Sure, I'll make the pitch. Tell me more about the audience, and how much time I'll have. It's a tough challenge, but thanks for the opportunity."*

FOUR LEVELS OF COMPETENCE

Your reaction to a specific speaking situation, like this one, depends on how you feel about speaking to groups in general.

In fact, your reaction--from the most negative (Fear), through the in-betweens of Anxiety or Willingness, to the most positive (Enthusiasm)--helps reveal the exact level of *competence* you expect of yourself as a speaker.[7]

Simply stated, emotions follow thoughts: If you think your competence is low, you're more likely to react (when asked to speak) with FEAR. If you think your competence is high, you're more likely to react with ENTHUSIASM.

Imagine, then, four Levels of Assumed Competence for speakers and the emotional reactions that would normally accompany each:

LEVEL:	ASSUMED *COMPETENCE*:	REACTION:
IV	HIGH	Enthusiasm
III	MEDIUM-plus	Willingness
II	MEDIUM-minus	Anxiety
I	LOW	Fear

Especially, catch the practical conclusion this idea must lead to . . . that you can directly raise your self-*confidence* by raising your sense of self-*competence*.

---

[7]In strict psychological terms, FEAR is considered the distressing emotional reaction to something *specific* or *known*; ANXIETY is the reaction to things *indefinite* or *unknown*.

In other words, the better you can do it, the more fun it becomes.[8]

Now ask yourself: What, in your opinion, is *your* current Level of Competence as a speaker: Level I, II, III, or IV? Sincerely and objectively--just how good are you?

As a guide, the following SELF-TEST will help you uncover your own suspected Competence Level for speaking to groups. From this SELF-TEST, you'll gain valuable feedback on where you stand now as a speaker and on what you need to improve.

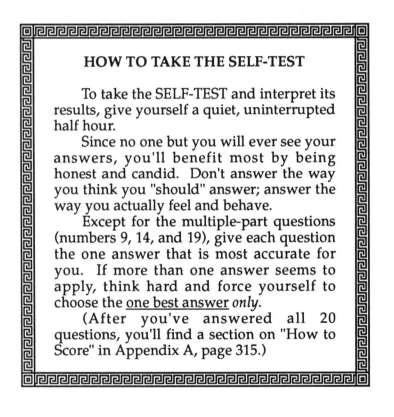

HOW TO TAKE THE SELF-TEST

To take the SELF-TEST and interpret its results, give yourself a quiet, uninterrupted half hour.

Since no one but you will ever see your answers, you'll benefit most by being honest and candid. Don't answer the way you think you "should" answer; answer the way you actually feel and behave.

Except for the multiple-part questions (numbers 9, 14, and 19), give each question the one answer that is most accurate for you. If more than one answer seems to apply, think hard and force yourself to choose the <u>one best answer</u> *only*.

(After you've answered all 20 questions, you'll find a section on "How to Score" in Appendix A, page 315.)

---

[8]On the connection between thoughts and emotion, see: Albert Ellis and Robert A. Harper, *A New Guide to Rational Living* (North Hollywood, Ca.: Wilshire Book Co., 1975). On the relationship of self-confidence to peak performance, see: Robert Kriegel and Marilyn Harris Kriegel, *The C Zone: Peak Performance Under Pressure* (Garden City, N.Y.: Anchor Press, 1984).

SELF-TEST

SPEAKING TO GROUPS:
TWENTY QUESTIONS

---

(1) The night before a major presentation:

    A. I often get so nervous I cannot sleep.
    B. I feel keyed-up, anxious, preoccupied.
    C. I rehearse my presentation to get my game plan clearly in mind.
    D. I forget about the talk and go out and enjoy myself.

(2) My voice is:

    A. Clear, powerful, dynamic.
    B. Better than most.
    C. Ordinary, untrained.
    D. Too high-pitched or too soft.
    E. Weak, monotonous, annoying.

(3) I feel perfectly "at home" speaking to an audience of strangers in an unfamiliar setting:

    A. ALWAYS.
    B. OFTEN.
    C. SOMETIMES.
    D. RARELY.
    E. NEVER.

(4) Once my talk begins:

    A. I often freeze, draw a total blank, and have to sit down early.
    B. I sometimes get brief "mental blocks" and temporarily lose my train of thought.
    C. I follow a carefully planned script and keep my ideas pretty well on track.
    D. I'm able to "think on my feet" well and can usually handle the unexpected with poise.

(5) If a speaker knows his or her subject well, the oral presentation will automatically be a success:

   A. STRONGLY AGREE.
   B. AGREE.
   C. NEUTRAL.
   D. DISAGREE.
   E. STRONGLY DISAGREE.

(6) When I need to plan an upcoming talk:

   A. I can't get started at all.
   B. I put everything off until the last minute.
   C. I procrastinate some, but once I get started I end up with an acceptable talk.
   D. I work hard, but there's never enough time.
   E. I get started easily because I have a step-by-step system for creating the entire talk.

(7) Other people compliment me on my abilities as a public speaker:

   A. ALL THE TIME.
   B. OFTEN.
   C. SOMETIMES.
   D. RARELY.
   E. NEVER.

(8) When speaking off-the-cuff in unexpected situations:

   A. I become totally speechless.
   B. I somehow say enough to get it finished.
   C. I do a good speaking job more often than not.
   D. I am seldom at a loss for words.

(9) When under pressure, I exhibit the following nervous mannerisms [ANSWER EACH]:

	YES	NO
A. The "uh" syndrome	?	?
B. Fidgeting, rocking	?	?
C. Nervous giggling	?	?
D. Stuttering, mispronunciation	?	?
E Verbalisms ("okay?," "y'know")	?	?

(10) While making a talk:

    A. I feel totally nervous before, during, and after.
    B. I feel nervous at the start, but settle down as the talk continues.
    C. I feel okay at first, but get more nervous as my talk goes on.
    D. I feel nervous only until the talk itself begins.
    E. I never feel nervous.

(11) When talking on a complicated technical topic:

    A I explain things in my own terms and hope everyone else can understand, too.
    B I get too wordy and over-explain.
    C. I am too brief and under-explain.
    D. I talk at the level I feel my audience can best understand.
    E. I do a detailed Audience Analysis, and tailor my talk exactly for that specific audience.

(12) When talking to people (especially groups), I find it hard to look them straight in the eyes:

    A. ALWAYS.
    B. OFTEN.
    C. SOMETIMES.
    D. RARELY.
    E. NEVER.

(13) When it comes to my ability to persuade others:

    A. I usually get "NO" for an answer.
    B. I get put on "Hold" a lot.
    C. I win some, I lose some.
    D. I usually move them to "YES."
    E. I can get a "YES" even from a hostile or unreceptive decision maker.

(14) I have used, and feel comfortable with, the following audio-visual aids [ANSWER EACH]:

	YES	NO
A. Chalkboard	?	?
B. Flipchart & Pointer	?	?
C. Handouts/Lapcharts	?	?
D. Overhead (Viewgraph) Projector	?	?
E 35mm Slide Projector	?	?

(15) While speaking, I can "read" my audience and sense their reactions to me and my topic:

    A. ALWAYS.
    B. OFTEN.
    C. SOMETIMES.
    D. RARELY.
    E. NEVER.

(16) When people ask me tough questions, I usually:

    A. Fall apart inside and respond poorly.
    B. Get angry and act defensive.
    C. Keep my head; only rarely do I lose my cool.
    D. Stay calm and answer all their questions as best I can.
    E. Correct their mistakes and show them who's boss.

(17) After my talks, I usually:

    A. Can't remember a word I just said.
    B. Feel only so-so and have no idea whether the talk worked.
    C. Know if the talk was a success or not.
    D. Know exactly how my audience reacted, plus what to do for follow-up.

(18) Given the choice, my bottom-line attitude is that:

    A. Whenever possible, I avoid speaking to groups.
    B. I don't mind speaking to groups; it's a necessary evil.
    C. I sometimes look forward to speaking to groups.
    D. I always seek new opportunities to speak to groups; I love it.

(19) I have gotten objective feedback on my speaking skills from the following [ANSWER EACH]:

	YES	NO
A. Boss or Peers or Family	?	?
B. Tape Recording (Audio only)	?	?
C. Speakers Club (Toastmasters, etc.)	?	?
D. Videotape Recording (VTR/VCR)	?	?
E Professional Trainer/Coach	?	?

(20) Overall, as a speaker, I am:

    A. Inexperienced, boring, and scared spitless.
    B. Semi-articulate but poorly organized.
    C. Better than most, if I take time to prepare.
    D. Experienced, colorful, and enjoyable.

ON-THE-LEVEL SCENARIOS

To find the results of your SELF-TEST, go to Appendix A and total your score. (Then return to this section to interpret the meaning of your score.)

 to Appendix A, "SELF-TEST SCORING," Page 315.

from Appendix A

HOW TO INTERPRET YOUR SCORE:

```
┌──────────────────────────────────┐------------▶ IV
│ Based on your SELF-TEST score, ◀┄┄┄           III
│ what is your personal competence ┤┄┄     ▶ III
│ LEVEL?                           │ ┄┄▶ II
└──────────────────────────────────┘  ↘ I
```

In speaking situations, each Competence Level has its own typical behavior.

In the following sections, find the descriptive Profile for your own Level (I, II, III, or IV). Read the comments and judge for yourself: How valid is this profile, overall? Does it accurately describe *you*? (You may feel you have some, but not all, of its characteristics.)

Find your own Profile now (on pages 28-31) and take time to read and evaluate it carefully.

PROFILE: **LEVEL I**   SCORE: **0 to 29 points**

As a speaker, your Competence score is <u>LEVEL I</u>. Your basic reaction towards speaking seems to be *FEAR*.

Typical behavior at LEVEL I is likely to be:

* to face any oral presentation with discomfort and dread--feeling nervous before, during, and after;
* to feel especially awkward talking off-the-cuff to groups of strangers in unfamiliar settings;
* to find it almost impossible to start organizing any talk in advance;
* to believe that good speaking is a natural ability, which you don't have;
* to get overly self-conscious facing a group and find it hard to look people directly in the eyes;
* to be afraid that tough, unexpected questions will get asked;
* to sometimes get "verbal paralysis" in meetings, with something to say but not finding the words;
* to display one or more habitual mannerisms, which in the past were rudely pointed out to you;
* to judge yourself as a speaker (if asked) as boring and unconvincing;
* to hold an uneasy feeling, once a talk is over, that it went badly.

QUESTION: How much (in your opinion) does this LEVEL I profile accurately capture *yourself* as a speaker?

0% .. 10% .. 20% .. 30% .. 40% .. 50% .. 60% .. 70% .. 80% .. 90% .. 100%

PROFILE: LEVEL II   SCORE: **30 to 55 points**

As a speaker, your Competence score is <u>LEVEL II</u>. Your basic reaction towards speaking seems to be *ANXIETY*.
Typical behavior at LEVEL II is likely to be:

* to feel nervous and distracted before the talk begins;
* to seldom feel truly "at home" when speaking to strangers;
* to tend to procrastinate and not organize your talks beforehand;
* to figure, what-the-heck, if you know your subject you'll pass the test;
* to be able to "read" the audience in some cases and sometimes not;
* to occasionally handle unexpected questions badly--by getting angry, defensive, or unsettled;
* to sometimes get mental blocks and lose your train of thought;
* to believe your voice is ordinary or that you have a slight voice problem;
* to have trouble with complicated, technical topics: either getting too wordy or under-explaining;
* to expect you can improve but will never be totally comfortable as a speaker.

QUESTION: How much (in your opinion) does this LEVEL II profile accurately capture *yourself* as a speaker?

0% .. 10% .. 20% .. 30% .. 40% .. 50% .. 60% .. 70% .. 80% .. 90% .. 100%

PROFILE: **LEVEL III**   SCORE: **56 to 79 points**

As a speaker, your Competence score is <u>LEVEL III</u>. Your basic reaction towards speaking seems to be *WILLINGNESS*. Typical behavior at Level III is likely to be:

* to get nervous (if at all) only before the talk starts unless something major is on-the-line;
* to feel sometimes at home in unfamiliar settings and sometimes not;
* to lack a systematic method of preparation--you'd rather avoid full outlines and just "wing it";
* to know your subject and feel good about yourself as a speaker, more or less;
* to talk directly to the audience with good eye contact, so you "read" them well;
* to stay calm under fire and rarely mishandle a hostile or unexpected question;
* to look forward occasionally to speaking to groups;
* to have a good voice, though you could still polish your speaking skills a bit more;
* to know how to talk on the technical level your audience can best understand;
* to usually get good results, but you'd like to be more consistent and get more ideas accepted.

QUESTION: How much (in your opinion) does this LEVEL III profile accurately capture *yourself* as a speaker?

0% .. 10% .. 20% .. 30% .. 40% .. 50% .. 60% .. 70% .. 80% .. 90% .. 100%

PROFILE: **LEVEL IV**   SCORE: **80 to 100 points**

As a speaker, your Competence score is <u>LEVEL IV</u>. Your basic reaction towards speaking seems to be *ENTHUSIASM*. Typical behavior at LEVEL IV is likely to be:

* to feel comfortable and confident in almost any speaking situation;
* to "think on your feet" well and handle the unexpected with poise;
* to get organized quickly, even under time-pressure, using a systematic method;
* to believe knowledge alone won't guarantee success: you also make a game plan and rehearse it;
* to look at your audience as unique individuals and "read" them very well;
* to handle tough questions without being awkward, angry, or apologetic;
* to study your audience in detail before you give any talk;
* to have a clear, powerful voice and body language that's expressive and dynamic;
* to have few, if any, nervous mannerisms;
* to know after a talk how you performed, how your audience reacted, and what to do next.

QUESTION: How much (in your opinion) does this LEVEL IV profile accurately capture *yourself* as a speaker?

0% .. 10% .. 20% .. 30% .. 40% .. 50% .. 60% .. 70% .. 80% .. 90% .. 100%

FOUR LEVELS OF COMPETENCE

SUCCESS FORMULA: HIT OR MISS?

From your Competence Level profile, you know more about yourself now as a speaker--in particular, how you feel about yourself as one.

And if you find yourself already at Level IV, you deserve congratulations. Perhaps this book can still offer you helpful tips on how to refine and improve your successful speaking skills.

But no matter what your current Competence Level, realize that with strong desire and hard work, it's possible for most people to reach the top--Level IV Enthusiasm-- where you're a dynamic, masterful speaker who truly enjoys the process and expects (and gets) good results.

The foundation for such positive expectations can be expressed in the three keystones of this SUCCESS Formula:

KNOWLEDGE
+
PREPARATION   =   *SUCCESS*
+
ATTITUDE

Chapter 3

THE RIGHT STUFF: THREE KEYSTONES

*"'He who fails to prepare prepares to fail.' A winner
thinks of winning while a loser thinks of losing."*
-- Chuck Norris

THE BORN SPEAKER

Why is one person a brilliant speaker and someone else
not? Often, those who dislike speaking to groups believe they
were simply "born" that way. They've decided some people
just have the gift of the gab and others (like themselves) don't.

Remarkably, though, no one ever attributes this magical
gift of in-bred eloquence to *himself*. It's always some *other*
lucky soul who is the natural, "born" speaker.

In reality, this notion is a destructive myth. The so-called
"born" speaker does not exist.

THE SELF-MADE SPEAKER

One inspiring example of how a bad speaker became
great is the career of Demosthenes, the orator of Athens in the
4th century, B.C.

Demosthenes was the opposite of a born speaker. As a
child, he had a weak and sickly appearance and an annoying,
bizarre way of speaking (for which he was ridiculed
mercilessly by playmates and given obscene nicknames).

Later, as a lawyer, he argued cases poorly in the same
irritating voice using a long-winded, involuted style. So, as
usual, he was brutally mocked and ignored by his peers.

Demosthenes was determined to succeed, however. He retreated into solitude, living alone for months, working to learn to speak better.

As is well-known, he created his own unique program for speech improvement. For clearer enunciation, he spoke with mouthfuls of pebbles. For better projection, he spoke against the roar of the Aegean Sea. To build more stamina and power, he spoke while running up and down hills.

As a result, he spoke better, but not well enough. He still had to practice every word in advance. In the Senate, he couldn't respond offhand to unexpected opposition. (Today, we'd say he was unable to "think on his feet.")

Nevertheless, Demosthenes kept speaking and improving. He taught himself to speak more spontaneously and sound more natural. Slowly, he won prominence as an orator.

In his last years, of all orators in Athens, the one chosen most often by popular acclaim to deliver important public addresses was Demosthenes. He was ultimately recognized in Greek history as a brave and honorable man, and today--24 centuries later--people still honor his memory and name, as symbolic of the world's greatest speakers.[9]

So, for anyone who feels that he or she is not a "born" speaker, the story of Demosthenes should give encouragement plus a fundamental lesson: Success in speaking to groups requires only commonsense skills that anyone (with desire and persistent effort) can master.

KEYSTONES FOR SUCCESS

At this point, though, you might ask a provocative question:

"Why pay much attention to style and delivery? I'm no Greek orator--I'm a citizen of the 20th century. Isn't it more important for me to know what I'm talking about?"

---

[9]For the life of Demosthenes, see: Plutarch's *Lives of the Noble Greeks* (Edmund Fuller, ed., New York: Dell, 1959). Also see: Will Durant, *The Life of Greece*, The Story of Civilization, Volume II (New York: Simon and Schuster, 1939).

In other words, forget delivery; isn't *mastery of the subject* enough in today's modern world?

The answer is "YES," subject knowledge is primary and always will be, but "NO," it is seldom enough. This wrong assumption (that for success as a speaker, *all* you need is to master facts and figures) will push you down a gauntlet of fearful outcomes and unhappy surprises.

In truth, any effective presentation is the result of the careful interplay of three critical keystones.

```
r------------------------------------------------1
!                                                !
!        KEYSTONE #1 - KNOWLEDGE                 !
!                                                !
L_____J
```

The first and foremost keystone is KNOWLEDGE.

Clearly, the heart of any presentation is its content--the *information* transmitted: actions, names, numbers, and details that tell your story.

KNOWLEDGE as a keystone demands *first* that you master the topic well enough to deliver a coherent talk, and *second* that you handle reasonable but unexpected questions from your audience. In capsule, you must "know your stuff."

Any speaker without solid knowledge is quickly seen as shallow--as more "show" than substance. Justifiably, he or she loses credibility, loses the audience, sometimes even loses the job.

If you've ever suffered the slow agony of facing a group yourself (on a topic you were expected to know well, but did *not*) you've already felt this lesson intensely, with deep embarrassment.

DOOR NUMBER FIVE

When the designated speaker for an upcoming talk is *you*, always ask yourself: "Do I know this subject well enough to speak on it, confidently, right now?"

If your honest answer is "No" (or even, "I'm not so sure"), you'll normally face four choices:

(1) to do more homework (even a fast "cram" course, if needed) in the time available;

(2) to check whether or not someone else--more knowledgeable than you--isn't really a better person to make the talk;

(3) to bring to the event one or more backup experts to cover your own gaps; or,

(4) to postpone the talk, giving yourself more research/study time.

At this point, if you're an experienced manager, you might be thinking: *"Yes, but . . . "*

Yes, but . . . in the real world, people are often forced involuntarily to choose *Door Number FIVE*. Choice five is: Make the talk anyway, right then and there on the spot, whether you're up-to-speed or not.

Often, in other words, your presentation can't wait; it's a command performance. Maybe the boss says, "Do it now!" Or maybe someone in your organization needs that information--incomplete or not--at that very instant.

What happens to our vital keystone of KNOWLEDGE then?

THE "NO-BLUFF" RULE

In that case, of course, you go ahead and make the presentation. You give the knowledge you have at the moment and do your absolute best to cover all bases.

And if your worst fears do come true? . . . if the great unanswerable question gets asked (that fearful, hard-to-handle zinger that exposes your lack of total knowledge)?

Your first instincts may urge you to try answering the question anyway, even with authority. Almost always, though, in awkward moments when you don't know the answer (but feel you should), your best bail-out is the "NO-BLUFF" RULE.

The NO-BLUFF RULE commands:

NEVER BLUFF!

Never bluff (i.e., don't "b.s.") an answer. Instead of giving some top-of-the-head, off-the-wall, out-of-the-air answer, just relax and tell the truth. Play it straight and admit (in an unapologetic, positive way) that you don't know the answer . . .

BUT . . . go one more step, too, and show them how you'll immediately *find* the answer. For example:

(a) *"I'm sorry, I don't know the answer to that question. But I'll be glad to find the answer and get back to you by close-of-business today."*

(b) *"I can't answer that for you right now. We expect that data in from the field by the end of the week."*

(c) *"I don't know the answer to that question myself-- but I'll tell you who does."*

THE JOYS OF IMPERFECTION

There's always an unanswerable question; it's part of life. No one has all knowledge on the tip his or her tongue--not even in his/her own area of expertise. No person, no matter how sharp, knows everything. Frequently, the worst thing you can do is blurt out an answer, under pressure, without careful thought.

Consider: Your questioner may be setting you up. He already knows the answer to his own question, so a trap is being laid . . . will you "fudge" an answer and dumbly help your opposition, who then shoots you down by exposing your bluff-answer?

Here's a solid antidote against fear, and a reliable self-defense for you against enemies and failure, in all your future oral presentations: To relax and win . . .

YOU MUST LEARN TO ALLOW YOURSELF TO BE (AND TO APPEAR) IMPERFECT.

Paradoxically, when you admit your shortcomings in a positive, professional manner, most audiences see you as more humanized, not less authoritative. Instead of losing respect, you'll usually gain credibility.

Honesty, then, is the best policy. Ironically, it's not only the best way to live, it's smart tactics![10]

Of course, if honesty forces you to keep admitting you know next-to-nothing about most questions asked, you either: (a) were the wrong person to give the talk in the first place, or else: (b) failed to do the right kind of advance preparation.

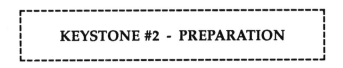

KEYSTONE #2 - PREPARATION

The second keystone is PREPARATION.

Before a presentation, most people worry about knowing *too little* about their subject. They work hard to accumulate the latest information, more facts, and better knowledge.

In some cases, though, the less-obvious reverse is more likely--a person can almost know *too much*. For example, a knowledgeable, experienced speaker can get careless or lazy. The typical comment is: "No sweat! I could talk *all day* on that topic!"

What this speaker fails to consider is: Do others need to sit and listen to YOU *all day*? Also, won't some approaches sell this audience, while others (on the same topic) turn them off?

Without good thinking beforehand, you run a big, unpredictable risk. For example, your audience may overlook your impressive mastery of the subject if you:

* jump right in with overwhelming details without first putting your facts in a meaningful context;

* talk on the wrong level (over the heads of decision makers or too elementary for the experts);

* project the wrong attitude (apathy, fear, nervousness, hostility);

---

[10]The pitfalls of "fudging" an answer were best captured in verse by Sir Walter Scott in his ballad, "Lochinvar," in *Marmion* (VI.17):
> *Oh, what a tangled web we weave,*
> *When first we practice to deceive!"*

* stop talking abruptly at the end without emphasizing the main points;

* try to sell ideas or products to people without understanding *their* concerns, without stressing benefits or consequences to *them*.

GET READY

Correct PREPARATION means thorough, step-by-step homework that goes beyond the content. You consider things like audience, message structure, visual aids, tough questions, persuasive approach, room logistics--everything.

Careful preparation, if done correctly, need not be long, hard drudgery. In-depth preparation saves you grief and wins results because you do things right the first time.

Prior planning is especially important when time is critical. For example, if you expect to face an ultra-busy, impatient decision maker (where every second is precious and intense), you must plan a bare-bones pitch that doesn't waste a minute.

That kind of presentation is no accident; it gets built carefully, by painstaking effort done in advance.

A successful talk does more than put your knowledge on display. Knowledge must be structured, to tickle the interests of your listeners and respond to their immediate needs.

With Knowledge and Preparation as a foundation, you'll then be ready to sustain a truly positive Attitude.

```
┌─────────────────────────────────────────────┐
│                                             │
│         KEYSTONE #3 - ATTITUDE              │
│                                             │
└─────────────────────────────────────────────┘
```

The third keystone is ATTITUDE.

Let's assume you already know your subject fully and have built a well-structured presentation. Is your success now guaranteed? Not at all.

Despite mastery of the subject and despite intelligent planning, you're still liable to fail if your ATTITUDE is wrong.

The great heavyweight champion, Joe Louis, once said:
"He can run, but he can't hide." He meant Billy Conn, his
opponent in a boxing ring, but the same idea applies to you
when talking to groups.

When you speak to most groups--unless you've trained
yourself inwardly to control all visible emotions (like an actor
or yogi)--you can *run* (trying to conceal your real attitude),
but you usually can't *hide* how you feel.

Consider your own past history. Haven't you felt less
persuasive when trying to sell an idea that, deep down, you
didn't really believe in, even if you never said so? Probably,
your lack of conviction was showing, too.

The Boomerang Effect

Your mood as a speaker--felt by your audience--has a
powerful BOOMERANG Effect. . . . What you send out comes
right back at you. What you expect is often what you get. So,
like self-expectations that breed "butterflies," your attitude
towards your audience is self-fulfilling, too.

Are you fearful or confident? Angry or calm? Uptight or
something else? No matter what, people usually "read" you
correctly. Your Attitude speaks silently, but louder than all
your spoken words.

Your attitude is contagious: it infects your audience. If
you feel hostile, so will they. If you are fearful and unsure,
they will distrust your ideas. If you are apathetic and
unenthusiastic about the topic, they'll get bored, too.

You thus possess the universal power to *create* a hostile
audience. Do you understand it? It's too easy.

To *create* a hostile audience . . . just "think hostile." Your
true attitude will scream out, even if not expressed verbally.
People will feel it and they will likely return it.

Yeah, that's it! Get mad and get mean! Imagine to yourself beforehand all the rotten questions they'll probably ask. Sure, and anyway, they hate this subject besides--and probably you and your stupid organization, too. What a bunch of flaming turkeys!

If you think hard enough, you can really work yourself up into a righteous rage at the whole gang of "Them" before the first so-and-so strolls into the room.

If you expect a bad audience, they'll accommodate you. It's truly all in your attitude, no matter what polite words you speak--they'll usually sense your bad vibrations at once, and react with equal negativity.

Fortunately, a friendly attitude can be self-fulfilling, too. *Especially* when your audience will likely be rough and hostile, your smartest move is to treat them as if they were *not* hostile.

If you could just learn to view difficult audiences in a different way--to expect from them simply a friendly challenge (not an angry, jugular attack), you'd often find, amazingly, that they live up to your positive expectations.

You really have the power to change the whole situation, then, just by changing your attitude.

A HOSTILE AUDIENCE

Will you soon face a hostile audience?

Then your best self-defense is a strong, positive attitude. Think friendly and you might arouse friendliness in return.

Do you need to lure people who already disagree with you?

Your best approach, again, is a positive attitude. Expect success and you might be nicely surprised.

But is this just storybook "wishful thinking," where you fall stupidly out of touch with reality? Not really. It's a universal and practical truth. You control your own reality through a powerful tool--your mind--more than most people dare to guess (or accept responsibility for).

You are seldom the helpless victim of circumstances. In a briefing or anywhere else, you can assert control over events by applying your own mental powers.

You shouldn't wait anxiously, then respond passively to whatever-happens-next. You can take control. You can actually *do* and not just be *done to*. Control your attitude and you control your world.

This good news is your secret for creating a more *positive* audience atmosphere. If what you transmit bounces right back at you--hostile or friendly--then you can turn that Boomerang around to your advantage.

If you act positive, self-confident, enthusiastic, and comfortable with your topic (and yourself), you'll likely create rapport and win agreement even from audiences who (at least temporarily) disagree with you.

THE PROFESSIONAL ATTITUDE

Countless books have been written and speeches made on the power of "positive thinking" and how to sustain a positive mental attitude. And positive thinking is, without doubt, vital for success as a speaker and as a human being.

An oft-repeated old saw about positive thinking concerns a half-filled glass as viewed by different people.

"Oh, my," says the pessimist, "the glass is half empty."

"Aha!" says the optimist. "You are wrong. The glass is half full."

The point, of course, is that we make things what they seem by how we choose to view them.

There is, however, a third possibility. The *realist* looks at the glass and says: "In reality, my friends, it is both. The glass is half full and the glass is half empty."

For a professional in any endeavor, the best positive attitude is grounded in reality, based on hard work, and fulfilled through positive (probable) expectations.

A true professional keeps a positive attitude, not by "psych-ups" or self-deception, but because he or she has genuinely earned the right to have faith. He's taken every possible step to ensure success; she's done her homework, solidly and thoroughly.

To master the keystone of Attitude, then, your target is to become a true professional--to have both inner calm and outward poise, and to experience this attitude as true and genuine, not faking it.

Beyond everything else, your attitude has a powerful and inescapable impact upon your entire presentation. In truth, of all aspects of a talk, the one that most affects your final outcome is found by looking within yourself: IT'S ALL IN YOUR ATTITUDE.

THE THREE KEYSTONES

Now, you know the three keystones for effective speaking:

KNOWLEDGE

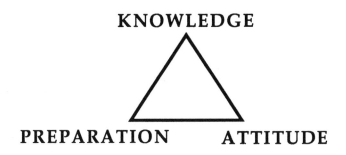

PREPARATION   ATTITUDE

They work together like the three legs of a tripod, and are mutually interdependent. Weaken any one and your whole substance can crash. But keep them all three strong and your platform will hold, steady and unshakable.

Chapter 4 ▬▬▬▬▬▬▬

A DOZEN DEADLY DANGERS

*"If a little knowledge is dangerous, where is the
man who has so much as to be out of danger?"*
-- Thomas Henry Huxley

THREE WHO SPOKE HISTORY

How important is the ability to speak in front of groups?
Consider a true example where the speaking powers of three
men changed forever the history of the world.

Let's begin in 1924 . . .

The first man (a German) had strong views on the power
of speaking in politics. In 1924, while confined in prison for
conspiracy against the local government, he started writing a
polemic book which contained this foreshadowing belief:

*"All great, world-shaking events have been brought
about, not by written matter, but by the spoken word."*[11]

The second man (an Englishman) also had strong views
on politics and speaking. In 1924, as a newly-elected
member of Parliament, he was sharpening the speaking
skills he would later command as an openly-declared,
worldwide enemy of the first man.

In 1924, the third man (an American) suffered privately.
His political career had ended from a crippling disability
with no hint that he, too, would eventually become a world
leader and speechmaker in a global war of good against evil,
words against words.

---

[11]*Mein Kampf*, trans. Ralph Manheim (Boston: Houghton Mifflin Co.,
1962), p. 469.

These three men were, of course: Adolf Hitler, Winston Churchill, and Franklin Roosevelt.

The hysterical speeches at mass rallies by Hitler, "Der Fuhrer," inflamed the madness of Naziism that swept Germany, engulfed Europe, and helped propel the world into the chaos of World War II.

In opposition, Churchill spoke as Prime Minister on the side of democracy and against Hitler with such inspiring eloquence that it was said he "mobilized the English language and sent it into battle" as a weapon.[12]

Finally, as 31st U.S. President, Franklin D. Roosevelt gave laudatory speeches and "fireside chats" so masterfully that he is now recognized as one of the most powerful public speakers in the history of the Presidency.

SECRETS OF THE SPELLBINDERS

Famous speakers like these are often *"Spellbinders"*--they grab and hold their audience's attention with electric intensity from start to finish. Spellbinders are dynamic and powerful. Their words are stirring and memorable. They possess an intangible "star quality."

To be a Spellbinder, however, means only that the person is outstanding as a speaker, not necessarily as a human being. Although many famous speakers (such as Churchill) have been Spellbinders, others (like Abraham Lincoln) have been great people but not spellbinding speakers in person. Some of the most evil people in history (like Hitler) were also Spellbinders.

The ideal speaker, of course, is someone who is *both* an outstanding human being *and* a Spellbinder.

If you hope to be a better speaker, Spellbinders can show you living examples of how to create talks that are effective and memorable.

Let's look at some of the basic techniques that Spellbinders display.

---

[12]Edward R. Murrow, I Can Hear It Now [1933-45]--quoted in *Familiar Quotations: John Bartlett*, 15th edition, ed. Emily Morison Beck (Boston: Little, Brown & Co., 1980), pp. 742-43, note 2.

PRINCIPLE #1 - FOCUS

Great speakers FOCUS their talks. Their best speeches are built around a single, central, important theme. This theme is often crystallized in one strong phrase or climactic statement that later comes to symbolize the entire speech:

Patrick Henry: *"I know not what course others may take, but as for me, give me liberty or give me death!"* [Speech, Virginia Convention, 1775]

Franklin Roosevelt: *"The only thing we have to fear is fear itself."* [1933, on the Depression]

For growing intensity, this thematic phrase is sometimes repeated throughout, as an echoing refrain with deepening meanings:

Marc Antony: *"Yet Brutus says he was ambitious; / And Brutus is an honourable man."* [William Shakespeare, 1599: *Julius Caesar*, III.ii]

Martin Luther King, Jr.: *"I have a dream!"* [Speech at the Lincoln Memorial, 1963]

PRINCIPLE #2 - SIMPLIFY

The most powerful speakers know how to SIMPLIFY. A truly memorable speech has clarity and simplicity, so its main ideas, no matter how complex, can be understood quickly and easily.

This quest for simplicity has a danger, of course . . . that the speech gets *over*-simplified, built of one-liner slogans alone, without true depth. Any speaker who stoops to manipulate a crowd by raw emotions only is merely a demagogue.

Nevertheless, the great speakers show us that--to be most effective--a *spoken* message must be more simplified than a *written* one. Generally when speaking, LESS equals MORE: less verbosity equals more clarity.

So, for most talks (heard by listeners in various states of attention or distraction), too much simplicity is normally less risky than the opposite peril--a befuddling morass of too much complexity.

The most profound speakers often delight and enlighten us with a deceptive simplicity that carries hidden meanings, ironic twists, and extra dimensions:

Jesus Christ: *"Blessed are the meek: for they shall inherit the earth."* [Sermon on the Mount, Matthew 5:5]

Mark Twain: *"Always do right. This will gratify some people, and astonish the rest."* [Speech at the Greenpoint Presbyterian Church, 1901][13]

William Faulkner: *"I believe that man will not merely endure: he will prevail."* [Acceptance Address for the Nobel Prize, 1950]

PRINCIPLE #3 - **ORGANIZE**

A typical audience can be a busy, impatient lot, who expect the speaker to tell a story so they understand it easily and get to the point quickly. To do this job right, a speech must go beyond mere eloquent words and memorable phrases--it must ORGANIZE ideas into a clear total design that fits together from start to finish.

Public speakers since at least the ancient Greeks and Romans have thus learned to organize their ideas using *idea patterns* (such as question-answer) for structure at every level: sentences, paragraphs, sections, and the total design.

For example, Abraham Lincoln's timeless "Gettysburg Address" draws its power not only from its verbal cadence and poetic expression, but also from its evolving logic and overall structure, which unifies the full meaning.

---

[13]As helpful tools in identifying or locating this and other quotations, I am indebted both to Bartlett's *Quotations* [See Note 12] and to *The International Thesaurus of Quotations,* compiled by Rhoda Thomas Tripp (New York: Thomas Y. Crowell, 1970).

Even at basic sentence level, ideas can frequently be formed in memorable ways by using *rhetorical devices* (like antithesis or parallel construction).

For example:

Benjamin Franklin: *"We must all hang together, or assuredly we shall all hang separately."* [At the signing of the Declaration of Independence, 1776]

John F. Kennedy: *"And so, my fellow Americans, ask not what your country can do for you; ask what you can do for your country."* [Inaugural Address, 1961]

PRINCIPLE #4 - DRAMATIZE

The greatest speakers are never dull nor boring. They possess a unique personality with a magic intangible--the power to inspire, surprise, and provoke--that indefinable something we usually call "charisma."

What is "charisma"?

Charisma means unpredictability, high energy, dynamic body language, an ability to shock and intrigue. Charisma is the talent, beyond cold logic, to DRAMATIZE a situation with intense fire and emotion:

Winston Churchill: *"This wicked man Hitler, the repository and embodiment of many forms of soul-destroying hatred, this monstrous product of former wrongs and shame."* [Radio broadcast, 1940]

John Kennedy: *"All free men, wherever they may live, are citizens of Berlin. And therefore, as a free man, I take pride in the words, 'Ich bin ein Berliner.'"* [Address at City Hall, West Berlin, June 26, 1963]

Barbara C. Jordan: *"'We the people.' It is a very eloquent beginning. But when that document was completed on the seventeenth of September in 1787 I was not included in that 'We, the people.'"* [Statement, House of Representatives, July 25, 1974]

Often, the charismatic speaker excites the audience's emotions with strong *visualizations*. Hitler, for instance, used pervasive visual symbols to promote Naziism (uniforms, swastika, banners)--most notably in carefully-staged outdoor pageants where he delivered his bombastic speeches.

Churchill, too, understood and used visual symbolism shrewdly--with his characteristic top hat and cigar, or the frequent "V"-handsign he flashed to signal "Victory."

For dramatic visualization to work, an audience need not be shown an actual picture. A colorful speaker using powerful language and delivery can often "paint a picture in their minds" with words and imagination alone:

William Jennings Bryan: *"You shall not press down upon the brow of labor this crown of thorns. You shall not crucify mankind upon a cross of gold."* [Speech at the National Democratic Convention, 1896]

PRINCIPLE #5 - HUMANIZE

The best speakers go beyond obvious generalities and trite abstractions. They HUMANIZE the topic by showing how an idea relates directly to *people*--even, when possible, to specific people by name.

These people are sometimes actually the audience present at the speech. Other times, the human connection is expanded symbolically to touch a larger group (even an entire nation). The human element may also be deep personal feelings expressed by the speaker himself or herself:

Winston Churchill: *"Never in the field of human conflict was so much owed by so many to so few."* [1940, in a tribute to the Royal Air Force]

Queen Elizabeth I: *"I am come amongst you . . . in the midst and heat of the battle, to live or die amongst you all, to lay down for my God, and for my kingdom, and for my people, my honor and my blood, even in the dust."* [Speech on the Approach of the Spanish Armada, 1588]

Masters of communication do not speak carelessly. They choose, thoughtfully and knowingly, the best way (place, time, style, examples) for relating to a specific audience at a given moment.

Thus, sometimes Franklin Roosevelt delivered oratorical addresses to the American people as grand public speeches, and other times he gave casual "fireside chats" in person-to-person style over radio like a guest in their living rooms.

Harry Truman was not an oratorical speaker with the gifts of a Churchill or Roosevelt, but he, too, was a highly effective communicator. Why?--because he talked straight to people in a human, down-to-earth way and *stayed himself*.

Ronald Reagan, also, has been called by many "the great communicator," in large part because of his ability to be a storyteller, using an anecdote to take a complex social problem and showcase its meaning in the life of a single citizen or family.

The instinctive question that all great speakers seem to ask of themselves constantly is: "What does this all really mean, in *human* ('people') terms?" The answer gives them a sure, powerful link between the events at hand and their listening audience--a link that the effective speaker is careful to point out directly:

> Abraham Lincoln: *"But, in a larger sense, we cannot dedicate, we cannot consecrate, we cannot hallow, this ground. The brave men, living and dead, who struggled here, have consecrated it, far above our power to add or to detract."* [Gettysburg Address, 1863]

ON-THE-JOB APPLICATION

Right now, though, maybe your own speaking chores don't rival those of Roosevelt or Churchill. You're not ready to run for President, yet. Your biggest problem today is just to brief the boss on why the GROK program is over budget and two weeks behind schedule.

Let's look at how *you* could successfully apply these five basic principles of the great speakers in your own on-the-job speaking chores:

PRINCIPLE #1 - **FOCUS**

When you plan your talk, concentrate on what's really important. Get right to the heart of things. What is the exact problem? What looks like the best solution? What is the "bottom line"? What does this mean for the future? (For best focus, unify your talk around a central idea or theme.)

PRINCIPLE #2 - **SIMPLIFY**

Support your main idea with just a few examples. In particular, follow the "Rule of 1-2-3," which says to highlight one, two, or (at most) three main points. Hold back the extra details. Skip the past history (unless asked). Be narrowly deep, not widely shallow.

PRINCIPLE #3 - **ORGANIZE**

Structure your talk from start to finish with a crisp five-part design:
> (1) State the main issue.
> (2) Develop your viewpoint with specifics.
> (3) End with a clear summary.
> (4) Handle any questions.
> (5) Make a last statement or request.

PRINCIPLE #4 - **DRAMATIZE**

Don't just tell it; *show* it! Find yourself some vivid, memorable way to get your point across. Can you tell this story in a visual--a chart, graph, photo, site visit, even a real demonstration? Use your creative imagination to add dramatic impact.

PRINCIPLE #5 - **HUMANIZE**

Remember: People are more important than things. So, don't get lost in numbers; tell this story in human terms. Cut out the jargon. Talk down-to-earth language with everyday examples. In a nutshell, ask: What does this mean to real people, on-the-job, in their own world?

THE DEADLY DANGERS

These five principles, all used successfully by great speakers for centuries, can help you speak better.

But you can't win them all! Even experienced, self-confident speakers sometimes find afterwards that they've survived the talk but failed to win the results they sought.

Here are the the "Deadly Dangers"--the twelve most common mistakes made by people when speaking to groups, which will likely cause *you* the most trouble, too:

A DOZEN DEADLY DANGERS

1 - NO CLEAR OBJECTIVE
2 - FORGETTING THE AUDIENCE
3 - ANTICLIMAX ENDING
4 - MYSTERY OPENING
5 - LOSS OF FOCUS
6 - NO SCRIPT
7 - POOR DELIVERY
8 - BAD VISUALS
9 - WEAK EVIDENCE
10 - NEGATIVE ATTITUDE
11 - SLIPSHOD PREPARATION
12 - NO FOLLOW-UP

From here on, this book will give you two things simultaneously: (1) the strategy and tactics for combating each Deadly Danger, and (2) twelve basic Rules for Success in speaking to groups.

Step by step, you will learn proven ways to avoid the "Deadly Dangers" so your future presentations will be outstanding exceptions to the common rule.

Practice these lessons faithfully and perhaps you can be a Spellbinder, too. People won't groan, sleep, or yawn when you stand up to speak--instead, they'll sit up straight and eagerly listen.

Chapter 5

RULE #1:

FIND YOUR ACTION OBJECTIVE

*"If you don't know where you're going,
you'll probably end up somewhere else."*
                                  -- David Campbell

SHOOTING BLIND

Ask enough people the question, "What's your objective for your next oral presentation?," and some will shake their heads sadly and honestly reply: "Just to get it over with."

Others who feel less nervous might say their objective is simple: "To stand up and tell all I know." They believe if you're a master of the subject, success is already guaranteed.

In either case, the first of the Dozen Deadly Dangers is at work: innocent people are scheduling talks with no clear objective or desired outcome in mind.

Making a presentation without a well-defined objective is like shooting a gun blindfolded . . . yes, you might accidentally hit something, but isn't it smarter (and safer) to look where you're trying to aim?

DEADLY DANGER #1 - **NO CLEAR OBJECTIVE**

A FORK IN THE ROAD

In the midst of her adventures, Alice in Wonderland encountered the grinning Cheshire Cat sitting on a tree bough at a fork in the road.

Should she go left or right?, Alice wondered.

'Cheshire Puss,' she began, . . . 'would you
tell me please, which way I ought to walk from
here?'
'That depends a good deal on where you
want to get to,' said the Cat.
'I don't much care where--' said Alice.
'Then it doesn't matter which way you walk,'
said the Cat.
'So long as I get *somewhere*,' Alice added, as
an explanation.
'Oh, you're sure to do that,' said the Cat, 'if
you only walk long enough.'[14]

THE ROAD NOT TAKEN

Suppose that soon, in the midst of your own life's daily
adventures, you encounter an oral presentation to be made
somewhere along the road.

Will you remember the lesson from the Cheshire Cat--
that if you don't know where you are going, any road will
take you there--and first identify a definite action objective?

Or will you begin by just beginning and assume, "Oh,
I'm sure to get *somewhere* . . . if I only *talk* long enough"?

In planning a talk, the smartest first step is usually to
pinpoint your destination. Ask yourself: "Where am I trying
to get to? Exactly what do I want to happen *after* my talk is
over?" See this end result as your ACTION OBJECTIVE and
target your desired outcome by *writing it down*!

You may resist this step--most people do. You'll think
you already know your own objective, so why bother to
write it? But try it and see.

If your objective is so clear, it won't take but a moment
to record it, right? You'll often find it's surprisingly harder
to capture than you think.

----

[14]Charles Lutwidge Dodgson (writing as "Lewis Carroll"), *Alice's
Adventures in Wonderland* (1865).

TARGETING THE OUTCOME

A habit of writing your action objective first, in a single sentence, is invaluable. It forces you to clarify your aim, helps simplify and focus your content, and uncovers hidden, unsuspected gaps in your argument.

Sometimes you'll feel no *action* is really involved--your objective seems simply to "convey information." Maybe you'll make a welcoming speech, or explain how to prepare a 171 Form, or give a status update on the FRAMMIS program. Where's the action?

But look farther down the road and you'll usually see an action, after all. Don't you want someone, some day, somewhere, to think or act differently based on what you'll tell them? The way to find your *action* objective, therefore, is to see that future difference now!

ACTION OBJECTIVE

Keep in mind that your desired outcome may be personal and unstated, thus unknown by the audience. For example, although your *stated purpose* might be simply "to give a status update on the FRAMMIS program," your *action objective* could secretly be "to get more visibility for this idea," or even "to come across as a sharp professional who's on top of my job."

In this light, your action objective may sometimes be your "hidden agenda."

KNOW WHEN YOU SCORE

Objectives that are overly broad (such as "to get my point across," or "to explain the topic well," or "to persuade my audience") are too vague and difficult to judge. How will you know exactly whether you've hit the target or not?

Better objectives are specific ones like "to get the go-ahead for phase two on the QRS project," or "to win approval for my $10,000 budget increase," or even "to lay the groundwork for a later agreement on Alternative B."

When writing your action objectives, then, be sure they are as definite, specific, and measurable as possible.

The key test for an action objective is . . . will it tell you clearly when (or if) you've hit the bull's-eye?

OBJECT OF THE GAME

To avoid the wasteful mistake of no clear objective, test yourself before your next presentation by answering three vital questions (preferably in writing):

---

(1) Why exactly will my audience be attending this talk?

(2) What outcome do I hope to accomplish?

(3) How can I measure my failure or success?

If you cannot give good answers to these, ask yourself another, tougher question . . . are you ready or eager to make a presentation for which you can find no clear objective?

Chapter 6

RULE #2:

KNOW YOUR AUDIENCE

"When in Rome, speak as the Romans do."
-- Proverb (paraphrased)

WHERE ARE THE RESULTS?

Suppose you don't care how you come across as a speaker. You don't need to sound like Joan of Arc or Socrates--your only interest is in getting *results*.

Fine, but ask yourself: How will you ultimately know whether you've won or lost? Where will these "results" of yours actually occur?:

(a) within your own mind, or (b) somewhere else?

For example, let's say a friend of yours conducts a briefing on-the-job and afterwards you ask: "How did it go?"

"Great! Fantastic!" says your friend.

"Good," you reply. "How do you know?"

"Oh, I talked like a real pro--had a strong voice, kept eye contact, used dramatic gestures, never said 'uh.' They asked tough questions but I stayed in calm control. You know--great!"

"That's excellent," you might persist. "But what about those decisions you've been seeking? Did you finally get their approval?"

"Well, uh, no," you are told reluctantly. "Actually, they vetoed all my ideas again . . . but, man, you should have seen me *talk!*"

What would you now think of your friend's brainpower, savvy, or ability to do a job right?

Clearly, the results that matter most to you usually occur *outside* yourself, in the thoughts of your audience.[15]

Whether you speak to one person, dozens, hundreds, or more, the key participant is never you (the speaker), always them (the listeners). *They* are your decision makers--even if their only decision is whether to keep listening to you or not.

So, avoid judging your presentation's final success by a subjective impression of "how well I did (or felt or looked)." Instead, judge your outcome by the "yes" or "no" answers you get.[16]

Your ultimate target--where your true success or failure always occurs--is the mind of your audience.

DEADLY DANGER #2 - FORGETTING THE AUDIENCE

TALKING TO YOURSELF

Speakers who've forgotten their audience signal it in countless ways. For example, they speak in a mysterious language of undefined terms, cryptic acronyms, and baffling gobbledygook. They talk on the wrong level--too elementary for the experts or too esoteric for generalists.

Sometimes, their visual aids are inappropriate (like nudes) or risky (like cartoons) or totally distracting--too small to be seen or too complex to decipher. Some tell misguided jokes that are unfunny, irrelevant, objectionable.

---

[15]This idea parallels what Peter Drucker once called the "business reality" that: "Neither results nor resources exist inside the business. Both exist outside." See: *Managing for Results* (New York: Harper & Row, 1964), p. 5.

[16]Philosophically, to measure actions by their outcomes only (not their intrinsic worth) is typical Western pragmatism. Other vital viewpoints (e.g., Zen Buddhism) suggest, however, that each act we perform (serving tea, shooting an arrow, doing motorcycle maintenance--or making a talk) should be done intently, with focused awareness on the beauty of the moment *now*, without thought to its practical consequences *then*. See, for example, the works of D.T. Suzuki, Alan Watts, and Sheldon Kopp; also: David K. Reynolds, *Playing Ball on Running Water* (New York: Quill, 1984).

Others (out of shyness, or rude arrogance?) seem to totally ignore their audience. They stand alone, speaking the speech, never looking at the crowd, never acknowledging that other human beings are in the same room.

THE ADMIRAL AND THE MERMAID

What happens when a dramatic ploy is sadly inappropriate for the audience faced?

Once, two young men in the Navy were assigned to deliver an "update" presentation on the status of a certain submarine program to a certain admiral.

Wanting to make a big splash, they chose to use color 35mm slides as the heart of their presentation, showing interior photographs of the submarine.

As an attention-getter, they decided (for reasons now forgotten) to grab attention by opening the briefing with a sexy photo of a reclining mermaid.

To get the photo, they hired a young female model who agreed to pose semi-nude, dressed only in a mermaid tail they rented from a costume-supply house.

The photo was taken and the day for their pitch arrived. In walked the admiral with a large entourage (men and women), expecting a formal presentation on submarines.

The presentation began and instantly--as soon as the mermaid slide appeared--the sailors knew they had made a big mistake! The admiral was not amused. Reportedly, you could see a blush of red start at his collar and boil slowly up his face, in slow anger like a human thermometer.

Then, to make things the absolute worst for our hapless crew, Murphy's Law chose to strike. The projector malfunctioned: the slide got stuck!

Now, already rattled, they panicked and--instead of calling a break or pulling the plug--they delivered the entire presentation with an embarrassing background (their "Mermaid of the Month") in constant view.

And the outcome?

Afterwards, they spent a painful half-hour in private with the admiral, who roared--not about submarines, but about "what *is* and is *not* appropriate in this command!"

SPEAK THEIR LANGUAGE

To get results, you must speak the language of your audience. In a foreign country, to communicate with others whose native language is different from yours, you could: (a) talk only to people who speak your own language (fellow countrymen or bilingual natives); (b) learn the native language (becoming bilingual yourself); or, (c) hire a translator (or use a very limited vocabulary).

To be understood best in China by a group of Chinese listeners, you would obviously make your speech in Chinese, not Swedish nor Spanish nor Swahili.

Nevertheless, time after time thoughtless speakers do befuddle and aggravate their audiences by lapsing into other "foreign" languages.

Sometimes it's jargon: *"Just access the network on-line via modem and download one meg off RAM in the remote CPU."*

Sometimes it's unexplained abbreviations, terms, or people: *"The new SECNAV DF states that every ICP in CONUS should get the C3PO's RFU, ASAP."* Forsooth!

If your audience speaks the same jargon, no problem-- but if not, it's not *their* problem, it's yours.

Note that to "speak the language of the audience" does *not* mean "just tell them what they want to hear." Your message can be good news or bad, discomforting or reassuring. The key factor always is to tell them *your* message in terms that are most meaningful and understandable for *them* (for that one person or specific group).

Often, it's better to explain the same thing to different people in slightly different ways. Take, for example, the concept of "effective time management":

For an AUDIENCE of: TIME MANAGEMENT is:

Engineers .... "minimum input for maximum output"

Accountants .... "budgeting a limited resource"

General Managers .... "doing more with less"

Schoolchildren .... "getting the most from a day"

THE REAL TARGET

Knowing your audience is an ongoing, total process-- before, during, and after the presentation. Beforehand, do a complete Audience Analysis (in writing) as part of your advance preparations, to help you structure your entire talk.

This Analysis should reveal whether you know your audience thoroughly or if you need more research to answer critical questions such as:

* what level (technical or non-technical) to talk on;
* how much past history to leave in or take out;
* what style of delivery to choose;
* which examples to give.

SOURCES OF INFORMATION

Suppose, though, you start an Audience Analysis but find some gaps in what you still need to know about your audience. What next?

Your next step is to exploit every possible source of information available--contacts, pipelines, networks, you name it. Use every method for intelligence-gathering you can think of, as long as it's legal and ethical.

Here are five prime sources of information for you about your audience:

1. CORPORATE HISTORY

For an on-the-job assignment, your first source for information is likely to be your boss, the client, or whoever gave you the assignment to speak. Set aside time to ask that person everything you can think of about the decision maker(s) you'll face. Get a clear picture of them in your mind; take notes.

Also, check the organization's grapevine. Smoke out the "hot button" issues (topics that are innocent looking but sensitive because other players have their own hidden agendas).

2. OTHER SPEAKERS

You can study your target audience through the eyes of colleagues (or others) who faced the same person or group earlier--even if their topic was unrelated to yours. Remember, what you're looking for is basic: a sense of how your decision makers behave in a typical briefing situation.

In essence, you want their psychological profile, to know what to expect: Do they interrupt often or wait politely? Are their questions broad-overview types or detailed and nit-picky? Do they send tell-tale signals of boredom (nail-biting, snorting, or pencil-tapping)? Do they prefer visuals or demand handouts? And so on.

3. KEY ASSISTANTS

Another excellent source for background on a decision maker is that person's own key assistants (his or her secretary, aide-to, executive officer, or right-hand helper). These people often have invaluable insights into the do's and don't's for presentations, based on daily experience. They also can give you an insider's version of the immediate situation.

Don't ignore those who surround your decision maker: keep friendly relations; show them courtesy and respect. Be sure that they, like your banker, learn to trust you *before* you actually need their help.

4. TARGET AUDIENCE

Whenever possible, go straight to the source--to the decision maker himself/herself. Ask for an advance "okay" of your agenda, approach, and level of discussion. Your basic question is simply: *"Am I on-track with you?"*

Some of us feel reluctant to ask such questions if, for instance, our target is an aloof, irascible person who enjoys intimidation and slaps down questions from subordinates as signs of weakness. This hesitancy is understandable but, nevertheless, why go in cold and find out too late you're off-base? You're not a mind reader, so take the risk and run it by your audience beforehand and then you'll be sure.

5. PROXIES (DRY RUN)

If you have no direct communications channel with the decision maker or group, try studying them by proxy in a dry-run simulation (where other people play the roles of your expected audience).

Be sure your proxies resemble the real audience as closely as possible. For example, if you're an engineer whose target audience is a non-technical manager (say, a financial officer), avoid choosing another engineer to act as audience stand-in.

This simulation technique is often used by prominent figures (executives and politicians), who've learned that a dry run helps them identify (and thus avoid) pitfalls and miscues before public exposure to the real event.

TIME CRUNCH

If "know thy audience" sounds time-consuming, you're right--it can be. Even granting that it's vital, most people have a counterargument . . . not enough time.

Here are a few shortcuts, to help you study your audience quickly and handle the time crunch:

(1) *Anticipate.* Don't wait until a last-minute "fire drill" strikes. Make it a point on a daily basis to know your decision makers better--especially how they react to new ideas.

(2) *Invest.* Try always to do an audience analysis, even under high-pressure deadlines: Time may be short but no other step will pay you bigger dividends. If necessary, find time by skipping something else.

(3) *Streamline.* Have a routine method for doing an audience analysis to reduce effort and save you time. Here's a well-tested 15-question format for Audience Analysis . . . .

AUDIENCE ANALYSIS

1. Who, specifically, will be your audience for this presentation?

2. Why will they be attending the presentation?

3. What will be your audience's general attitude?

   FRIENDLY?
   　　RECEPTIVE?
   　　　　NEUTRAL?
   　　　　　　UNPREDICTABLE?
   　　　　　　　　HOSTILE?

4. What general level of knowledge (technical or otherwise) will your audience have--compared to your own--on this topic?

5. What information in your presentation will already be well-known or familiar to them?

6. What information in your presentation will be new or surprising to them?

7. What is the main PURPOSE for this presentation?

8. Keeping your audience in mind, what technical (or "specialist") aspects of this topic should you present in a simplified, *non*technical way?

9. What are the key points you would like your audience to understand and accept?

10. What--in *their own* terms and from *their own* viewpoint-- would it take to convince them of your key points?

11. What main objections are likely to be raised against your position?

12. What questions might be particularly difficult to handle?

13. What visual aids could you add to get your point across more vividly or to make your case more persuasive?

14. Who among your audience will be the principal decision maker(s)?

15. What specific ACTION would you like to see happen as a result of your presentation?

ON-THE-SPOT ANALYSIS

As a last resort, with a totally unfamiliar group, do an audience analysis on-the-spot. For example, open a speech on white-water rafting with an exploratory question like: *"How many of you have ever rafted on Class VI rapids?"* Then be ready to adjust your talk, based on their response.

Just be sure you can adjust quickly to the situation--no matter what kind of answers you get.

Although audience analysis can be time-consuming, it's always worth it. It's not a luxury, it's a necessity, since you can be a brilliant expert in your field and still fail, easily and absolutely, by talking to the right audience in the wrong way.

HOW TO DEAL WITH HIGHER AUTHORITY

Some speakers do well talking to most groups but face a unique set of problems when they talk to higher-ups (people with authority or clout, famous people, and such).

Here are a few quick tips for dealing with intimidating people at higher authority:

* *Be Thoroughly Prepared* - Top management people often act impatient because they are bright, quick, and over-worked. Don't waste their time (or yours): walk in fully up-to-speed.

* *Do A Careful Audience Analysis* - With higher-ups in particular, the more you know about them and their agendas, the better. When in doubt, go ask. Never guess--find out for sure.

* *Stay Flexible* - Avoid getting too set on any one answer to a problem. You might inadvertently allow other solutions to slip past you. Expect surprises; roll with the punches.

* *Don't Get Psyched Out* - Higher-up's are human, too. Learn to treat them as individuals--not a menacing, collective "THEY." (Remember that somewhere they also have their *own* "They" to answer to.)

THE GOLDEN RULE

Maybe this final advice goes without saying, but honor the Golden Rule. Always treat your audience with sensitivity and kindness--just as you yourself would expect and want to be treated.

At every moment, stay tuned in to their feelings and reactions. Do everything possible to keep rapport with them and to deserve their respect.

"Wait a minute!" you say. "Even with mean and angry, *hostile* audiences?"

Yes, *especially* with unreceptive people whom you need to win over. In those cases, just apply the well-worn Southern expression: "You'll catch more flies with honey than with vinegar."

Here are a half-dozen recipes for sweet success to avoid the sourness of failure:

1. STEREOTYPES: Above all, avoid implying *any* stereotypes by what you say or picture. Never seem to suggest that everyone of the same race, sex, or nationality (including your *own*) thinks and acts alike.

2. NICKNAMES: Likewise, avoid using all forms of derogatory nicknames for groups, professions, or individuals.

3. PRONOUNS: Be aware that you may offend women listeners by using only masculine pronouns ("he-his") all the time. Make everyone feel included by considerately using "he or she."

4. BOSS-EMPLOYEE: Be careful not to portray leadership roles in your organization as if they are open exclusively to one category. For example, avoid the careless use of only male references for bosses ("the manager--*he*") and only female references for assistants ("the secretary--*she*").

5. JOKES: When it comes to humor, avoid *all* humor at the expense of anyone else--in other words: no mother-in-law jokes; no race, age, sex, ethnic, or occupational jokes. The most acceptable humor is self-deprecatory (it makes fun of *you*, the speaker--not someone else).

6. WHEN IN DOUBT: Finally, if a joke, story, or reference has you worried whether to use it or not, the best advice is . . . *when in doubt, leave it out!*

SILENCE IS GOLDEN

Once, in a large organization, a hapless speaker's first slide showed a picture of six people--all white men--sitting around a table, under this heading:

"EXECUTIVE DEVELOPMENT"

Instantly, before his talk even began, the speaker was sidetracked by noisy controversy. The audience shouted their outrage over his apparent, symbolic message. *Did he really mean to suggest* (they asked him) *that women and minorities were excluded from the opportunity to be executives?*

Before you say such feelings are ridiculous overreactions based on "over-sensitivity," put yourself in the other person's mind, heart, and skin.

If these points sound like self-evident truisms, recall recent U.S. history . . . where not one but two Cabinet officials--Earl Butz and James Watt (former Secretaries of Agriculture and Interior)--were both fired from their high-level jobs after telling questionable "jokes" in public.

So, why alienate anyone by your own insensitivity? Don't tarnish good ideas with bad judgment. Practice the Golden Rule . . . it's not only an ethical and moral way to treat other human beings, it's much wiser, too.

THE CARDINAL RULE

In truth, if you garnered all the world's wisdom on how to communicate best with people and compressed it into one single, tiny capsule of *only three words*, then the cardinal rule for speaking to groups--and the major cause of failure when ignored--must emphatically be:

KNOW YOUR AUDIENCE!

Chapter 7

THE TECHNICAL-NONTECHNICAL DILEMMA

*"If we go on explaining we shall cease
to understand one another"*

-- Talleyrand

SPEAKER: LISTENER

Let's suppose you're talking on any topic, anywhere, to only one other person:

SPEAKER ◄────────────► LISTENER

Think for a moment about your listener. How likely is it that on this topic his/her knowledge, experience, or understanding will be identical to your own? . . . very likely, not very likely, or what?

The only answer is: not very likely. The uniqueness of each human being makes it virtually impossible that anyone (even a twin or clone) is exactly identical to anyone else in all particulars.

Further, add just one more person:

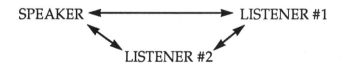

How likely is it now that Listener #2 will have the same amount of knowledge, experience, or understanding of the topic--no more, no less--as you (the Speaker) or as Listener #1?

It's obvious but important to know that every person in your audience has his/her own unique level of understanding of (and interest in) what you say. So, neither you nor Listener #1 nor Listener #2 (nor even Listeners #3, #4, #5, and so on) will each know, think, or feel exactly the same about your chosen topic.

This awareness (that no audience is a homogenized mass, but rather a multi-minded congregation) highlights a dilemma often faced by speakers . . . that of choosing the correct technical or nontechnical level to talk on.

THE TECHNICAL-NONTECHNICAL DILEMMA

Sometimes, talks are difficult to organize because the topic itself is technical and complicated.

Worse, the audience may be a mixed group of all levels: with specialist-experts (who know the field better than you) sitting next to generalist-managers (who don't need or can't grasp all the "nuts and bolts"):

TECHNICAL

(Specialists & Experts)

MIXED

(Generalists & Managers)

NONTECHNICAL

LEVELS OF UNDERSTANDING

As the speaker, your problem is often that you must somehow reach all members of this audience. You must: (a) convince the technicians that your idea is technically valid, yet also: (b) sell the decision makers on giving the go-ahead or providing the funding.

In addition, you must frequently do all that (and more) within a single briefing, without antagonizing, boring, or confusing anyone.

This perennial problem of the "Technical-Nontechnical Dilemma" can be resolved, however, if you anticipate it and organize your briefing correctly beforehand for a multi-level audience.

JABBERWOCKY

One possible solution to the Technical-Nontechnical Dilemma (the solution used too often by unthinking speakers) is simply to talk on your own high-tech level and let your listeners catch up with you as best they can.

Just stay on your own purely technical level throughout (it keeps them guessing, doesn't it?), and, shucks, if those less-informed generalists can't keep up with you . . . well, heck, if they get confused, that's *their* problem, isn't it?

Of course, the problem quickly becomes yours.

The danger when you stay purely-technical is that you talk over the heads of critical higher-ups (who inescapably tend to be more generalist than specialist), or that you lose the money people (who need to understand your proposal in their own, everyday terms).

So: "Eschew obfuscation and disdain the bamboozling gobbledygook of jabberwocky."

In plainer words: Don't let important people in your audience get snowed, lost, or alienated because you foolishly talked "Totally Technical."

SEE SPOT RUN

On the other hand, a contrary, extreme solution to the Technical-Nontechnical Dilemma is to talk throughout on the absolutely simplest level--that is, to intentionally bring everything from start to finish down to the infamous "lowest common denominator."

Everyone can surely understand it then, right?

Yes, but the danger is that you may sound so ultra-simplistic, aiming *under* the heads of the technical experts. You'll damage your credibility by making your knowledge sink to the elementary primer level of: "See Dick; see Jane; see our technical proposal. See Spot run."

Your risk in staying "Entirely Nontechnical" is that you'll dilute the essence of your technical discussion and lose another important segment of your audience (the expert technicians).

It's a dangerous trap either to stay Totally Technical (too obtuse) or to go Entirely Nontechnical (too simplistic).

SOLVING THE DILEMMA

So, what's the answer . . . some kind of a magic soup where you intermingle the Technical and Nontechnical together and hope each point is somehow comprehensible on everyone's level all at once?

The ideal solution to this Technical-Nontechnical Dilemma is a happy compromise, which structures your entire talk so everyone's needs get met.

The answer is to use an *HOURGLASS* Structure.

THE HOURGLASS STRUCTURE

Whenever you must convey technical information of any kind--on nuclear physics, laser technology, robotics, high-speed photography, or NBA basketball--your best pattern of organization is normally the HOURGLASS Structure.

Even for talks on less-technical topics, it's smart to treat your whole audience as a cross-mixture of individuals, some of whom understand more (and some less) than each other or than you.

As a basic model for a factual briefing, you should always begin with the HOURGLASS and depart from it only for good reason.

Let's now look at the HOURGLASS and learn how to make it work.

(1) OPENING: General *PRE*-View

In any talk, the OPENING must gain attention and set the stage for what's to come. The worst-possible first move is to lose part of your audience immediately--by jumping in too technical, throwing around buzzwords and jargon without an overall context:

POOR APPROACH: *"Good morning. Since a number of important liquid mixtures are azeotropic systems, we've had to apply a separating agent using either extractive or azeotropic distillation. The agent is critical as it influences the relative volatility of the components."*

This sample gets too specific, too soon. Already in a multi-level audience, at least some of your listeners are wondering: "What's an 'azeotropic system,' and why are you telling me this, anyway?"

If your tendency is to say, "Well, they should know that already or they shouldn't be in the room," think again.

Usually, the larger your audience or the higher-up your decision makers, the less likely it is that everyone knows all the technical details. That, in fact, is why they came to listen and learn from you.

So, before getting into nitty-gritty specifics, be sure to open your briefing in general, *non*technical terms:

BETTER APPROACH: *"Good morning. Today, we'll evaluate how our company plans to use distillation to separate liquids. We'll look especially at the need for special treatment of 'azeotropic systems,' which are liquids that cannot be separated by conventional methods of distillation."*

A good OPENING should (to repeat the old truism) "tell 'em what you're going to tell 'em"--and why--in terms that are general, nontechnical, and clearly understandable.

By giving everyone a PRE-view of what's to come, the opening is valuable for all your listeners, including the most experienced, most "technical" people there.

(2) **CLOSING:** General *RE*-View

For similar reasons, the CLOSING should back off from nuts and bolts, and make some overall sense of the talk--in terms that are again general, nontechnical, and clear. The worst CLOSING just stops--plop!--with no wrap-up, no climax: the audience feels caught off-guard, surprised, and let down.

You may think the "facts speak for themselves," but more often the specifics speak louder when they're packaged in a neat RE-view (and reinforcement) of what's been said.

> GOOD APPROACH: *"In summary, today you've seen our plans for distillation to separate liquids--in particular, for the treatment of 'azeotropic systems.' We're confident this plan is sound, and we welcome your agreement to fund the project for next year. Thank you. Any questions?"*

Your CLOSING is a review that closes the loop, ending in general terms to ensure that all listeners understand very precisely what you think the main point is and what you're asking for.

(3) **BODY:** Specific *VIEW*

Thus, the overall HOURGLASS structure starts *general*, gets *specific* in-between, and ends again *general*:

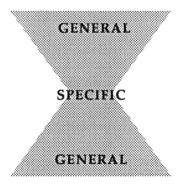

HOURGLASS STRUCTURE

If both the OPENING and CLOSING stay general and non-technical, you'll clearly need to cover the more technical details somewhere . . . by giving *specifics* in the talk's BODY.

This HOURGLASS image looks deceptively simple. Suppose, however, your talk consists of more than one point?

In that case, instead of moving simply from general to specific and back, your talk must vary its levels, with a smaller hourglass for each SUB-POINT within :

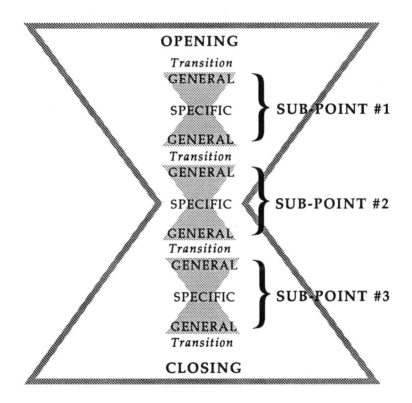

HOURGLASS: WITH SUB-POINTS

The General opening and closing of each key point need not be elaborate nor long. As an example, you might start KEY POINT #1 by saying simply: "First, let's look at the electrical system," and ending with: "So, the electrical system is in fine shape; now let's look at the cooling system."

In summary, whether you're looking at the main pattern for the talk as a whole or at the discussion level for any sub-point, your basic "Technical-Nontechnical" formula is the same: start general, end general, and cover the specifics in-between.

THE DILEMMA OF AUDIENCE

Here is a helpful list of more practical tips on how to present <u>technical information</u> to a multi-level audience:

* Be sure to define key words--especially jargon terms like acronyms, abbreviations, and technical shorthand.

* Bring your generalizations to life by adding well-chosen, specific examples.[17]

* Whenever appropriate, use the tool of *analogy*: explain what they *don't* understand in terms of something they *do* know.

* Reinforce key points with strong visuals, and add color for emphasis and clarity.

* Use handouts wisely--both to give fuller details to technicians and to give more basic information for generalists.

* When you answer questions, stay aware of differences in audience level: talk technical when necessary but still be sure to define key terms.

* Above all, recognize the challenge: Each mind in your audience is separately unique. Stay aware of your audience, use good judgment, and welcome every question.

---

[17]For more on the relationship between the GENERAL and the SPECIFIC, see Chapter 10, "Rule 5: Keep a Sharp Focus," pp. 92-97.

Chapter 8

RULE #3:

BUILD FROM THE CLOSING

"The last shall be first."

-- Matthew 19:30

WITH A BANG, NOT A WHIMPER

Sometimes at the wrap-up, a speaker seems to get stuck in verbal flypaper. Everyone knows the presentation is over, but the hapless speaker just can't seem to stop talking and get offstage:

"So, uh, in conclusion, uh, I'd like to say, uh,
in summary, uh, as I said, uh, in conclusion--"

The whole presentation just sputters off to an awkward close--no clear resolution, no precise summary of the main idea, no real climax. It's embarrassing for the speaker and uncomfortable for the audience.

This mistake is especially devastating because the most important moment in your entire presentation is usually your CLOSING!

At the closing, your audience listens with a special intensity. At the closing, they (rightfully) expect you to bring all key points together and showcase your main idea. The thing they remember best is often whatever they hear last.

A feeble, weak ending--which goes 'round and 'round, like a wheel stuck in snow, or just STOPS! abruptly without warning--is one of the worst mistakes you can make.

```
DEADLY DANGER #3 - ANTICLIMAX ENDING
```

PLAN THE CLOSING FIRST!

Why do anticlimax endings ever occur, anyway? Don't people who speak want strong, upbeat endings?

Usually, an anticlimax happens when a speaker starts talking with no ending at all in mind. He or she just drifts along as if stumbling through fog, with no clear and final destination in view.

How can you start a journey well if you have no idea where you're trying to end?

Yet, few speakers start organizing their talks at the most important place--the ending. Most who write scripts start at the beginning (it's the logical place), then work forward in normal sequence: first the Opening, then the Body, finally the Closing.

In practice, however, a linear approach--working forward from beginning to end--has many pitfalls. For example, if planning time is short, you may do the opening first, then scramble the rest but run out of time, and suddenly there you are, already speaking before a group and wondering how to get off and . . . oh, no--the anticlimax ending again.

To prevent an anticlimax ending, you must plan ahead. Know the last words you plan to say, before you utter the first ones. Capture that ending in writing and, if possible, rehearse it beforehand.

To repeat: Before you face any audience--if you know nothing else!--you should at least know the main point you're trying to get across, and that main point should be the heart of your CLOSING.

This is one of the simplest, yet most powerful timesavers for you, and the best way to ensure your talks always have a strong, clear focus . . .

PLAN THE CLOSING FIRST!

THE ONE-SENTENCE BRIEFING

Do you want brevity, clarity, and focus? Next time you make a talk, try this . . . pretend you've been strictly warned that your entire presentation must be only *one single sentence,* 25 words or less! What would your "one-sentence briefing" say?

Distill all your ideas into one concentrated "golden nugget" of information (your focus point). Make this focus point the heart of your closing. Then aim the rest of the talk towards your focus point, and the presentation should track crisply from start to finish.

For almost all presentations, the best sequence in which to prepare them is:

> *first* .... the CLOSING   (your focus point);
> *second* ...... the OPENING   (an audience "link");
> *third* .... the BODY   (specifics and examples).

THE SURPRISE WRAP-UP

Knowing your CLOSING also helps during presentations when you need an emergency bail-out. Specifically, let's consider two situations that are not farfetched: (a) "FREAK-OUT," and (b) "SHUT-OUT."

SITUATION A: *"FREAK-OUT"*

Suppose--in the middle of making a presentation--you suddenly freeze and forget everything you'd planned to say. What now? (You're only halfway through.)

If you hopelessly draw a total blank, the best solution usually is . . . go to the CLOSING. Yes, you'll leave out half of what you meant to say, but frankly most audiences seldom know the difference: they'll assume your talk went as planned, even if it didn't.

If your closing gives a neat capsule of your main point, it's a much smoother bail-out than any other choice: standing stone-silent, telling giraffe jokes, repeating the first half again, or just babbling more words.

Once you start to wrap up, if it triggers your memory and everything you meant to say comes back--never mind!-- go ahead and close, nevertheless. (If you retreat to where you left off, you'll usually foul it up worse.)

SITUATION B: *"SHUT-OUT"*

As another scenario, suppose you've been asked to brief an important, high-level decision maker. This person runs at so brutal a work-pace that any time with him at all is precious. Normally, you see him only once every quarter.

The time and place for this particular briefing were scheduled weeks in advance, and for the total presentation you are allotted 30 minutes.

So, you work hard: You develop a crisp briefing with solid structure, dramatic visuals, and a persuasive argument. You rehearse in dry runs (where your boss and boss's boss act as "devil's advocates"). With their help, you've created a finely-tuned talk that (allowing space for some questions) should run exactly 30 minutes--no more, no less.

Finally, the day for this briefing arrives. As you walk into the decision-maker's office, you feel reasonably relaxed and confident. You're certainly well-prepared and you're anxious to begin your talk.

Without warning, just as you're starting to speak, an assistant rushes in, interrupts, and whispers something into your decision-maker's ear.

After they huddle, the decision-maker looks up at you and says woefully: "I'm terribly sorry but I've been called to an urgent meeting with Congresswoman Gerrymander and must leave immediately. Could you wrap this up in five minutes?"

What now? (Your talk, remember, is carefully polished and 30 minutes long):

OPTION #1: Suggest that, rather than proceeding, you come back another time when he can listen to your whole presentation.

RISK: You may have to wait too long. Ultra-busy people like this can get sidetracked for weeks (but, they'll say, "We'll get back to you").

OPTION #2: Try to give the entire presentation right then anyway, hoping to hold his attention for the next half-hour.

RISK: You'll end up talking to an empty chair.

OPTION #3: Resort to "speed-talking," trying to cram in as many words as possible before he leaves?

RISK: It's silly. The talk would be unintelligible and unconvincing. You want to communicate for results, not be an auctioneer.

OPTION #4: Go to your CLOSING.

RISK: You're giving the "bottom line" without the in-between.

What's the most desirable solution? In most cases, OPTION #4 works best: Go to your CLOSING.

By telling your closing (the FOCUS POINT), you hope to pique his interest so he'll want the whole story later. You seek a reaction like: "That's interesting. I've got to run, but get on my docket for tomorrow and come in early, would you? I want to hear more about this."

There are two main exceptions, when you'd avoid going straight to the closing: (1) when the point is so complex it can't be explained in a quick capsule; and, (2) when you're dropping very bad news and want more time to prepare (or soften up) your audience.

Usually, when you get caught in a surprise wrap-up (the "SHUT-OUT"), your best option (at least, the lesser of evils) is to go to your closing.

FOUR FUNCTIONS OF A CLOSING

In a factual presentation, the closing might fulfill any or all of four standard functions:

(1) **SUMMARY** - To restate the main idea ("just the facts") with no discernible slant, no effort to persuade.

EXAMPLE: *"In summary, radio waves that are transmitted by frequency modulation (FM) produce less static than those sent by amplitude modulation (AM)."*

(2) **ALTERNATIVES** - To spell out two or more different items (things, people, approaches) from which a choice is to be made.

EXAMPLE: *"So, as you have all seen, there are now three alternatives: (a) expand the scope; (b) continue as is; or, (c) terminate the program."*

(3) **CONCLUSION** - To state an actual conclusion based directly on the facts presented.

EXAMPLE: *"From our investigation, we conclude that the potential melt-down at Three Mile Island was the result of human error."*

(4) **RECOMMENDATION** - To give a specific call to action, where a definite step (or steps) is unmistakably advocated.

EXAMPLE: *"We therefore strongly urge the start of a new Employee Assistance Program for our employees, to include counselling in stress management and substance abuse control."*

Remember that these four functions of a CLOSING are not mutually exclusive. More than one of the functions could be combined in the same closing.

WHEN IN GREECE

As your final guidance on closings, consider this advice from Aristotle in his handbook for Greek orators, the *Rhetoric*. To be successful, according to Aristotle, the ending of any speech must do four things:

(1) make your audience feel good about you and bad about your opponents;

(2) highlight (or downplay) the proven facts;

(3) excite the emotions of your listeners; and,

(4) repeat the main points that you've already developed.[18]

---

[18]Aristotle, *Rhetoric*, trans. W. Rhys Roberts (New York: Random House, 1954), Book III, Chapter 19 (paraphrased).

Chapter 9

RULE #4:

HOOK YOUR AUDIENCE INSTANTLY

> *"Yes, but first you have to get his attention!"*
> -- joke punch line about a stubborn mule

ATTENTION! ATTENTION!

The first moments of a presentation are crucial: They set the tone, lure attention, and put things in context. A "lost" audience can be impossible to win back, so your OPENING must quickly get them personally involved.

Sadly, many presentations get off-the-track immediately. The speaker opens his or her mouth, and already listeners feel confused, get frustrated, and even wonder angrily, "What the [BLEEP] are you talking about?"

By failing to introduce the topic well, the speaker has stumbled into the trap of a "Mystery Opening"--since it's a mystery what's being talked about, or why.

DEADLY DANGER #4 - **MYSTERY OPENING**

IN SEARCH OF AUDIENCE

What does it take to catch an audience's attention instantly? Audience excitement will seldom pop up automatically or accidentally. You must think and plan for it with care.

Start with an in-depth Audience Analysis. But go beyond "know your audience"--that's only step one. You must next convert your awareness of them into action. Find a quick way to gain rapport, and build a solid bridge between audience and topic.

FIND THE MISSING "LINK"

To build an opening that really pulls in your audience, look at the world through their end of the telescope--that is, see the topic as seen by *them*. Why should *they* care? What is the meaning or relevance for *them*? Constantly keep asking yourself this challenging question (on behalf of your audience) . . . *"So what?"*

Here are ten proven OPENING techniques that should help you find a useful "link" to gain immediate audience attention:

1. **AGENDA.** One solid way to open is simply to sketch for your listeners a brief overview of exactly what the talk will cover and what you expect to be the final outcome. (This direct AGENDA opening is very common and often best for formal briefings.)

   EXAMPLE: *"Good morning. Today, we'll look at the status of the R2D2 project. We'll review the planned schedule, point out a few slippages, and--at the end of my briefing--ask for guidance on how you prefer to proceed."*

2. **VISUAL.** The strongest impact on an audience is often what it sees. (Visuals generally carry about three times more power than words alone.) So, you can usually get fast attention by opening with an intriguing VISUAL (like a photo, chart, model, or slide).

EXAMPLE: A Marine Corps officer in uniform stood erectly before an audience and proudly announced: *"Ladies and Gentlemen, today my topic will be: 'How to Decorate a Cake.'"* The visual contrast between the cake he displayed and his military image was an immediate attention-getter.

3. **A QUESTION.** To get quick involvement, ask an opening QUESTION. Without fail, questions engage the mind more forcefully than bald statements. Questions can be *rhetorical* (posed only for thought, or for the speaker to answer himself/herself) or *interactive* (intended to solicit an actual audience response, such as to raise their hands, speak, or stand up).

EXAMPLES:

[Rhetorical]: *"Have you ever stood on solid Earth but glanced skyward, to dream of bold new journeys into space, exploring other worlds?"*

[Interactive]: *"How many people here tonight own a foreign-made car, camera, or stereo? Let's see a show of hands, please."*

4. **THE DRAMATIC.** People pay attention instantly to the DRAMATIC, which can be anything that startles. Usually, but not always, it is visual or physical: a loud noise, a sudden movement, a demonstration of an actual event. "The dramatic" surprises or shocks us and stirs our emotions: its key element is the unexpected.

EXAMPLE: To demonstrate why motorcyclists should wear safety helmets, a young man took off his own helmet and lofted it into the air. As it cracked hard onto the pavement, his first words were: *"Now imagine that, instead of a helmet, that projectile was your bare head."*

BEWARE OF "I" TROUBLE!

5. **"YOU" EMPHASIS.** Most dull speakers suffer from incurable "I" trouble. They talk only about (and to) themselves. For a stronger opening, avoid the self-centered "I" or "WE," and instead focus on your audience. Keep a *"YOU"*-EMPHASIS. Use the word "YOU" itself and keep a "YOU"-attitude. (In a briefing, your "YOU" opening might refer back to what the decision-maker originally asked for.)

   EXAMPLE: *"Ms. Kirkwood, last week you expressed personal dissatisfaction with the repair service on your mainframe computers. You directed us to look into this matter immediately--which we did. This morning I'd like to report the major findings to you."*

6. **QUOTATION.** You may occasionally choose to kick off your talk with a sparkling QUOTATION. In most instances, a quotation works best when it is witty, relevant, opinionated, memorable, and said by a famous person.

   EXAMPLE: *"According to Will Rogers, 'Politics has got so expensive that it takes lots of money to even get beat with.'"*

7. **FACT OR STATISTIC.** Sometimes a provocative FACT or well-chosen STATISTIC alone can shock or intrigue an audience. You could simply state it or might put it in the form of a question.

   EXAMPLE: *"Did you know that an automobile driven at 30 miles per hour will--in one second--cover a distance of 44 feet? In football, that's more than enough for a first down. But on the road, it may be too far and too late."*

8. **THE PERSONAL TOUCH.** Opening to a friendly audience, you might tell a PERSONAL anecdote they're all familiar with, or acknowledge some positive accomplishments of people in the audience, by name. (If you embody the main theme or situation yourself, you could use that fact, too.)

EXAMPLE: *"I'm delighted and honored today to talk about space exploration with this group, since two people in this room--you, John and Alan--were already active pioneers in the space program when I joined NASA as an upstart engineer."*

9. **HUMOR.** A joke or funny story, if it works, can be the perfect "ice-breaker." With HUMOR, just be sure that: (a) the humor reinforces your main point (in a formal briefing, avoid humor for laughs alone); (b) the humor is appropriate for the audience; and, (c) the butt of the joke (if there is one) is the speaker, not anyone else.

EXAMPLE: *"When they first met in 1959, President Kennedy asked Premier Khrushchev about a medal on the Russian leader's chest. Told it was the Lenin Peace Medal, Kennedy quipped: 'I hope you do nothing to make them take it away from you.'*[19] *Well, today, I'd like to discuss the serious concern behind his droll remark--namely, war and peace between East and West."*

10. **SELF-INTEREST.** The best way, above all others, to gain people's immediate involvement is to appeal directly to their own positive SELF-INTEREST. Show them a legitimate promise of benefits to themselves, to their organization, or preferably to both, and invariably they'll perk up and listen to you.

---

[19]Pierre Salinger, *With Kennedy* (Garden City, N.Y: Doubleday & Co., 1966, p. 178).

EXAMPLE: *"Ladies and gentlemen, this afternoon I
intend to show you a proven new method we can use
to cut our operating costs by at least 15 percent, while
at the same time doubling profits with no new
expenditures by this division."*

COME TO THE POINT!

Usually, your best opening is straightforward and direct,
like the Agenda opening. You tell your audience up-front
exactly what the topic is, and why you're talking about it.
You mention if a decision will be sought from them. You seek
to "link" your audience with clarity and undisguised appeal
to their self-interest.

EXAMPLE: *"Good morning, ladies and gentlemen.
Today, as you requested, I'll address the current status of
the Rainbow Project. We'll look at the options at hand,
and--at the end of my talk--I'll ask you for a 'go/no-go'
decision on the future of Rainbow."*

In general, beware of the indirect ("mystery") opening.
Instead, be direct. Come right to the point! Why are we
here? As a rule, if most of your talks convey factual
information (like on-the-job briefings), you should prefer the
direct approach at least 95 percent (or more) of the time. It
hooks attention quickly, avoids perplexity, and points
everyone towards a common outcome.

Remember that the direct opening does not tip off all
your positions or conclusions prematurely. It gives your
listeners only a preview of coming attractions--not a full
glimpse at your conclusions before-the-fact.

To you, the direct opening may look less creative than
the indirect ("mystery") opening, but it's also safer and more
reliable.

WHEN TO USE SUSPENSE

As a rule, you should attempt the indirect ("mystery")
opening in talks only 5 percent (or less) of the time. To avoid

the indirect approach altogether, however, would be overly cautious.

In Shakespeare's play, *Julius Caesar*, Marc Antony displays a masterful example of the indirect approach for public persuasion in his oration to the Romans at the funeral of Caesar. He comes, he says, "to bury Caesar, not to praise him." Yet, word by word, he weaves a verbal web of emotion, innuendo, and accusation that inflames the mob against Caesar's assassins, openly but indirectly.[20]

When done well, the indirect opening can effectively create suspense, blunt skepticism, and arouse curiosity: it's just very tricky. The main danger is that, by keeping your audience in the dark, you also risk getting them confused, frustrated, or turned off.

Unfortunately, the mystery opening (like the anticlimax ending) often happens inadvertently because a speaker hasn't bothered to create a well-planned OPENING and, instead, just starts saying the first things that come to mind.

> **WHEN TO BE INDIRECT**: Your best times for an indirect opening seem to be:
>
> * for more *casual* kinds of talks: where audiences are usually more willing to play a guessing game;
>
> * to lay *groundwork* before you deliver bad news: since you may need to prepare someone before you "drop the bomb"; and,
>
> * for a *"sales pitch"* approach: where a too-direct beginning ("Good morning, I'd like you to buy our software--sign here!") would be guaranteed to fail.

Whenever you have doubts (will an indirect opening start you off on the right foot or not?), you're probably better off to go straightforward, unambiguous, and direct.

---

[20]William Shakespeare, *Julius Caesar*, act III, scene ii, lines 78ff. (Anyone interested in the use of persuasion in speaking to unfriendly groups should study this speech.)

TAKEOFF AND LANDING

The most important part of your presentation--for *immediate* impact on your listeners--is usually the OPENING. (For *long-term* impact, the most important part is the CLOSING.)

So if, as suggested in this and the last chapter, you always carefully plan both your OPENING and CLOSING in advance, you'll have three big advantages:

(1) you'll have an overall structure for your ideas (a road map on how to start and stop the journey) before you begin;

(2) your self-confidence should consequently be higher, as an antidote to nervousness; and,

(3) you'll avoid making a deadly presentation that prompts your audience to secretly think (at first): "What's this all about? Get to the point!"; or, worse (afterward): "So what? What did any of that have to do with *me*?"

REMEMBER

Silently . . . but constantly,
   your listeners are always thinking to themselves . . .

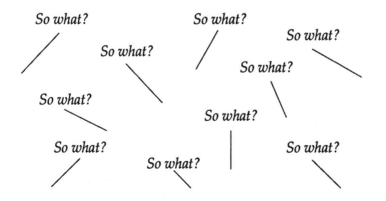

So what?
So what?
So what?
So what?
So what?
So what?
So what?
So what?
So what?
So what?
So what?

Chapter 10

RULE #5:

KEEP A SHARP FOCUS

"A fool uttereth all his mind."
                                    -- Proverbs 29:11

THE FUZZY BLOB

Every photographer (amateur or professional) has taken shots that turned up out-of-focus. Yes, somewhere in there, amongst the hazy shapes of blurry things, it's Aunt Maude, isn't it?--or maybe that's Mount Rushmore? The fine details are hard to discern.

Too many oral presentations display the same blurriness. The speaker seems to drift and wander. Ideas don't track. Some statements are like tangents, others are off-the-subject entirely. Past history is regurgitated while the main point gets lost or obscured.

In a nutshell, watch out for another deadly yet common mistake . . . a presentation that lacks clear FOCUS.

DEADLY DANGER #5 - LACK OF FOCUS

WHERE'S THE MEANING?

When you talk, where does the meaning come from? In most oral presentations, your listeners catch the meaning from a combination of two major ingredients: the general and the specific.

Compare each of these versions:

GENERAL:	SPECIFIC:
Grigori Rasputin was hard to kill.	On Dember 29, 1916, Rasputin was first poisoned, then shot three times, then plunged (still breathing) into an icy river, before he finally died.

GENERAL:	SPECIFIC:
Due to a number of factors, our most recent results were notably significant.	With a 30% increase in sales of our DORFTECH machine, profits for the third quarter were up by $275,000.

Inevitably, if you bypass either the general or the specific, you risk losing FOCUS. Your talk can fail to strike at the heart of things. As a result, your listeners may miss the whole point of your message.

Thus, your formula for a well-focused talk is:

GENERAL + SPECIFIC = MEANING

Speakers lose their focus in three basic ways:

1. A FOREST WITHOUT TREES: You'll lose focus if you give the listener only abstract *generalizations* (all forest), without support by concrete facts or vivid examples (no trees).

2. TREES BUT NO FOREST: Likewise, you'll lose focus if you flood the listener with an overwhelming sea of *details* (all trees) without demonstrating any unifying principle or larger meaning (no forest).

3. LOST IN THE FOG: You could blend both the specific and general, yet still lose focus by information overload--addressing so many *secondary points* that your vital few primary points get missed.

Let's look at each hazard in detail . . .

1. A FOREST WITHOUT TREES

Some varieties of presentation are notoriously boring and uninspiring--for example, commencement addresses at school graduations sometimes sound, regretfully, like this:

> *"And as you young people go forth into that bright new future, let me remind you that the world will only be what you make it. I urge you therefore to accept this challenge for a new tomorrow. Let your horizons be as high as your mind can lift them. For, yes, you are our planet's next generation of citizens, and your many choices will fashion our collective destiny for all the years to come."*

Noble sentiments, but . . . did you hear snoring in the bleachers? How many people were looking at their watches?

The major shortcoming of this talk is easy to spot: it's too abstract, too full of generalized platitudes without any vivid specifics. It's so unoriginal it even makes its own meaningful ideas sound trite.

And here's another flawed gem--an orientation, welcoming new employees (first day on-the-job) into the organization where they've chosen to work:

> *"Good morning, and welcome to a dynamic, forward-looking organization where we contribute to a truly vital need, meeting the technological demands of a unique segment of the industry we serve. You have joined an upwardly-mobile team of bright, highly dedicated professionals who are striving together to fulfill our important mission. Look around, and you will find both challenges and rewards. As we like to say, we are totally dedicated to the quest for becoming a center of excellence in all things."*

Sounds good, but . . . any questions?--like: "But what do people actually do around here?"; or even: "Where's the bathroom?"

Audiences love the speaker who can breathe life into bloodless generalizations. The best speakers do this with everyday examples, exotic facts and figures, down-to-earth anecdotes, eye-catching visuals, and more.

Since bald generalizations, by themselves, are usually meaningless, a good rule of thumb for any speaker is this . . . every time you make a *generalization*, follow it immediately with at least one specific, well-chosen *example*:

GENERALIZATION

└─────────▶ **EXAMPLE**

Make this GENERALIZATION-EXAMPLE pattern a habit. After any generalization, you want to hear yourself saying things like:

for example . . .	*to illustrate* . . .
such as . . .	*for instance* . . .
that is . . .	*in other words* . . .
namely . . .	*specifically* . . .

These helpful trigger phrases nudge you into telling specific examples. (Be sure your examples are good ones, since a poor example can confuse or mislead people as badly as a vague generalization.)

If unsubstantiated generalizations are so obviously weak, though, why don't all speakers go the extra mile and clarify all of their general statements with examples?

Apparently, we don't always realize how terribly "general" our own generalizations really are. After a while, a person gets so knowledgeable that, to him or her, the generalization is simply a truism that captures the (unstated) specifics of a larger experience--say, a full week's work, an entire project, or even a whole lifetime.

To the helpless listener, however--who lacks the sensory detail and memory of the actual event--that generalization is still nothing but a vague generalization.

You must, therefore, be certain to show the trees, not just the forest, to prevent confusion and avoid the trap of boredom.

2. TREES BUT NO FOREST

Specifics alone--despite their tremendous power--are not enough, either. Your talk can also lack focus if you spout nothing but isolated facts, with no clear relationship among them (that is, "trees but no forest").

This phenomenon--which is "DATA DUMP"[21] --usually exposes the speaker who is poor at logical communication or who just speaks at a ramble, without forethought.

Some presenters, for instance, unleash a rapid-fire barrage of small details (illustrated by flashing slides or viewgraphs), not bothering to relate these items to some larger point or bigger picture. In other words, they never put the facts into any *context*. For example:

"Good morning. The Coanda effect is also sometimes called the wall-attachment principle. The simplest kind of fluidic amplifier is one that uses cross-directed fluid jets. Some machine tools can be controlled by using both fluidic logic systems and proximity sensors. All fluidic devices share the same general characteristics."

Already, the audience is straining and guessing: "Yes, yes, but what's the point? . . . Why are you telling me this?"

To tell your story well, therefore, means to help your audience build a meaningful pattern from all the disparate facts you're feeding them, one by one. You must impose this pattern on the facts first in your *own* mind.

Remember: You have the advantage over your listeners. You--presumably--know how these facts fit together to start with; your audience doesn't. Your ideas will never be clearer in their mind than in yours, always less.

Most people find it hard to keep focus when they speak off-the-cuff (even on topics they know well). So, unless you can spout a cloud of logic while thinking on your feet, don't improvise. Find your theme, know your structure, and remember:*"It takes a lot of careful planning to make a good extemporaneous speech."*

---

[21]"DATA DUMP": *Noun (Indefinite).* An indistinguishable string of seemingly unrelated facts in search of some overall meaning.

3. LOST IN THE FOG

The best framework for success, then, is always double-edged: (1) show the larger GENERAL meaning, and (2) amplify it with SPECIFIC details and examples.

Yet, even if you do show an overall meaning while blending all the separate facts, you can still blur the total focus . . . if you try cramming in so many extra details that the issue is overwhelmingly "fogged."

Too many details spoil the focus. They also make you more vulnerable to the twin jeopardies of counterattack and sidetracking by your adversaries.

Here's how: Every new (presumably weaker) argument that you introduce is also a new (more favorable) target for your opposition. More details also bring new distractions to shift attention away from your main, best arguments. So, don't try to cover *all* reasons and points in your favor (unless asked).

FOCUS means to target for the bull's-eye, rising above the "trivial many" and pinpointing the "vital few" points.[22] Ideally, for clearest focus, build your talk around no more than *three key points.*

A good professional talk keeps a narrow focus. On one hand, it reduces the general scope to the few most important ideas; at the same time, it develops these specific points in rich, full detail.

SUMMARY: Typically, for a talk to be well-focused and to work simply yet persuasively, it must:

(a) clarify each key point with one or more *concrete examples;*

(b) have a *unifying main theme,* structured into an overall idea pattern; and,

(c) concentrate primarily on the *few, most critical points* (usually, no more than three).

---

[22] According to R. Alec Mackenzie, the phrases "vital few" and "trivial many" (to distinguish the important from the unimportant) were originally used by Joseph M. Juran in his book, *Managerial Breakthrough* (New York: McGraw-Hill, 1964). See: Mackenzie, *The Time Trap* (New York: McGraw-Hill, 1975), pp. 52 & 179.

Chapter 11

PLAN A SCRIPT

> *"I always work from a script. Speaking
> extemporaneously is simply too exhausting."*
> -- Lee Iacocca

THE TWILIGHT ZONE

For many people, speaking to a group is a nightmare
from the Twilight Zone. They struggle helplessly as if
detached and adrift, while their real selves become
transformed (by alien forces?) into monstrous "Others" who
resemble them physically but who--inside their brains--act
uncontrollably slow-witted, boring, silly, or dumb.

True daredevils, of course, love on-the-spot decisions and
improvised victories. There's fresh joy in facing the
unknown, a challenge from the unexpected, a thrill in being
spontaneous. We all honor brave explorers like Columbus--
and ignore the fact that he ended up in the wrong place.

But, when speaking to a group, it's no adventure, it's an
excursion into disaster if you walk straight towards the
unexpected, willingly unprepared--that is, "wing it."

The truth is that shrewd professionals in all fields (ball
players, negotiators, opera singers, mayors) do meticulous
planning and infinite preparation, and for one main reason:
to control the outcome.

If possible, they'd prefer to eliminate the unpredictables
altogether. They've learned painfully that the more
unpredictable things are, the greater the risk. So their
watchword is: "(Please, God) No surprises."

A vital key for winning consistent results in your own presentations, then, is to control the outcome in advance as firmly as possible.

In other words, to raise your probability of success, you'll need a clear vision, going in, of how you want things to turn out--namely, a SCRIPT.

DEADLY DANGER #6 - **NO SCRIPT**

SCRIPTS: PRO AND CON

If a script offers so many advantages, why don't all speakers always create one?

People usually propose five arguments against making a script:

(1) ARGUMENT #1: *"It's worthless!"* . . . A script is a waste of time because life is too unpredictable; reality won't follow your script. After Murphy's Law strikes, the script is quickly forgotten anyway.

ANSWER: Your goal is not to control every detail--just the total situation and its final outcome. Even with a script, you'll still need flexibility to know when to discard your best-laid plans.

With no script, however, you have no road map, no step-by-step plan of attack, no navigation guidelines. How could you possibly control the outcome better with no plan at all?

(2) ARGUMENT #2: *"It's not spontaneous!"* . . . A truly good speaker is free, natural, unpremeditated. Having a script just doesn't feel right: it's like cheating; it's too inhibiting; it makes things too structured.

ANSWER: Of course you should be spontaneous, not so rigidly programmed that you can't respond that moment. But, are you really more spontaneous under-the-gun in tough surprises? Most people are least creative under pressure, so having a script actually frees you to be more spontaneous.

A script lets you think out your alternatives beforehand, coolly. And, if the unexpected strikes, you can always abandon the script and change your plan on the spot.

(3) ARGUMENT #3: *"It's too hard to follow!"* . . . A script is awkward and distracting: If you read it, you lose eye contact; if you depart from it, you lose your place. Either way, it separates you from your audience.

ANSWER: A script works tremendously well, if you know how to use it well. Being able to build and apply a script is a skill you can master. A script is not like an actor's monologue in a play, to be recited word-for-word; it's only a guide to give you an ideal but flexible scenario for the overall talk.

Most people who prefer to speak off-the-cuff, without forethought, use this unscripted approach as a habit rather than a well-chosen strategy. For consistent success, the habit of prior scripting must be cultivated.

(4) ARGUMENT #4: *"There's no time for it!"* . . . All our presentations get thrown together at the last minute, anyway--that's normal. You hardly have time to get the facts straight, much less to create a planned script.

ANSWER: Very few jobs actually require the atmosphere of ceaseless "fire drills." If *all* your talks are last-minute hurry-ups, something may be wrong (procrastination by you, or "management by crisis" in your organization).

It's a cliche', but true, that planning time saves time. Major foul-ups, on the other hand, usually cost extra time. Remember Meskimen's Law of Bureaucracy: "There's never enough time to do it right, but always time to do it over."

(5) <u>ARGUMENT #5</u>: *"It's not needed."* . . . Why make a script? You're a total master of the subject, right? You're experienced; you're comfortable thinking on your feet; you're always a winner; etc., etc. Who needs a script?

ANSWER: Are you absolutely, positively certain that you're that good? Life is full of amusing and perverse surprises for us speakers who get overconfident.
Why live dangerously, when a little planning can reduce uncertainty, head off the imponderables, and put you--not chancy Dame Fortune--back in control of your situation?

When it comes to structure and idea development in your talks, therefore, avoid unplanned spontaneity. Having no script at all does not make you more flexible; it makes you more vulnerable to greater chaos.

WHAT IS A SCRIPT?

Actually, a SCRIPT is nothing more than a projected model of how you'd like your talk to go.
Whether your presentation is a one-hour briefing, ten-minute sales pitch, or quick statement delivered on short notice, you should consider at least these items before you speak:

(a) What is your *desired outcome*?
(b) What *main idea* are you driving towards?
(c) What will you *say first*?
(d) What *specifics or examples* can you give?
(e) How can you *amplify* your message (handouts, etc.)?

These five items give you the heart of your strategy from which you'll build your basic SCRIPT. When you identify them in advance, you force yourself to think, respectively, of your:

(a) ACTION OBJECTIVE .... *"desired outcome,"*

(b) CLOSING .... *"main idea,"*

(c) OPENING .... *"say first,"*

(d) KEY POINTS .... *"specifics/examples,"*

(e) AUDIO-VISUAL AIDS .... *"amplify."*

If you have a well-thought-out plan and follow it, your presentation is much more likely:

* to come across as well-organized and professional,
* to stay focused on the main topic, and
* to lead your audience directly towards granting the results you desire.

HOW TO USE A SCRIPT

Here are a few practical tips on how to use a script:

WHEN TO READ

> Never read a speech verbatim, unless it's essential for some reason that you express it exactly word-for-word.

Examples of when a person might wisely read a text verbatim include:

(1) as an opening statement before a press conference or prior to Congressional testimony (to set the stage and tone for the subsequent give-and-take);

(2) if your boss (who orchestrates presentations by your team and hates "surprises") requires you to use a pre-screened, verbatim text;

(3) if you are a highly trained speaker (or actor), who can deliver a written text in a dynamic and natural way (as could, for example, President Ronald Reagan).

(4) when every word counts, and the slightest mistake or misunderstanding could be catastrophic (such as President John Kennedy's address to the nation--and implicitly to the leaders in the Kremlin--during the Cuban Missile Crisis in October 1962).

Otherwise, avoid reading a text verbatim: It tends to make you sound artificial, reduces your eye contact (since you're looking down to read every word), and gives your whole talk a "canned" feel.

WHEN TO MEMORIZE

> Never memorize any portion of a speech, word for word, except short passages of poetry or quotes used for dramatic effect.

As with verbatim texts, memorized talks tend to sound too mechanical, less natural, and thus insincere. If you ever lose your place while reciting a memorized piece, it's also very hard to regain sequence. (You often have to think all the way back to the beginning!)

WHEN TO USE NOTES

> Most speakers deliver their best presentations in their own words, talking from an outline script that gives *key words* and *highlights only*-- not a letter-perfect recital.

This KEY WORD script is usually the best strategy for most people in most situations . . . it keeps your thoughts on track while also keeping your delivery natural--especially if you become familiar with your script in advance by rehearsing.

If you're afraid you'll leave out vital points or must cite many numbers, you can capture these on a pre-arranged visual (for example, flipchart or overhead transparency). Then, you'll be confident they're available whenever you need them.

Even when you're an absolute master of the topic, it's always a good idea to sketch out a rough game plan of how you'd like a talk to go, in the form of written notes.

DO'S AND DON'T'S FOR NOTES

Here, in summary, are the "DO's" and "DON'T's" on how to prepare and use good NOTES:

DON'T . . .

   * Memorize the talk.
   * Read the speech verbatim.
   * Make notes too sketchy.
   * Make notes too detailed.
   * Look at your notes (instead of audience) too long.
   * Assume you talk better without notes.

DO . . .

   * Use key words/phrases only.
   * Write very BIG.
   * Write on one page-side only.
   * Highlight key points with color.
   * Draw yourself pictures (if it helps).
   * Number each page, in sequence.
   * Keep notes loose (not bound or stapled).
   * Record critical facts on a visual aid.
   * Practice with notes and aids beforehand.
   * Keep notes out-of-sight, inconspicuous.

HAVE A GAME PLAN

It may sound boring (if you consider a higher probability of success to be boring), but normally the less unexpected things that happen in your presentation, the better.

Of course, if you prefer the high-risk excitement of danger, if you need an uncertain outcome to make your blood run, then don't do your homework: Walk in cold.

But if you want the best chance at getting what you want: *Get prepared!*

The best way to assert control over the situation--to communicate your ideas clearly and persuasively and to channel the minds of others towards the fulfillment of your action objective--is by having a plan of execution for your entire presentation . . . that is, a script.

PRACTICAL EXAMPLE: *"Spellbinders"*

The author once used chapter 4 of this book[23] as the basis for a one-hour talk titled "Spellbinders." Its theme joined two questions:

(1) What is different about speakers who are great, charismatic, or famous?

(2) What useful lessons can everyday speakers learn from them?

The next page shows a condensed version of the actual notes used for this presentation, as an example of how a set of "key word" notes might look.

---

[23]"A Dozen Deadly Dangers," pp. 44-52.

SCRIPT FOR TALK: *"SPELLBINDERS"*

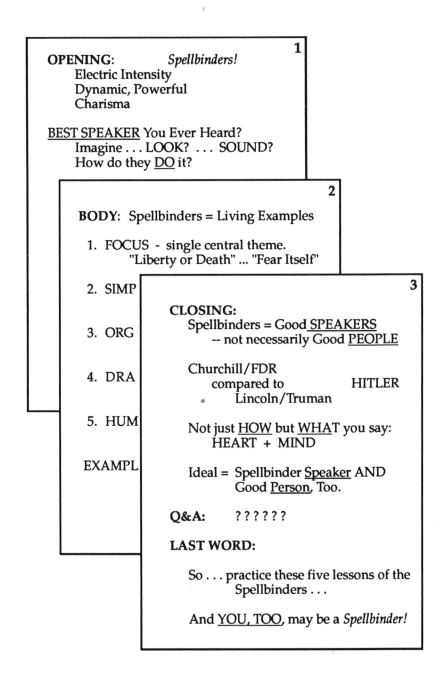

1

OPENING: *Spellbinders!*
    Electric Intensity
    Dynamic, Powerful
    Charisma

<u>BEST SPEAKER</u> You Ever Heard?
    Imagine . . . LOOK? . . . SOUND?
    How do they <u>DO</u> it?

2

BODY: Spellbinders = Living Examples

  1. FOCUS - single central theme.
        "Liberty or Death" ... "Fear Itself"

  2. SIMP

  3. ORG

  4. DRA

  5. HUM

  EXAMPL

3

CLOSING:
    Spellbinders = Good <u>SPEAKERS</u>
        -- not necessarily Good <u>PEOPLE</u>

    Churchill/FDR
        compared to   HITLER
            Lincoln/Truman

Not just <u>HOW</u> but <u>WHA</u>T you say:
    HEART + MIND

Ideal = Spellbinder <u>Speaker</u> AND
    Good <u>Person</u>, Too.

Q&A: ? ? ? ? ? ?

LAST WORD:

    So . . . practice these five lessons of the
        Spellbinders . . .

    And <u>YOU, TOO</u>, may be a *Spellbinder!*

Chapter 12

PUTTING YOUR IDEAS TOGETHER

*"True eloquence consists of saying all that
should be said, and that only."*
-- La Rochefoucauld

FIVE MOTIVES FOR SPEAKING

People normally choose to speak to a group for any of five basic motives:

1. To INFORM - to transmit information to others so they understand it quickly and accurately (examples: a Status Briefing, a Conference).

2. To PERSUADE - to go beyond explanation and get people to reach a decision or to take an action (examples: a Decision Briefing, a Sales Pitch).

3. To INSTRUCT - to impart specialized knowledge or practical skill to others as a teacher (examples: a How-To Lesson, an Orientation).

4. To ENTERTAIN - to bring amusement and diversion with fun for the sake of fun (examples: an After-Dinner Speech, a Story-Telling).

5. To INSPIRE - to reach people on a loftier level and stir them to bigger and greater things (examples: a Sermon, a Presidential Address).

Few speeches, of course, are pure models of only one of the five motives; most good talks are a mixture.

Some talks are flops precisely because the speaker speaks from only one motive and neglects the others.

Two classic examples of failure are:

* the tedious teacher who spouts boring facts (to INSTRUCT) but neither adds any human interest (to ENTERTAIN) nor sparks the students' desire to learn (to INSPIRE);

* the hard-line salesperson who goes straight for the sale (to PERSUADE) but skips the need to first answer all objections (to INFORM) or show how the product works (to INSTRUCT).

The best talks, therefore, are multi-dimensional--not telling us "just the facts," but also making the process enlightening, memorable, and enjoyable.

IT'S LOGICAL

In addition, most listeners find well-organized talks easier to understand and follow than haphazard ones. As a rule, the best speakers learn to communicate their ideas in the form of *idea patterns.*

An idea pattern is nothing more than a logical framework (a clear structure) that organizes the talk into a cohesive, unified whole. The pattern allows your audience to digest your ideas (which they are being fed, a bite at a time) with less effort: it makes everything fit together easier.

When you attempt to impose a logical framework on your material, however, you face a number of nagging questions and judgment calls: how to structure, how to position, how to simplify and clarify, and so on.

To help give you a head start (either towards putting together the whole talk, or for organizing one or more of its subdivisions), here are eight time-tested LOGICAL FRAMEWORKS you might choose from.

(1) QUESTION-ANSWER

This framework is built logically, from answers to one or more key questions. To create the structure, first identify: (a) all major questions you feel need to be answered, plus: (b) any extra questions your audience will likely want answered. Then, simply consolidate both lists of questions into one unified sequence (which becomes your QUESTION-ANSWER framework). For example:

[OPENING]   *"Today, we'll answer three basic questions: First, how did the project begin? Second, how has it evolved? And third, where does it stand today? . . .*

[BODY]   *"Let's start with how the project began . . .*
              "Now, let's see how it has evolved . . .
              "Finally, where does it stand today? . . .

[CLOSING]   *"So, in summary, we have now answered three basic questions . . . "*

(2) PROBLEM-SOLUTION

This framework first defines a problem, then explores its possible solutions. It may or may not actually advocate a single solution. Normally, the opening states the PROBLEM and the remainder of the talk addresses the SOLUTION(S). For Example:

[OPENING]   *"Our group's task was to assess the environmental, human, and cost impacts of using automated spray-painting by robots in our assembly process. This briefing will show the apparent benefits, define the problems foreseen, and propose acceptable solutions."*

The PROBLEM-SOLUTION approach is very common for people in technical or scientific fields--where briefings are often given to explain findings or results of a study, experiment, survey, or test.

(3) STATEMENT-PROOF

This framework is straightforward and bold: you make a direct assertion, then back it up with evidence. For example:

> [OPENING] *"The income tax system of the United States should be totally scrapped and rebuilt. Let me show you why ...."*
>
> *"I plan to vote in favor of the proposed bond referendum for new school construction. Here are the reasons. ..."*

In classical Greece, STATEMENT-PROOF was considered by Aristotle to be the basic pattern for all argument. This approach can be applied in most situations today, too (especially debates). However, its success depends upon the topic, audience, and skill of the speaker.

You should avoid the directness of the STATEMENT-PROOF framework if: (a) your audience is hostile, resistant, or very skeptical; or, when: (b) your evidence is weak or inconclusive. In those cases, you'll often need to "soften up" their minds and overcome their objections first, before you make your forthright statement.

(4) TIME SEQUENCE

The TIME SEQUENCE framework (also called "chronological order") is used to explain something in the exact same order as it happened or happens in real time. For example:

> *"Operating a personal computer starts with three easy steps: first, plug it in; second, turn it on; third, boot the system. Now, let's look, step by step, at how to get ready for word-processing and number-crunching."*

TIME SEQUENCE is especially good for topics like case studies, "day-in-the-life" vignettes, incident reports, and instructions (such as how to operate equipment, or how to fill out a form).

(5) GENERAL/SPECIFIC

GENERAL-to-SPECIFIC. The GENERAL-to-SPECIFIC framework starts with a general rule, law, or principle, whose meaning then grows richer and fuller through specific examples.

EXAMPLE: You might start by explaining a *general* model of economic behavior (for example, supply and demand), then show the concept in action at a *specific* business (say, The W&D Group, Inc., which manufactures and sells widgets and doodads).

SPECIFIC-to-GENERAL. Its counterpoint, the SPECIFIC-to-GENERAL framework, works in just the opposite way--by starting with one or more specific examples, then developing towards a general conclusion.

EXAMPLE: You might start with a *specific* incident of personal terror (say, a robbery or mugging), then move towards a *general* theme of the need for better crime prevention.

The GENERAL/SPECIFIC framework is especially well-suited for a religious talk or sermon. From a general tenet of faith (*"You are the salt of the earth"*), you might bring clarity and meaning by specific examples (of real people in everyday service to others today). Or, you might take a specific scriptural event (Abraham's willingness to sacrifice Isaac) to help explain its relevance to some larger general principle (wholehearted faith).

(6) CAUSE/EFFECT

The cause-and-effect pattern shows how or why one thing is a direct result of something else. Like the GENERAL/SPECIFIC framework, CAUSE/EFFECT may operate in either of two ways: (a) You can start with a Cause as your opening, then develop the Effect(s) in detail in the body; or (b) vice versa (Effect-Cause).

EXAMPLE (CAUSE—►EFFECT): Starting with the OPEC oil boycott in 1973 (CAUSE), you might show the impact upon a country when it is dependent upon foreign sources for a vital resource (EFFECT).

EXAMPLE (EFFECT—►CAUSE): Starting with the near-catastrophic accident at Three Mile Island nuclear plant in 1979, or the tragedy at Chernobyl in 1986 (EFFECT), you might talk about the dangers of ignoring "human factors" in the design of high-tech facilities (CAUSE).

(7) COMPARISON-CONTRAST

When you're presenting a choice between two or more alternatives (people, approaches, equipment), an excellent framework to use is COMPARISON-CONTRAST. The COMPARISON-CONTRAST gives your audience a detailed, side-by-side comparison and contrast of each alternative (such as showing the advantages/disadvantages of all key criteria or characteristics). For example:

"Alternative A has these advantages . . . but these
    disadvantages . . .
"Alternative B has these advantages . . . but these
    disadvantages . . .
"Alternative C has these advantages . . . but these
    disadvantages . . ."

COMPARISON-CONTRAST also makes a good visual display--especially in the form of a matrix chart showing the details of each choice side by side against all competitors. For example:

	Alt A	Alt B	Alt C
(a) Cost: under $1 million		X	X
(b) Radius: 300+ miles	X	X	X
(c) Fuel capacity: 250 gal's	X		
(d) Payload: 1 ton, minimum	X	X	X
(e) Recreation: HBO/CNN	X		

(8) TOPICAL GROUPING

If your topic is large and no other framework seems exactly right, you might try a TOPICAL GROUPING. The TOPICAL GROUPING is created simply by dividing the total topic into several smaller sub-topics, each of which is discussed in turn. As examples:

You might organize the topic, "Structure of the Federal Government," in terms of its three main sub-units: Executive, Legislative, and Judicial.

You might discuss "The Human Body" by looking at each of its major subsystems: skeletal, circulatory, digestive, etc.

TOPICAL GROUPING is a very common pattern and usually easy to create (all you do is subdivide the whole into smaller parts), but it's also less original and less compelling than other options. Given the choice, you might consider another framework first.

SPEAKING RHETORICALLY

In earlier periods, the art of speaking was called the "Art of Rhetoric." By studying other people's most effective speeches, orators learned to use a number of "rhetorical devices" and "figures of speech" to improve their own success.

Both Rhetorical Devices and Figures of Speech are simply powerful arrangements or uses of words that have been proven, over time, to strengthen the impact of a delivered speech.

With *Rhetorical Devices* (such as Antithesis), the words generally tend to keep their literal meanings, while *Figures of Speech* (such as Metaphor) tend more towards making poetic "plays" on words.

Here is a consolidated list of rhetorical devices and figures of speech that are most likely to make your next speech more colorful, powerful, and memorable.

(1) *ANALOGY* uses a likeness between two things to explain to an audience something unfamiliar (what they *don't* understand) in terms of something familiar (what they *do* know).
EXAMPLES:

> *"I'll explain cost-effective accounting in terms of managing your family budget."*

> *"Let's understand electrical current by relating it to water flow through the pipes of your house."*

ANALOGY is an especially valuable tool for explaining technical information to an audience that is at least partially *"non*-technical" (such as Bertrand Russell did by using a train to explain Albert Einstein's concept of relativity[24]).

(2) *SIMILE* makes a comparison between two things that are not the same and may not normally be considered alike. The key words that distinguish a simile are "like" or "as."
EXAMPLES:

> *"How like a winter hath my absence been."* [William Shakespeare]

> *"Thou hadst a voice whose sound was like the sea."* [William Wordsworth]

> *"Doing that is like shooting yourself in the foot."*

(3) *METAPHOR* (unlike SIMILE) makes a comparison directly, as an equation, by talking about one thing as if it were another.
EXAMPLES:

> *"An aged man is but a . . . tattered coat upon a stick."* [William Butler Yeats]

---

[24]Bertrand Russell, *The ABC of Relativity*, rev. ed., Felix Pirani, ed. (London: George Allen & Unwin, 1958). In addition, see: George Gamow, *One Two Three ... Infinity* (New York: Bantam, 1961), Part II, pp. 43-114.

"Clouds are hills in vapor, hills are clouds in stone."
[Rabindranath Tagore]

"My new computer is an absolute cream puff."

The principal difference between simile and metaphor is that SIMILE makes a comparison ("this is *like* that") while METAPHOR jumps directly into symbolism ("this *is* that"). Compare:

METAPHOR: "All the world's a stage."
SIMILE: "All the world is *like* a stage."

As with this example (from Shakespeare's *As You Like It*[25]), metaphor is often a prime tool of the poet as well as the orator.   Many phrases in our everyday speech are really similes and metaphors: *"She's crazy like a fox"*; *"my new car's a lemon."*

SYNEDOCHE is a specific kind of metaphor where a part symbolizes the whole or the whole a part--for example: *"To move that material, we're going to need more wheels* [i.e., transportation]."

Note that for figures of speech that show similarity (Analogy, Simile, or Metaphor), the "alikeness" of things compared must be easy to see, appeal to common sense, and be defensible.

(4) *PERSONIFICATION* is a figure of speech that attributes human characteristics to either inanimate objects, animals, or ideas.
EXAMPLES:

"Death be not proud." [John Donne]

"The White House said today that no tax increase was planned."

---

[25] Speech by Jaques, *As You Like It*, act II, scene vii, line 139.

METONYMY is personification that adapts a term closely associated with a person or object to symbolize that person/object itself--for example: *"They died defending the flag [i.e., the country]."*

(5) *REPETITION* is the technique of using the same phrase over and over, or of restating the same idea in more than one way.
EXAMPLES:

"Blessed are the poor in spirit . . .;
Blessed are those who mourn . . .;
Blessed are the meek . . .;
Blessed are they which do hunger and thirst after
righteousness . . . ." [the Sermon on the Mount][26]

"But Brutus says he was ambitious;
And Brutus is an honourable man;
* * *
Yet Brutus says he was ambitious;
And Brutus is an honourable man . . . ."
[Marc Antony, in *Julius Caesar*][27]

Repetition is powerful and should be used often in your speaking--not avoided, as some people believe. In fact, psychological research shows that repetition makes your ideas more memorable, for a longer time, even if the audience gets tired of hearing the same thing more than once. (That's why the exact same commercial seems to appear 14 times during the Super Bowl.)

But, isn't there a danger of diminishing returns, where repetition just "turns off" people? Yes--when you restate the obvious, when you become redundant, or when you sound patronizing or nagging.

In most presentations, though, your main point should be reinforced at least three times (at the beginning, middle, and end) and often even more (some psychologists suggest as many as 7 to 21 repetitions to insure retention).

---

[26]Matthew 5:3-5:11ff.
[27]William Shakespeare, *Julius Caesar*, act III, scene ii, lines 91-92, 98-99 (& 103-104).

So, variety may be the spice of life but repetition is the relish of the spoken word.

(6) *PARALLELISM* means to use identical patterns of syntax (phrases or sentence structures) to express ideas that are closely related--for instance:

PARALLEL: *"I came; I saw; I conquered."* [Julius Caesar, *Commentaries on the Gallic Wars*]

NOT PARALLEL: *"I came; I saw; and along the way we also did some conquering."*

Parallel construction is always a vital and powerful tool of oral communication: it makes your random ideas fit together better in the minds of your listeners.

If you introduce a numbered list of ideas (#1, #2, #3, and so on), be sure to identify all items in your list as you talk--not just the first few. In other words, don't make the confusing mistake of starting off by-the-numbers (1, 2, . . .), but then neglecting to number each later item ("Whoa," thinks the listener, "is this point 5 or maybe 6?"). Stay parallel and help your audience keep on track with you.

Parallel construction is stark and straightforward, so it may look less creative, but it's invariably effective and (unless you have a good reason for avoiding it) you should adhere to it rigidly.

(7) *ANTITHESIS* is a rhetorical balancing or contrast of one item against another. Since antithesis can be so effective, it's commonly used by speakers to capture memorable ideas in their oratorical addresses. Some of the most famous lines from speeches of the past are built from antithesis--for example:

"Not that I loved Caesar less, but that I loved Rome more." [Marc Antony, *Julius Caesar*]

"We will never negotiate out of fear, nor will we fear to negotiate." [John F. Kennedy]

You need not be an orator to use antithesis: you can use it (preferably in moderation) to bring force and clarity to your own talks, too.

EXAMPLES:

"Don't just think of the costs, think of the benefits."

"We can pay them now, or we can pay them later."

(8) *HYPERBOLE* is intentional overstatement for the sake of emphasis.

EXAMPLE:

"When tillage begins, other arts follow. The farmers therefore are the founders of human civilization."
[Daniel Webster]

As with metaphorical language, we often use such blustery exaggerations in everyday speech: *"That would never happen in a million years!"* Or: *"I'll die if I don't get that promotion!"*

Hyperbole, however, is an old-fashioned, out-of-style way of speaking and should be avoided unless you have a strong reason for using it. In an era when people are bombarded daily by overstated commercials and inflated advertising claims, you'll find the opposite of Hyperbole (namely, *UNDERSTATEMENT*) to be much more effective with a modern audience.

(9) *APOSTROPHE* is the device of addressing a people or personified abstractions as if they were present.

EXAMPLES:

"And, you, oh Pericles, what would you have to say about the state of things?"

"What would Tom Watson, Sr., think of this industry, if he were alive today?"

Like Hyperbole, Apostrophe should be used sparingly, if at all, by a modern speaker.

(10) *IRONY* is the use of words or statements carrying the opposite of their literal or intended meaning, such as in sarcasm, which is an everyday form of Irony: *"Oh, sure, we'd love to work overtime, Martha."*

Irony is invariably tricky and treacherous--especially when you intend it to be funny--because people often miss the irony, take you literally, and thus get confused or angry. Normally, clear communication and understanding are difficult enough between human beings without the added dangers of purposefully saying the opposite of what you mean.

To prevent potential backfires against yourself in your own talks, then, avoid Irony altogether and just talk straight.

(11) *RHETORICAL QUESTIONS* are questions posed for the audience to think about, but not answer out loud. As shown earlier (in Chapter 9), questions can be an excellent way to structure your talk, as well as to provoke thoughts and stimulate audience involvement.

Since the answer to a rhetorical question is assumed to speak for itself, the speaker normally lets each listener answer it silently for impact:

"Now, how can we turn this policy into action? Let's think about that, before we all vote 'yes.'"

On other occasions, the speaker may ask a rhetorical question, then offer his/her own answer to it:

"What is the worth of all [history]? The only guide to a man is his conscience; the only shield to his memory is the rectitude and sincerity of his actions." [Winston Churchill]

(12) *CLIMAX* is the arrangement of words, phrases, or clauses in a sequence of increasing impact, with the strongest element (the climax) coming last. Climax is powerful: it builds in rising intensity with a "punch line" effect at the end:

"We tried diplomacy, but it didn't work. We tried economic sanctions, but they didn't work, either. So, now we are forced to take military action."

THE HUMAN FACTOR

The best-laid foundation--of your structure, rhetorical devices, and figures of speech--will always be too weak to support your message if you neglect the still-all-important factor . . . the *people* in your audience.

A member of the U.S. Defense Department had the job of visiting foreign countries to discuss with their leaders what the American government could and couldn't provide as military aid.

The man who gave these briefings was troubled because he felt that, by the end of his presentations, his audiences were always hostile. He couldn't figure out why, because sometimes the news was bad, but sometimes good: "You'll get *more* than you asked for."

"How long do you talk in these presentations?" he was asked.

"Oh, about three hours or so," he replied.

"Three hours, huh? That's pretty long. How many question-and-answer periods do you have throughout?"

"None--well, not until the end. I always tell them to hold any questions until I'm finished. (I don't want to get off the track.)"

"I see. And how many breaks?"

"Breaks? Not any. If I give them a break, they might not come back!"

"So, let's see . . . you have them sit there for over three hours . . . without a break . . . and prevent them from asking any questions?"

"Yes, yes, yes . . . I see what you mean."

Do you see the point, too? A solid logical structure, built from an idea pattern, is important. But the logic that you give your presentation is not an abstract thing: to be truly effective, you must also fully consider the human factor.

Chapter 13

BUT FIRST . . . GETTING STARTED

"A journey of a thousand miles
Starts from beneath one's feet."

-- Lao Tsu

THE FIRST STEP

Many speakers suffer the torture of nervousness before (and often while) facing an audience. Others, however, face an even more paralyzing struggle beforehand--the "EMPTY PAGE" syndrome, which inhibits them from even *getting started* in their actual preparation.

Has it ever happened to you? A rush presentation is assigned and must be created by you, the speaker-to-be. You know you must prepare this talk but you put it off. Why can't you get "up" for it?

There's no option--the talk must be done. Yet, as the deadline closes in, the words and ideas stay frozen in your brain at an elusive standstill; they just refuse to flow. You *must* produce, but you *can't!*

So you sit and suffer under pressure, staring at that blank page (which, after an unpleasant half-hour or so, just stares back), and no progress is made except your own mental anguish and emotional turmoil. Sound familiar?

What's the problem? And how can you escape it?

A STARTING BLOCK

First, let's recognize that few people avoid doing the things they truly enjoy.

If you're invited to watch a vibrant rainbow from a distant beach, or swap funny stories with a longtime friend, or taste your favorite birthday cake, or share tender moments with your sweetheart . . . then, getting started will be easy.

If, on the other hand, you're working to organize your next oral presentation and it's the *opposite* of easy--you try to get started but it feels torturously hard, even impossible-- then maybe something is fundamentally wrong. Maybe you're the victim of disguised (and self-inflicted) procrastination.

Your mysterious "starting block" may be only an unspoken signal that, for whatever reasons, you really do not want to give this talk at all.

To help break your inertia, first do an attitude check. Ask yourself questions like:

(1) Do you secretly feel incompetent to talk on this subject right now?

(2) Have you been asked to defend a position that you, in fact, disagree with?

(3) Do you simply lack the fiery spark of enthusiasm for this particular topic?

Any "yes" answer to one of these questions and you've pinpointed an attitude that could be provoking your troubles in getting started.

INTENTIONAL DELAY

Incredibly, a few people actually claim they procrastinate on purpose and that such inaction is not only intentional but wise! They explain how they deliberately put a thing off until they *have* to do it--until the absolute last minute-- because (they say): "I work *best* under pressure."

However, most people who think they work best under high-tension, last-minute pressures are terribly wrong.

As mentioned in Chapter 1, all recent research shows that human beings operate at their "peak performance" level while in a state of alert relaxation.

Truly, the more we stay inwardly relaxed, the better we attain high-performance results.

So, what these "last-minute" performers have actually done is simply to form a bad habit . . . the habit of avoiding things until they can no longer be postponed and *must* be done, ready or not--as seen, for instance, in the frantic, tardy rush to file tax forms every April 15th.

What these last-minute dawdlers are saying, in other words, is not: "I work best under pressure," but really: "Under pressure, I *work!*"

THE LOST OUTLINE

Do you typically create your own talks with rapid ease or with a hard dose of grief?

If you seldom have trouble getting started--just now and then, for a few talks only--the thing that stops you could just be selective procrastination: you're somehow, at those moments, resisting the whole assignment itself.

On the other hand, if it's hard for you to get started often or even all the time, the most likely cause is either that you: (a) have limited experience in speaking to groups, or (b) have a past history of negative experiences that poisoned your attitude towards all stand-up talks, or (c) are using the wrong method (perhaps you lack a systematic approach).

In school days, most of us also found getting started to be a painful chore--especially if part of the product was the dreaded *outline.* Remember? Your homework assignment was to write a paper or talk. "Start with an outline," you were told. So, you diligently worked to make an outline first, but nothing much seemed to happen.

Still, an outline was clearly part of the assignment, so (even if you couldn't see things clearly) you struggled at it. But, hard as you tried, it wasn't working and time kept passing, running out, until finally . . . oh, forget it!--you just wrote the paper and copied the outline *afterwards,* because good old hard-nosed Ms. McGillicutty had demanded: *"Don't forget your outline!"*

(Never have so many students suffered so painfully for so long as when trying to make an outline!)

HOW TO GET STARTED

If you've recognized yourself in this hard-luck scenario, then here are seven specific suggestions to help you overcome the problem of "Getting Started":

1. *ACCEPT THE INEVITABLE.*

People sometimes respond to a new challenge in a human, predictable way . . . they deny the problem exists. It's as if a task will disappear if only we ignore it well enough. Unfortunately, though, in the day-to-day world of business, unsolved problems seldom go away blithely; they linger or even get worse.

You can't escape briefings or talks, either, by ignoring them. Time keeps passing and getting shorter, eventually making the final pressures worse. So, to get started, accept the inevitable . . . you're going to go through with it and make a presentation: don't fight the problem--start making a solution.

2. *TAKE ACTION.*

Likewise, inaction breeds inaction. Procrastination feeds on itself and inertia takes hold stronger, the longer you avoid that first step. Once you accept the inevitable, one of the best cures for procrastination is to take action immediately-- almost any action.

Even when you can't get started exactly right, do not wait--*do* something, anything! Write your closing, plan the opening, create a visual, analyze your audience, build some notes, find a logical framework, or something else. Never mind how you feel. Don't wait for inspiration. Move into action and you'll soon fall into the swing of a fresh momentum.[28]

---

[28] A parallel viewpoint is seen in Morita therapy, which suggests that in life we should just "see the next thing that needs to be done" and do that. See the books of David K. Reynolds: *Playing Ball on Running Water* (New York: Quill, 1984), *Even in Summer the Ice Doesn't Melt* (New York: Quill, 1986), and *Water Bears No Scars* (New York: Quill, 1987).

3. AVOID PERFECTIONISM.

One way we all keep ourselves from getting started is by striving for idealized "perfection." Since true perfection is impossible, you're doomed to fail before you start (CATCH-22)--so why begin at all? You haven't taken the first step but you're already demoralized: you sit and suffer or just waste time.

Paradoxically, the perfectionist is *less* efficient and *less* effective than his/her colleagues, whose personal standards appear slightly lower, because they've figured out the truth: perfection is impossible . . . excellence is usually good enough.

A big step towards getting started, then, is to abandon your perfectionism: risk being imperfect. Just jump in and do the job. You'll find you *can* get started and--to your surprise--your work's quality will be very good, too.

4. DIVIDE AND CONQUER.

If you've had trouble getting started, make your first step a small one, based on a time-tested technique for effective time management--Divide and Conquer. The basic idea is that you can make any large, complex task more manageable by dividing it into smaller, simpler sub-tasks.

This approach has been called the "salami" technique (first, cut the big salami into smaller slices) or the "swiss cheese" method (first, punch holes in the large cheese, then work outward from there).[29]

By any other name, the principle is a sound management tool. It was adapted into decision-making processes such as Gantt charting, critical path method (CPM), and program evaluation and review technique (PERT), and is vital in major, complex challenges like the building of Polaris submarines or transporting of human beings from Earth to the moon and back.

---

[29]These tasteful time management approaches are suggested by Edwin C. Bliss, in *Getting Things Done* (New York: Charles Scribner's Sons, 1975, pp. 84-85) for "salami"; and Alan Lakein, in *How to Get Control of Your Time and Your Life* (New York: Signet, 1973, pp. 100-108) for "swiss cheese."

When "blocked" from starting your next talk or briefing, try applying the same idea . . . just divide your full feast of ideas into smaller, bite-sized pieces; then, stir the tidbits together into a tasteful blend that gets your points across effectively.

And once you've started on that first small step, be sure not to stop; just keep working, accomplishing each sub-task one at a time until you've finished.

5. *SET INTERIM DEADLINES.*

As you're dividing the task, also think about the time factor. How long do you have until you meet your audience face-to-face: a month, two weeks, ten minutes? Given "x" amount of time between now and then, what must be accomplished by *when*? You needn't draw up a total schedule, but you should at least identify the key milestones, with interim deadlines.

These self-imposed deadlines will help you get started in two ways: (1) as a "kick-in-the-pants," to let you know quickly if you're already behind the curve; and, (2) as a positive reinforcer, to give you intermediate feedback while you fulfill the steps along the path towards completion.

6. *BE CREATIVE.*

If you can't get started, maybe it's because you're trying to organize your topic by thinking in the wrong way: you're being too logical! Too many people firmly believe that there's only one approved way to build an outline, and thus they deny their natural creativity.

However, you have the power to think in other, startling ways besides conventional logic. In the next chapter, you'll learn ways to organize your thoughts by using an alternative, creative method (like "brainstorming"). These methods can be superior to traditional, analytical logic--especially in helping you get started. So, when you somehow can't get started, maybe you need a fresh boost of creativity.[30]

---

[30]For a fresh look at creativity and original thinking, see: David Campbell, *Take the road to creativity and get off your dead end* (Niles, Ill.: Argus, 1977), and any book by Edward de Bono.

7. HAVE A SYSTEM.

Getting started is a harder burden if, every time you begin again, you must reinvent the wheel. If you learn a careful, step-by-step, systematic approach instead, you won't have as hard a time beginning--it becomes more habitual, less difficult.

Once you have a dependable system, you'll find getting started to be more natural and to come quicker.

CHANGE YOUR HABITS

Everyone at times encounters a tough assignment where things don't magically flow and getting started is painful agony. If you *always* struggle to get started, however, you should know that your condition is not inevitable--in truth, it may be only an emotional habit.

Most good speakers do *not* writhe in pain to produce a top-flight talk: they've learned better, smarter ways of working.

So, if you suffer or procrastinate every time you're called upon to make a presentation, check your behavior patterns: it could just be a bad habit. With deep desire and hard effort, you can break your old choking habits, and learn to get started with ease.

Chapter 14

BRAINSTORMS AND FLURRIES

*"Thinking often proceeds as drift
and waffle and reaction."*
-- Edward de Bono

THE OUTLINE PROCESS

Let's suppose you're struggling to organize a talk, using a conventional "outline" approach in the time-tested pattern of:

```
I.                          |    II.
        A.                  |    III.
        B.                  |
              1.            |              etc. . . .
              2.            |
                    a.      |
                    b.      |
```

When you build a traditional outline this way, the end-product flows onto your page from left to right, so it looks like a consecutive sequence (1-2-3-4), from start to finish.

What you're actually doing, however, is dividing a whole into its parts. To choose items "I," "II," and "III," you must really slice the total topic into three smaller sub-topics:

I
II
III

Likewise, as you move from item "I" to items "A" and "B," you're just subdividing the larger "I" into two smaller pieces (I.A and I.B):

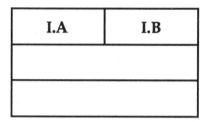

On and on, this process of subdivision continues as far as the outline is carried, to ever-smaller and lower levels:

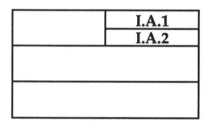

This realization explains why teachers always insist that if an outline has a "1" it also needs a "2" . . . because you cannot *divide* anything into just one part.

This traditional method of outlining is very logical. It is also (most of us are taught) the official, "correct" way to outline.

For many people, however, it is actually this demanding, logical pattern that seems to freeze their minds and get them slowed down, hung up, and deadlocked so they can't get started.

Yet why, when conscientious people try building outlines the good old-fashioned way, does logic so often seem to fail or abandon us? Perhaps our thinking itself makes it so.

Let's realize that this traditional method of outlining is what's now called a "*left*-brain" (i.e., highly analytical) process. This fact shows why outlines are so often a pain.

LEFT BRAIN, RIGHT BRAIN

Recently, scientists and researchers have learned new, remarkable things about the human brain.[31]   One of the most important findings is that people don't think in just one way. Each of us thinks in at least two different prime modes of thought: (1) logical, and (2) intuitive.

(1) The *logical* mode is analytical and specialized. It is systematic, deductive, linear, self-conscious. Typically, it reasons from the general to the specific, working things out step by step. Such logical thinking is used by an engineer to do mathematical calculations or by an architect to render a final blueprint.

(2) The *intuitive* mode is creative and holistic. It is organic, inductive, lateral, subconscious. Typically, it reasons from the specific to the general, often jumping to the solution in one leap. Such intuitive thinking is used by a musician to compose a new song or by an artist to create a fresh vision on canvas.

Within the brain's two halves, the logical mode operates in the *left* hemisphere and the intuitive mode operates in the *right* hemisphere. (At least, that's so for right-handed people: for left-handers, there is evidence that the reverse is likely true.)

For convenience, people talk about these differences in shorthand, saying that logical thinking is "LEFT brain" and intuitive thinking is "RIGHT brain."

Everyone has the capacity to use both modes of thinking, and everyone does--as when the architect thinks up a wholly new design for a building (RIGHT brain) or when the musician balances his checkbook (LEFT brain).

---

[31]Foremost in the study of split-brain theory is Roger Sperry, who won the Nobel Prize for medicine in 1981. For more on "whole-brain" thinking, see: Jacquelyn Wonder and Priscilla Donovan, *Whole-Brain Thinking* (New York: William Morrow, 1984). For whole-brain applications, see: Betty Edwards, *Drawing on the Right Side of the Brain* (Los Angeles: J.P. Tarcher, 1979), and Gabriele Lusser Rico, *Writing the Natural Way* (Los Angeles: J.P. Tarcher, 1983). Also, the works of Edward de Bono are always worthwhile-- especially see his *New Think* (New York: Basic Books, 1968).

Each person also tends, by preference or habit, to favor one mode over the other. Thus, virtually everyone's thinking style tends to be dominated by either the logical or the intuitive.

The ultimate goal is, of course, for all of us to think flexibly--using both modes as complementary tools, either of which we can rely on, depending on the needs of the moment. In other words, we should be WHOLE-brain thinkers.

All right, but how is all this "Left-Brain, Right-Brain" stuff relevant to you when you're plodding away, hoping to crank out a nice, workable outline for your own next talk?

THE PARALYSIS OF LOGIC

As we've seen, the traditional outline is intentionally *analytical*--it shapes your disorderly ideas into a unified form by dividing a whole into smaller pieces.

That's fine when it works . . . but what if, in the first place, you can't yet see that larger whole? What if, in your mind's eye, your overall topic has no divisible form, no boundaries yet: it is only a nebulous, inchoate blur of isolated fragments?:

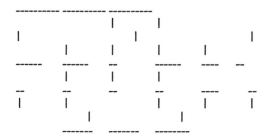

How can you divide something if you don't yet know its scope, its outer limits?

Here's where the conventional approach often fails to get your outline built. "Left-brained" logic not only doesn't get you moving, it even drives you into a worse, more frustrating paralysis . . . you cannot subdivide and organize your topic, it seems, until you've already organized it!

ESCAPE FROM LOGIC

Analytical logic is just one way to think, and sometimes it's actually the wrong tool for the task. So, to break a mental logjam, become creative and think backwards: Rather than working deductively from general to specific (i.e., LEFT-brain), try going inductively from specific to general (i.e., RIGHT-brain).

In other words, instead of logic, try something else. Quit struggling to divide an unknown whole by traditional outlining. Instead, try uncovering those things already known by creative brainstorming.

In particular, when no logical framework (such as Time Sequence or Question-Answer) is immediately obvious, you can use Brainstorming as a way to create a good organic structure for your talk, or simply to get started.

BRAINSTORMING

You know the term "Brainstorming" already as a group process for creative thinking--to unshackle people's minds from the inhibitions of everyday thinking and stimulate the free flow of fresh ideas (no matter how crazy or impractical they may at first seem).[32]

A spin-off of group Brainstorming can also be applied by one person, working alone, and can help you quickly organize a difficult topic for an upcoming oral presentation. This alternative way of organizing has definite advantages:

1. You *get started immediately.* No time is spent doing logical thinking first, so no time is wasted by agonizing.

2. You may discover a *more creative* approach to the topic. The process often gets you moving in new, fresher ways.

---

[32]The term "Brainstorming" was first introduced, and the concept systematized, by Alex Osborne in the 1940's for the advertising industry. See his book, *Applied Imagination* (New York: Charles Scribner's Sons, 1953).

3. For many people, it's a *more natural* process, closer to the way they really think.

4. By starting with the known and building outward, you sometimes get *a better outline,* which fits together without serious revision.

HOW TO "BRAINSTORM" AN OUTLINE

Having proclaimed its virtues, let's examine the five steps of Brainstorming when used to create a major outline:

Step #1 - BRAINSTORM
Step #2 - CLUSTER
Step #3 - LABEL
Step #4 - REFINE
Step #5 - ORDER

We'll now look at each step in detail . . .

STEP #1 - BRAINSTORM

First, get yourself into a calm, relaxed state of mind (preferably alone in a quiet room), with writing materials handy, and get ready to concentrate.

Then focus your attention and don't hesitate; don't even think--act! Immediately, just write the first thing about your topic that comes to mind . . . not complete sentences but words, phrases, names, numbers. Anything!

Also, don't censor yourself. Let every idea come by stream of consciousness, no matter what. You're trying to break the inertia, to build momentum. So first, write it *all* down. Even if it seems irrelevant or off-the-wall, write it.

Your goal is to get all the information you can out of your head and onto paper, quickly. Never mind how the next thing relates to the last. Just let it flow and keep doing it until you run out of ideas.

APPLICATION (Step #1): Suppose you plan to make a 20-minute talk on the topic, "Investing in the Stock Market," and decide to create it by using Brainstorming.

By doing a quick BRAINSTORM, you might spawn a number of various items, like:

Stocks	New York Stock Exchange	
Risk	NASDAQ	Safety
Common/Preferred		Bonds
Blue Chips	Mutual Funds	Amex
P-E Ratio	Over-the-Counter	Cost
Options	Dividends	Exxon
IBM	Interest	Yield
General Motors	Price Appreciation	

These items, produced by Brainstorming, next become the building blocks from which you'll fashion your presentation.

STEP #2 - CLUSTER

Next, look at all the items you've generated. (You'll often be happily surprised at how much material you've thought of and written.)

In Step #2, you start to organize this "brainstormed" information by finding meaningful relationships: You CLUSTER the data, assembling all items into fewer, smaller groupings.

Instead of leaving all items clumped together in one all-inclusive group (called, for instance, "Investing in the Stock Market"), your goal here is to sort the pieces into three, four, five, or more related groups.

At this point, logic will likely urge you to pigeonhole immediately--to start with preconceived headings (say, "MARKETS") and work to fit the separate items under these headings. For example:

MARKETS .... New York Stock Exchange
Amex
Over-the-Counter

Contrary to your instincts, you'll find it's best *not* to start with general categories but rather with specific items. Use your gut feel and intuition--just *feel* that certain items fit together and join them without any categorizing.

For instance, grasp directly (without bothering to say how) that a relationship exists among the items "New York Stock Exchange," "Amex," and "Over-the-Counter," and combine them for now as an unspecified cluster: *New York Stock Exchange . . . Amex . . . Over-the-Counter.*

For the moment, in other words, resist giving them a label. For now, keep thinking in your creative, uncategorical (RIGHT-brain) way.

APPLICATION (Step #2): For your talk on "Investing in the Stock Market," your CLUSTER step might result in groups like these:

New York Stock Exchange	Blue Chips
Amex	General Motors
NASDAQ	IBM
Over-the-Counter	Exxon
	Mutual Funds
Stocks	
Bonds	Safety
Options	Cost
Common/Preferred	Yield
	P-E Ratio
Dividends	Risk
Interest	
Price Appreciation	

```
┌─────────────────────────────────────┐
│                                     │
│          STEP #3 - LABEL            │
│                                     │
└─────────────────────────────────────┘
```

After you've clustered all items, look carefully at each cluster and (as Step #3) ask yourself this question: "What is the unifying relationship among these items?" Once you see a unifying theme, find a precise word or phrase (a LABEL) that somehow captures that relationship and write a label to identify each group.

APPLICATION (Step #3): For the talk on "Investing in the Stock Market," each of your clusters might now be given a LABEL as follows:

New York Stock Exchange.......... *MARKETS*
Amex
NASDAQ
Over-the-Counter

Safety.................... *INVESTMENT FACTORS*
Risk
Cost
Yield
P-E Ratio

Stocks..............................*ALTERNATIVES*
Bonds
Options
Common/Preferred

Blue Chips........................ *SPECIFIC ISSUES*
General Motors
IBM
Exxon
Mutual Funds

Dividends............ *RETURN-ON-INVESTMENT*
Interest
Price Appreciation

```
┌─────────────────────────────────┐
│                                 │
│        STEP #4 - REFINE         │
│                                 │
└─────────────────────────────────┘
```

You've now brainstormed a healthy amount of information on your topic (Step #1), grouped it into clusters (Step #2), and labeled the clusters to show how they fit together (Step #3). These clusters will form the sub-sections (key points) of your talk's BODY, when finally presented.

If you haven't already done so by this point, you should also:

(a) Capture your main idea in a capsule <u>FOCUS POINT</u>--which becomes the heart of your CLOSING. For example: *"Investing in the stock market can be fun and rewarding--if you are smart, careful, and can afford the risk."*

(b) Find an appealing way to grab the attention of your audience up-front as a <u>LINK</u>--which becomes the heart of your OPENING. For example: *"Do you now invest in the stock market? If not, would you like to?"*

The Brainstorming process thus starts intuitively, then moves gradually more and more towards logic. At this point in building your outline, you must shift your thinking fully back into logical mode and analytically *refine* all the random information you've developed so far.

Specifically, you'll now improve what you've already done by performing any or all of these six major functions:

(1) *ADD* anything that was overlooked earlier or forgotten.

(2) *OMIT* anything that now seems irrelevant, unnecessary, beyond the scope, or off-the-wall.

(3) *SHIFT* items from one cluster into another, where they appear to fit better.

(4) *DUPLICATE* items to be discussed under more than one sub-topic.

(5) *COMBINE* two or more items that cover the same or a unified idea.

(6) *DIVIDE* a too-large cluster or item into two or more smaller ones.

APPLICATION (Step #4):   As you REFINE your talk, "Investing in the Stock Market," you might do the following:

ADD...the names of more securities (*AT&T, Johnson and Johnson*, others) to SPECIFIC ISSUES.

OMIT.....*Common vs. Preferred* from the ALTERNATIVES cluster, to reduce the talk's scope to fit the allotted time.

SHIFT......*Mutual Funds* out of SPECIFIC ISSUES and into ALTERNATIVES.

DUPLICATE...*Mutual Funds* (instead of Shifting) and treat it both in SPECIFIC ISSUES and in ALTERNATIVES.

COMBINE.......*Over-the-Counter* and *NASDAQ* into one sub-group within EXCHANGES.

DIVIDE...*Bonds* (under ALTERNATIVES) into more specific sub-topics (U.S. Treasury Bonds, Corporate Bonds, Municipal Bonds).

```
┌─────────────────────────────────────┐
│           STEP #5 - ORDER            │
└─────────────────────────────────────┘
```

Once all clusters (and items inside) are refined, you must set the final sequence of ideas before you deliver the talk to your audience. Step #5, therefore, is to ORDER the information.

First, count the total number of clusters, then block out a planning format with positions for that many numbers. For example, for a talk with five sub-topics, the format (including opening and closing) would look like this:

OPENING
1 -
2 -
3 -
4 -
5 -
CLOSING

Now, to order the sequence of ideas in the talk's BODY (points 1 through 5, in this example), ask yourself exactly why you'll be speaking to this audience--to persuade or merely to inform? (For help, review your written-down Action Objective and Audience Analysis.)

Typically, the order of sub-topics in your talk will be different for PERSUASION sequence versus INFORMATION sequence.

PERSUASION SEQUENCE

If you're speaking to *persuade*, the position of greatest impact in the BODY will be at the end. So, find your best, strongest "bottom-line" point and put it *last* in the BODY, with a tie-in to the CLOSING.

Then, find your second-strongest point (which should grab the audience's attention, set up the coming argument, and dovetail with the OPENING), and place this point *first* in the BODY.

APPLICATION (Step #5-Persuasion): Let's look again at the talk on "Investing in the Stock Market." You'll recall that the sub-topics are: MARKETS, INVESTMENT FACTORS, SPECIFIC ISSUES, ALTERNATIVES, and RETURN-ON-INVESTMENT.

Suppose you intend to make a direct argument in favor of investing in common stocks. Which of these topics would then support your point best?

Probably it's RETURN-ON-INVESTMENT, to emphasize the benefits of regular interest or dividend income plus the potential for price appreciation. If RETURN-ON-INVESTMENT looks like your "bottom line," you'll place it *last* in the BODY (position 5).

Then, which topic would grab their attention and set up your argument best? Perhaps it's SPECIFIC ISSUES, where you might choose an attractive security that has recently made outstanding, well-publicized gains in the current market.

So, you block in SPECIFIC ISSUES as your "grabber" *first* in the BODY (position 1). At this point, therefore, the planning format for your talk on the Stock Market looks like this:

| OPENING |
1 - *SPECIFIC ISSUES* ("grabber")
2 -
3 -
4 -
5 - *RETURN-ON-INVESTMENT* ("bottom-line")
| CLOSING |

If you were arguing *against* investment in the market, on the other hand, you'd likely choose different sub-topics for these positions. You might, for example, put INVESTMENT FACTORS *last* in "bottom-line" position (and emphasize the risks), and keep SPECIFIC ISSUES *first* as a grabber--but now portray a horror story about some volatile stock that went kaput or a company that went bankrupt.

INFORMATION SEQUENCE

Occasionally, you'll be speaking only to *inform*. Your main objective is simply to get facts across clearly with no persuasion whatsoever required (or so it may appear).

Then and only then, it may be preferable to use the inverted pyramid--to position your bottom-line point *first* in the BODY. In this case, your second-strongest point should come *last*, so the BODY still delivers a strong final note.

The inverted pyramid is frequently good for writers but seldom for speakers. It is recommended only when you have a solid reason to prefer it (since persuasion--whether you realize it or not--is almost always a silent factor in every presentation).

APPLICATION (Step #5-Information): Suppose your talk on the Stock Market is purely educational. You'll explain the market, and have no desire to influence anyone to invest or not to invest.

Your bottom-line point (put *first*, in position 1) might be MARKETS. You could open by describing stocks and markets, and how they operate. Your wrap-up point (put *last*, in position 5) might be ALTERNATIVES. You could mention where people invest, how to track values, or who to seek for help.

[Continued Page 142]

[*Continued: APPLICATION, Step #5-Information*]

Thus, we get:

| OPENING |
1 - *MARKETS* ("bottom-line")
2 -
3 -
4 -
5 - *ALTERNATIVES* ("wrap-up")
| CLOSING |

THE REST OF THE BODY

After you've set the first and last points of the BODY, you won't need to keep inching towards the middle from both ends (from the OPENING down and the CLOSING up). Usually, you'll see a logical sequence for the leftover points and the rest of the body will track very clearly.

APPLICATION (Step #5-Body): For "Investing in the Stock Market," you might block the remaining clusters into the BODY in this sequence:

. . .
2 - *MARKETS*
3 - *ALTERNATIVES*
4 - *INVESTMENT FACTORS*
. . .

and your overall format is complete.

The structure for your talk on "Investing in the Stock Market" is now done.

THE FINISHED TALK

If you've chosen the persuasive approach, the sequence of your entire talk might look like this:

"INVESTING IN THE STOCK MARKET"

OPENING: *"Do you invest in the stock market?*
If not, would you like to?"

  1 - SPECIFIC ISSUES: Companies for growth/dividends
     IBM, Apple Computer, AT&T - technology
     Johnson & Johnson, Exxon - basic business
     Blue Chips
     Mutual Funds (esp. for small investors)

  2 - MARKETS: Where to buy stocks?
     New York Stock Exchange
     American Exchange
     Over-the-Counter (NASDAQ)

  3 - ALTERNATIVES: Ways to invest?
     Stocks (Common/Preferred)
     Bonds
     Other (Options, Warrants, Commodities)

  4 - INVESTMENT FACTORS: Things to Consider
     Safety/Risk
     Yield
     Cost (P-E Ratio)

  5 - RETURN-ON-INVESTMENT: Payoffs! ($$$)
     Dividends
     Interest
     Price Appreciation

CLOSING: *"Investing in the stock market can be fun and*
rewarding--if you are smart, careful, and can
afford the risk."

BY ANY OTHER NAME

Do you recognize what you now have?--

(pardon the expression):

. . . an OUTLINE.

It's an outline with a difference, however, for this one was developed unlike the traditional approach. Rather than starting with logical subdivision, this outline was started by creative brainstorming (step #1), and only later (steps #4 and #5) was logical analysis used to refine and order the final product.

Does "brainstorming" your outlines really work?

Yes, absolutely. Many happy people find this approach not only gets them moving, it also gives them a superior, more organic structure than the ordinary way of outlining.

Nevertheless, the approach is not the only (nor for some, the best) way to create an outline; it's simply an alternative, when you need it.

But it's a fresh approach and often (in the BRAINSTORM step itself), you'll think of so many things you hadn't before that sometimes the brainstorm "runs away" with you, and you're astounded at the wealth of information you have.

So, when you must organize a major talk in a hurry, if you know *anything* about the topic, you should now be able to get started and finished fast: just jump in, don't ruminate, take action, start writing, and follow the five steps.

With systematic BRAINSTORMING as a tool, you should never again sit in agony, staring at an empty page, trying to get started. You can get started painlessly every time.

Chapter 15

Q&A STRATEGY: TEN COMMANDMENTS

"Ask me no questions, and I'll tell you no fibs."
                                        -- Oliver Goldsmith

TRIAL BY FIRE

Of all danger spots in a presentation, the one most feared by most speakers is the Question-&-Answer (or "Q&A") period.

Given enough time, almost anyone can create, rehearse, and deliver a polished, well-structured talk. But the Q&A is unrehearsed and unpredictable: it introduces new on-the-spot threats . . . mainly, fear and uncertainty over the unexpected.

As we all know, it's usually during the Q&A period when the speaker really begins to feel like a moving target.

Nevertheless, it needn't be that way. The Q&A can be the most valuable part of your whole presentation--the time when you really sell your ideas best.

You should, in fact, actually *welcome* the Question-and-Answer period, since it's your best opportunity to engage minds with the audience and learn without guessing what they're really thinking.

HANDLING QUESTIONS: TEN COMMANDMENTS

Here, to help you master the art of answering questions, are ten basic principles for success at Q&A:

COMMANDMENT #1: *ANTICIPATE*

The best defense against tough, unexpected questions is to *expect* them beforehand ("fore-warned is fore-armed") and be ready for them.

So, in advance try to identify every tough question that might be asked, then plan a good answer for each--even if it's only: "I'm sorry but I don't know."

Don't memorize exact, word-for-word answers. That would be phony and ineffectual. Just give prior thought to each hard question and find a basic theme or strategy for your response. You want to avoid blurting out some foolish top-of-the-head answer in the rough, high-pressure atmosphere of the Q&A itself.

Proper anticipation gets you ready in two ways: (1) If that hard question is asked, you'll already have a well-considered reply; and, (2) even if it's never asked, you'll still walk in feeling more confident and relaxed because you're ready for the imagined worst.

COMMANDMENT #2: *LISTEN*

Before you speak, listen! Be absolutely certain that you understand the question. If necessary, repeat it, reword it, or ask the questioner to restate it.

Listen with all your senses, too: Watch body language; hear tone of voice. In every way, catch the real point of the question.

Don't interrupt and start answering too soon, either-- unless it's clearly just a "windbag" tirade and not a true question. First, listen: it may *not* be the usual question you think (to which you'd automatically give some standard answer); it might be different.

COMMANDMENT #3: *BE BRIEF*

Make it a habit to give short, crisp answers to most questions. The more you know or care about a subject, the greater you'll be tempted to give wordy over-explanations. But save your words.

Just answer each question directly, concisely, and to the point. Then stop talking. If they want more, let them ask a follow-up.

Also, stay off your soapbox. Don't spin off a question to make a speech. Most audiences will appreciate your quiet restraint and it may keep you out of trouble, too--since (like a suspect on the witness stand) you don't want to open a fresh can of worms by saying too much.

COMMANDMENT #4: *TALK STRAIGHT*

Go directly to the gist of the question. Truly answer it as best you can. Don't play games. If the question confuses you, ask for a clarification. If it's ambiguous, ask: "Do you mean [this] or [that]?"

Avoid those round-about circumlocutions (typically heard from guests on TV-panel forums), which evade the point, skirt the issue, or even answer a question that was never asked. For example:

QUESTION: *"Senator, do you think a tax increase will be required to balance the Federal budget?"*

UN-STRAIGHT NON-ANSWER: *"Larry, I feel the American people deserve the right to economic freedom without undue restraint from government. Our nation now faces the urgent need today to budget for the challenges of tomorrow. Although we can expect foreign competition, we must continue to practice internal fiscal restraint. Consequently, I am confident that, if we work together as a nation, we can solve this important tax problem and our great democracy will prevail."*

FOLLOW-UP: *"I see. Uh, was that a 'yes' or a 'no'?"*

In Q&A, if you absolutely must give a long explanation, state the "bottom-line" answer first--then, explain in detail. For example:

"I don't think so, Larry. Let me explain why . . ."

COMMANDMENT #5: *BE RESPONSIVE*

A successful Q&A often allows for energetic give-and-take. You must be willing to clarify your answers and have two-way involvement with the group. Let people ask follow-up questions if they desire. Be willing to say, "That's a good question"--*if* you sincerely mean it.

Be responsive not only to the question, but also to the person who asked it. In particular, keep eye contact with your questioners: you must "read" their reactions, to be sure they've grasped your answer.

If you aren't sure whether you've been understood, don't silently wonder--ask them directly: "Does that answer your question?"

COMMANDMENT #6: *GIVE SPECIFICS*

When you answer questions, talk in concrete language: in facts and figures, names and numbers, not abstract platitudes nor vague generalities. Be specific!

Remember that MEANING arises best from the juxtaposition of both (a) the *general* relationship of a set of facts, and (b) the *specific* facts themselves, such as:

GENERAL:	SPECIFIC:
"The initial outcome of our market testing was very encouraging."	*"We project a potential sales volume of more than twenty million."*

If you answer a question with a generalization, always back it up immediately with a phrase like: "for example," "that is," "for instance," or "such as"--followed by hard specifics that amplify your point.

Likewise, be careful to relate any answer of isolated facts or random details to a larger context--to the main issue or big picture. Specifics alone, without a unifying theme, are just as meaningless as a bald generality.

COMMANDMENT #7: *ADMIT YOUR GAPS*

Your best approach to Q&A is positive, self-confident, and not apologetic. The attitude is: "I'm ready; send in the lions."

But should you ever apologize? Yes, of course . . . when you make an obvious, perilous mistake--by numbers that don't add up, a mispronunciation that confuses, or even a plain misstatement of fact--you must plead guilty.

Even then, don't grovel--just admit your mistake in a straightforward, professional way, and correct it with gracious finesse.

The best protections against unexpected questions are: (1) anticipate them if possible, so they become "expected"; (2) when caught by surprise, just relax and do the best you can; and, (3) under total shock attack, be honest--say: "You know, I've never thought of that!"

Most of all, when for whatever reason you truly can't answer a vital question, don't fake it: simply admit your gap and offer to find the answer. In other words, remember the "NO-BLUFF Rule" (from Chapter 3).

COMMANDMENT #8: *STAY POLITE*

Always be polite to your audience, no matter what--no exceptions. It's common courtesy and smart tactics.

But, what if . . . what if, during Q&A, you face some fire-breathing mob of anger-mongering nay-sayers? What then?

Still, stay cool. Watch your negative emotions; control your temper.

But, what if . . . what if they are rude, and stupid, and (worst of all) wrong?

Then take a deep breath; control yourself; stay polite.

Does this mean be a saint?!

No, it means stay adult and be the winner.

Undoubtedly, you may think, there must be some exceptions--some argumentative hard-ball questioners whose inflammatory blatherings could force *any* self-respecting speaker to unleash his or her inhibitions and meet hostility with anger, fight fire with fire.

Surely, in *this* outrageous scenario, you'd say, a person could counterattack and cleverly put those fools in their proper place, right?

Well, wait a moment. Before you jump into battle one-on-one, ask yourself what's at stake . . . once you go on the angry offensive (no matter what the outcome), what will you win and what will you lose?

As public examples, recall the time Ronald Reagan (as President) shouted "Shut up!" at a White House heckler; or the incident where Nelson Rockerfeller (as Vice President) gave a symbolic middle-finger gesture to an abusive audience.

Those were amusing, human, memorable moments.

The question is: Does anyone remember anything that Mr. Rockerfeller *said* that day--or only that the Vice President of the United States "shot a bird" at somebody? Did he elevate the office of the Vice-Presidency?--or did he just divert his own message?

Nevertheless, it somehow "feels wrong" to stay adult and control your bubbling inner emotions in the face of uncivilized provocation, doesn't it? What about "saving face" and standing up for yourself and keeping your self-respect?

Sure, defend yourself! But do it smart, with controlled intensity--not in emotional high gear at a fever-pitch rage, reacting mindlessly, not wisely. Usually, your momentary release of anger will cost you more in the long run than any brief self-satisfaction you'll ever gain.

One more point: Whenever you are tempted to counterattack, stop and think first: "Am I about to become a sucker for the opposition?" Some people, as a calculated ploy, will deliberately try to provoke you into an argument to sidetrack bad news they'd rather avoid.

When you next face a rough-and-tumble audience, your best tactics are to restrain your natural urge for childish fury. Remember that *"Stay polite"* really translates into *"Stay adult"* (and thus stay in control of the situation).

Instead of fighting fire with fire (which only inflames the atmospheric temperature), be cool: Fight fire with water . . . quench your audience's angry heat with your own calm inner strength. You'll then control *them*--and not vice versa.

COMMANDMENT #9: *BE FIRM*

Let's underscore emphatically that "staying polite" does *not*, however, mean to become a wimpy marshmallow or a smiling punching bag.

The strategy of self-defense by self-control is not a disguised retreat or surrender. It still requires you (in an alert, controlled way) to hold your ground and be firm.

In answering questions, you're clearly expected to give your own viewpoints a vigorous defense. Some briefings seem, in fact, designed to be more or less adversarial as a test of your true depth of commitment: Will you fight for the idea or fold?

The Q&A gives you a chance to "smoke out" (and overcome) objections that others have against your idea. So, go for victory: support your key points forcefully. Don't back down just because tough questions suggest opposition or lukewarm acceptance.

Your basic objective, though, is to give a response that is well-measured (something like what Macchiavelli called an "iron hand inside a velvet glove"). In other words, your best move is neither an aggressive overreaction nor a weak acquiescence . . . yes, stay polite but also be firm.

When appropriate, be ready to compromise. If you can stay flexible--not rigidly dogmatic--you're more likely to win consistent success among people.

COMMANDMENT #10: *CHALLENGE DISTORTIONS*

Clearly, then, your basic strategy for Q&A in most cases is to be "firm but polite . . . polite but firm." But, still, what about antagonistic questions that contain obvious distortions or frontal assaults?

Some questions are "loaded" with a hidden premise (phrased as a prefatory statement) like this one:

"Look, John, all your past numbers were off-the-wall, out-of-the-air, and totally unreliable. So, what about these new ones you're feeding us today? Can we finally trust your numbers to be accurate?"

Clearly, as with its ancient prototype (*"John, have you stopped beating your wife?--yes or no?"*), your handling of such a loaded question calls for caution.

This maneuver is often a disguised bullying tactic, and (as with most bullies) the best response is *not* to gently ignore the attack, and *not* to dismiss the question merely with a derogatory label (that it's "hypothetical" or it's "loaded"), but to challenge it directly.

Do you see why a simple answer ("Yes, these numbers are very accurate") to such a question is inadequate? Tacitly, it appears to agree with the hidden false premise (that your past numbers were always wrong).

The correct way to handle loaded questions is to give a two-part answer: First, *CHALLENGE* their wrong premise (ideally, in a spirit of friendly self-confidence); second, *ANSWER* the explicit point, matter-of-factly. For example:

> *"Wait a minute, Harvey. You know that my numbers are always solid* [CHALLENGE]. *So, I'm confident you can trust the ones you'll get today, as usual* [ANSWER]."

THE KENNEDY WIT

The first U.S. President to allow his regular press conferences to be broadcast "live" to the American public by television was John F. Kennedy.

His decision to answer questions on live TV (done first on January 25, 1961) was at the time considered bold, even risky. What if the President should slip up, under the questions of probing reporters, and reveal some vital secret of national security?

In practice, however, these dangers were proven to be overstated. The U.S. ritual of holding nationally-televised press conferences has continued, more or less regularly, with every President since Kennedy (and, more rarely, elsewhere by some heads of state in other countries).

Kennedy proved to be a master of the question-&-answer process. Not only could he "think on his feet" deftly, he also frequently used quick wit (and careful preparation) to deflect questions that were tricky or potentially damaging.

As one example, when a reporter told Kennedy that the Republican party had just voted a resolution calling him "a failure" as President, he replied: "I am sure it was passed unanimously."[33]

John F. Kennedy, then, gives you a model for how to handle the Q&A format effectively because, in answering questions, he often used each of the Ten Commandments for Q&A.

THE LAST WORD

Let's say, finally, that your Q&A is about to end. The last question has just been answered . . . now what? If you want the biggest chance for success, don't just sit down.

With rare exceptions, in fact, never end a presentation simply on your answer to a question. Instead, expect and plan to have "The Last Word."

Recall that whatever your audience hears at the end will, as a rule, have strongest-lasting impact on their minds. People not only pay most attention to the last thing, it's also what they remember longest.

Clearly, then, if your Last Word only reacts to someone else's question, you risk an exit with a backfire result.

Suppose, for example, that the last question is trivial or irrelevant. It might raise a side issue, which appeals to the questioner but strays off the main topic. If you merely answer the question (and say nothing more), you risk shifting your audience's attention--at the strong, last moment--away from your own central point.

Worse, suppose the final question is overtly hostile or insulting. It may be untrue, plus unfair, but--if it's the last exchange the audience hears--it may raise an indelible cloud of lingering doubt against you or your position.

Therefore, always be careful to allow yourself time, after the last question during Q&A, to have The Last Word.

What exactly do you say as that "last word"?

---

[33]Theodore C. Sorensen, *Kennedy* (New York: Harper & Row, 1965), p. 324.

The Last Word is not a full restatement of the CLOSING. It's simply a shorter capsule of your talk's *main point*, often with a call for action, like the following example:

> *"So, to recap, we see robotics as the most desirable solution, and we look forward to getting your go-ahead."*

For speakers who work in service jobs (like a Personnel office), the last word can be an offer of further help:

> *"So, my name is Marlene Meredith, and if you ever need assistance, please call me on Extension 496."*

The Last Word is critical. It allows you to regain center stage for three reasons: (1) to *re*-focus the audience's attention upon your talk's main point; (2) to repeat and thus reinforce your desired outcome; and, (3) to offset any damage done, if the final questions were hostile or insulting.

After your next Q&A, therefore (unless your decision makers immediately shout in chorus: "Great idea! We'll do it!"), be prepared to go that one extra, persuasive step and have The Last Word.

Chapter 16

Q&A TACTICS: ESCAPE AND EVASION

"I'm glad you asked me that question!"
-- Richard M. Nixon

HOW TO PREPARE FOR Q&A

You can prepare yourself for the Q&A by doing a number of fruitful things. Here are a half-dozen suggestions for you:

1. **HARD QUESTIONS:** Make a list in advance of the most difficult hard questions that might arise and plot your responses. Typical rough questions might be:

   (a) **QUESTION:** *"What happens if we don't do what you suggest? Could we still perform our mission? Can we still survive?"*

   SOLUTION: Always ask *yourself* this fundamental question before you face an audience: What is the realistic impact on them if they *do not* accept your idea? The better your answer, the stronger your case (and vice versa).

   ? ? ? ? ?

   (b) **QUESTION:** *"Can you give us a 100% guarantee that things will occur the way you suggest?"*

POSSIBLE ANSWER: *"No, sir. But I can guarantee that our profits will continue to plummet if we do nothing. And I sincerely believe my solution offers us the best chance for a turnaround."*

? ? ? ? ?

(c) **QUESTION:** *"What if we try your idea and it fails?"*

COMMENT: Your questioners may feel anxiety over making a wrong decision. As an antidote, reassure them by showing that: (1) even if the "worst-case" outcome happens, the damage is tolerable; (2) the consequences of *not* taking action are significant; and, (3) the potential payoffs are worth the risk.

? ? ? ? ?

(d) **QUESTION:** *"Suppose we could only give you half of what you're asking for? What then?"*

PITFALL: Think twice before you nobly "bite the bullet" and say okay. This question may be a test of your firmness. If you agree you'd take half--and just do the best you can--the harsh reply may be: *"Done! Now, suppose we only give you half of that?"* [Gulp!]

? ? ? ? ?

(e) **QUESTION:** *"What makes you competent to propose this idea, anyway? What are your credentials?"*

PITFALL: Don't feel you have to justify yourself in detail, quoting your whole life history. Just pause, relax, think, and give a one- or two-sentence explanation of your involvement in the topic, then move on. (If they sucker you into a long, emotional self-defense and you take the bait--guess what: you've been sidetracked.)

2. **WHAT IF's:** Create a "WHAT IF" Scenario for every Q&A catastrophe that might reasonably occur. Then, make a "Plan B" for handling each one if things *do* go wrong. For example, what if you lose control of your audience--say, they get into a hot argument with each other and forget or ignore you, the speaker? What's the best way to deal with it?

3. **WEAK-POINT PROBE:** Probe your argument analytically to spot its weak points or inconsistencies. You need to pinpoint any holes or soft spots, so you can "bone up" and bolster your knowledge in anticipation of rough questions.

4. **DRY RUN:** Do a full-scale, dry-run rehearsal (sometimes called a "murder board") with colleagues there to act as devil's advocates, asking you every hard question they can imagine.

5. **BACKUPS:** Consider any "backups" that you can take along for Q&A. For example, is there a strong visual you might use to help explain a complex issue? Would it help to have a reference manual or the latest printout, if a certain question gets asked?

6. **ATTITUDE CHECK:** Before the Q&A, do an attitude check on yourself: Can you accept hard questions without taking them personally? Are you confident enough to admit you don't know everything? Breathe deeply and relax, to raise the threshold level where your ego gets bruised.

WHEN TO ALLOW QUESTIONS

Given that Q&A is valuable and often inescapable, when is the best time in a presentation for answering questions? Should the Q&A be postponed until the end or should you allow questions throughout?

This choice normally depends on three aspects of your presentation--its length, type, and specific audience.

1. *Length*: For a short talk with limited time, you may need to hold questions until the end. Since time is precious, an ongoing barrage of questions may eat up time needed to cover the rest of your presentation. On the other hand, for a long talk (say, one hour or more), you should probably insert one or more breaks for audience questions, to keep listeners involved and on the right track.

2. *Type*: The type of talk is also a major consideration. If, for example, you're in a teaching situation (giving a lecture, orientation, or workshop), you must be open for questions throughout so people can clarify their misunderstandings and "learn as they go." A formal briefing, too, may require Q&A along the way, depending on the audience. Often, however, it's more desirable--when possible--to develop your ideas first without interruptions, followed afterwards by the Q&A.

3. *Audience*: You may decide to request up-front that all questions be held until the end, although your audience may not always honor your request. If they outrank you, especially, they may prefer themselves to dictate how the Q&A is handled. Some decision makers, in fact, have a trademark of interrupting, almost as if to test the speaker's poise and degree of conviction. In these cases, you can't control it--but you can at least be ready for it based on Audience Analysis and control your reaction.

One last, obvious point . . . if you feel very ignorant about the topic (or have something to hide), you might opt for self-defense against full exposure and decline to allow any questions at all.

Avoiding the Q&A is typically a weak, defensive tactic-- to be chosen mainly when you'd rather let people *suspect* your ignorance (or perfidy) than open your mouth and *confirm* it for them yourself.

HOW TO HANDLE INTERRUPTIONS

One of the toughest problems faced by speakers during a presentation is a question that is also an interruption. Say, for example, you're giving a talk and it's going along well, according to plan, when (without warning) you're interrupted by a question on some point you intend to cover *later*, not now.

This interruption-question creates a dilemma for you: (a) you would prefer not to answer it because it's out of sequence and might scramble the logic of your presentation--yet at the same time: (b) you'd like to be responsive by answering the question directly (especially if it's from some higher-up decision maker).

What's the solution?

You might reply, as some people do, *"I'll answer that later,"* and return to your script. Such a tactic is okay, but it carries obvious risks. From that moment on, your questioner may sit listening, waiting, preoccupied with his/her unanswered question, feeling shut off and frustrated. Or the questioner may even just obstinately respond: *"No, answer it now!"*

Your best tactic, then, would do two things: (1) not make the questioner feel you've been evasive or unresponsive, yet still: (2) keep you on your game plan.

How? . . . give the interrupter only a "snippet" answer-- one that, as briefly as possible, answers the question in *part* but not in whole. You thus avoid slipping into all the details while you're showing that--if the questioner will be patient and listen--you'll explain things fully later.

Here's an example of how a "snippet" answer to an interrupting question might sound:

> *"In a nutshell, the answer is 2,500 rpm. And later I'll show exactly how we derived that figure. For now, I'd like to get back to the propulsion system."*

After the "snippet," don't hesitate but get immediately back on-track and continue, firmly but politely.

Sometimes during Q&A, an interrupter will blurt out a question at you while you're still answering someone else's question.

Here, just follow our basic Q&A strategy and be polite but firm. Never let an interruption detour you off one question onto another until the first question gets answered.

What if your answer to an interrupting question were interrupted by a *third* question? Would you again shift gears? No, hold the line against interruptions by saying something like: "Excuse me, let me answer the first question, then I'll come right back to you." And do so.[34]

"NO COMMENT"?

If you can't or won't answer a particular question, just say so directly and respectfully, and explain why.

Generally, avoid using the literal words "*NO COMMENT*." To most people, an answer of "No Comment" sounds devious and evasive.

A better substitute for not answering a question is to explain why you cannot. For instance, instead of "No Comment," you might say:

> "I'm sorry but I can't answer that question today. As you know, an investigation is under way and legal action may result. So, I'd prefer to get all the facts first. I assure you, as soon as we have the whole story we'll share it with you immediately."

To protect your future credibility, of course, be sure to keep this promise: Follow up with all the facts as soon as possible.

HOW TO DEFLATE WINDBAGS

Sometimes, instead of a question, you get a "windbag tirade"--a long-winded "question" that is really a haranguing speech in disguise. On and on, the questioner will go, talk-talk-talk, while the audience fidgets and you stew inside,

---

[34]For excellent guidance on assertive coping with difficult people and situations in general, see: Manuel J. Smith, *When I Say No, I Feel Guilty* (New York: Bantam Books, 1975).

wondering how to diplomatically regain control. Long-winded questioners are especially tough for the speaker who remembers Q&A Commandment #2, which says to *listen* while a question is being asked.

So, what's the solution to this dilemma?

This one is a judgment call. At first, you must listen patiently and politely, without interruption, and assume the person is just naturally verbose.

However, once it's clear that no question is being asked, wait for the windbag to take a breath (that's your opening), then jump in and--politely but firmly--say: *"Excuse me, what is your question?"*

Normally that's enough to force the issue: Either the windbagger will finally ask a real question or will admit, *" I just wanted to make that point."* In either case, you then just thank the person, reply if needed, and move on.

A similar problem is the "repeater"--a questioner who asks you the same question over and over. You answer the question once; later he asks it again. You answer it again; he asks it again later, for the third time.

At this point, unless you just haven't understood the question correctly, a reasonable answer might be:

> *"Sir, my answer would be the same as before, so we must have a basic disagreement on this point. Let me ask that, for the sake of time, I finish my presentation. Then afterwards, I'll be happy to join you one-to-one, so we can explore this topic fully, as it deserves."*

Be sure you mean it, too: You must be ready and willing to meet and talk as promised. (Most times, though, you'll discover that--once the audience is gone--such people lose their desire to explore the issues further.)

HOW TO ENCOURAGE QUESTIONS

Maybe your real fear is of *not* getting any questions. You dread that empty, awkward pause that falls at the end of a presentation, when the speaker says, *"Now, are there any questions?,"*--and the only reaction is deadly silence: nothing moves, no one speaks.

For those cases, there are three things you can do to encourage people to ask questions:

1. *A PLANT:* Arrange in advance for an audience member to be ready (if needed) to ask the first question. You do *not* "plant" any specific, self-serving question, but just have someone break the ice to start other people asking questions. (It usually works.)

2. *UNASKED QUESTIONS:* To provoke questions, mention the ones you had expected to hear--for example: *"No questions? I thought some of you might be curious about why we chose wood instead of aluminum to build the hull."* (Typically, someone will follow your lead: *"Yeah, why did you?")*

3. *YOU ASK THEM:* Ask direct questions for comments by your audience, to get them talking-- for example: *"Okay, let's see what you think. Is this a good idea or not?"* (Avoid this tactic, however, with higher-level audiences: they seem to feel it's too peremptory.)

HOW TO SOFTEN HOSTILITY

Suppose (based on Audience Analysis or past experience) you realistically expect your audience to be hostile towards your topic, conclusion, organization, or even you personally.

You're certain you'll get plastered by questions that are unmistakably unfriendly, even openly antagonistic.

Is there anything a speaker can do to offset or soften such genuine hostility?

The best advice here is to respect and apply the BOOMERANG EFFECT: What you send out comes back at you. Remember, even if you're only *reacting* to someone else's negativity, your own attitude still "boomerangs" like a ricochet at you: First they act; then you *re*-act; then they react to your reaction; then you start to *over*-react . . . on and on it escalates--a chain reaction!

Be smart enough to break the chain yourself. The best cure for overt hostility usually is to ignore it. Be strong and be careful because *all* emotions are powerful and usually infectious. So stay friendly, positive, professional. Let the other guy take the "low road"--never you.

If you're asked a question that's blatantly hostile, HEAR NO EVIL: simply cut through the emotional garbage and answer the factual point within the question. And if it is a diatribe--not a question at all--with no redeeming factual point, then simply say, *"Thanks for your viewpoint"* (politely but firmly), and move on to something worth hearing.

Even when you're *certain* that you'll face a mean-spirited, combative group of angry dissidents, learn to guard against building up your own whirlwind of fear or anger inside. It's self-defeating.

Your attitude has incredible power; it can make your worst nightmares come true. Instead of getting up-tight, channel that energy into conquering their needless hostility, to overcome their resistance and (the real key) to accept *them* so they'll accept *you*.

AD HOMINEM: THE PERSONAL ATTACK

Of all questions, the most distressing are those that openly insult or attack the speaker personally--for example, a vitriolic zinger like: *"Mary, what can a <u>woman</u> possibly know about a subject like this?"* (You don't have to be a woman to be victimized by such a challenge.)

Each of us, in one way or another, is vulnerable to being prejudged on the basis of a single personal characteristic, such as:

AGE: *"Look, I've been in this business forty years. How in blazes could you find anything worth saying to me?"*

"It's time for a fresh approach. Why can't we get some younger ideas around here?"

SEX: *"How could a woman ever understand this kind of situation?"*

"I always expect that kind of attitude from a man!"

RACE: *"You people all think alike, don't you?"*

                     *"Isn't that just a typical comment, coming
                     from someone like you?"*

OCCUPATION: *"How could a Government worker
                     understand what it takes to run a
                     business?"*

                     *"What's a civilian know about life in the
                     Air Force?"*

                     *"You're just a businessman--you don't have
                     a first-hand understanding of how Congress
                     really works, do you?"*

POSITION: *"Out there in the field, we do the real work.
                     You headquarters desk jockeys just make
                     rules and push papers, right?"*

                     *"You field people never look outside your
                     own tiny bailiwick at the bigger picture, do
                     you?"*

Let's first say unequivocally that any personal attack upon you--based on prejudgment or prejudice--is fallacious, malicious, and hateful; that's self-evident.

Nevertheless, it sometimes happens. The problem that you as speaker-victim may face is: What's the best way to handle an *ad hominem* (personal) attack on-the-spot when it occurs?

If you have ever been wounded by such a personal attack, you know that the first reaction is normally shock and outrage: "Did that person really *say* that?" you wonder, "and did he *mean* it, that way?"

Immediately, no matter who the perpetrator is, your own instincts are urging you either to: (1) justify yourself, (2) lose your poise, or (3) fight back in anger--maybe all three at once. However, each of these three options is a treacherous pitfall that you should avoid.

To learn how best to defeat a personal attack, let's take as an example the flagrant violation: *"What's a woman know about a subject like this?"*

Let's look pragmatically at your options for responding to such an overt attack, and learn three pitfalls to avoid . . .

PITFALL #1 - *DON'T GET DEFENSIVE*

When a question assaults your credibility ("What's a woman know about a subject like this?"), your natural reflex may be to start justifying yourself. For instance:

"Well, let me tell you what a woman knows! . . . I have a Masters degree and seven years' experience and they must've thought I know what I'm talking about or they wouldn't have sent me here . . ."

You may be totally correct but it sounds weak. You are now on the defensive. You've lost the momentum. At times you may need to spout your credentials, but in this situation (the true *ad hominem* attack), there's a better way to validate your credibility.

PITFALL #2 - *DON'T GO TO PIECES*

Besides being insulting, the *ad hominem* ploy is also often a "surprise attack." It can be especially unsettling for the speaker who is inexperienced. Adult speakers under attack have been seen to babble, whimper, cry, go blank, run out of the room, or otherwise beg for mercy (they didn't get it).

Don't *you* let that gargoyle rattle your cage. In other words, don't let one ugly-thinking person ruffle your entire professional poise in front of everyone else. Take a deep breath and--if nothing else--stay silent until you're ready to reply. Even if inside you feel an emotional volcano, don't "go to pieces" for them to see. There's a better way to respond.

PITFALL #3 - *DON'T COUNTERATTACK*

The most common (and, of course, most self-satisfying) instinct when attacked is to counterattack--with such sweet utterances as:

"Step outside, doodle-brain, and you'll find out!"

Or maybe:

*"Oh, yeah?   Well, I know your mother and you're one,
too!"*

Feel better?   Fine, but is this the most effective way to
react--by trading insults?

The normal argument in *favor* of a counterattack is that,
since it's provoked by your attacker, it's justifiable self-
defense.   Furthermore, the argument goes, being polite or
staying adult are poor moves because *"they don't work against
an S.O.B. who uses intimidation tactics.   You'll only appear weak
if you 'blink' or back down!"*

However, if you ever feel tempted to trade insult for
insult, ask yourself: "Who's wagging what--the tail or the dog
(and which one are *you*)?"   Is your angry insult likely to stop
the back-and-forth exchanges?   Probably not.

Unless handled deftly, your counterattack will only
inflame more anger in return.   You'll end up prolonging the
conflagration, escalating into a noisier "Round Two," and
getting yourself sidetracked.

So, what should you do, then?   Smile meekly and turn
the other cheek?   No, without a doubt you must defend
yourself when under attack . . . the only question is, "How?"

DEFENSE AGAINST S.O.B.'s

As a general principle when personally attacked, defend
yourself *intelligently* with *dignity*.   In practice, that means to
stay adult and unflappable, and you'll win far more
skirmishes.

As already implied, the best defense against an
intimidating S.O.B. is *not* to "fight fire with fire"--by mirroring
the behavior of your antagonist--but to act exactly *opposite* his
scare tactics and widen the obvious difference between you
both.

Does your S.O.B. act hostile and shout, growing louder
and meaner?   Then act the opposite: the more rudely he acts,
the more calm and controlled you should appear.   Speak
slowly but firmly and talk facts.   Keep your professional
poise; avoid a head-to-head battle.   Fight fire with ice water.

This move is fatally disarming to an S.O.B. adversary because, instead of making you both look alike, it builds up a clear *contrast* to spotlight his/her very "S.O.B.-ness." While you appear reasonable and mature, your adversary looks more childish and foolish.

Your refusal to counterattack directly need *not* conceal your natural and legitimate outrage. You are simply focusing your anger, with smart intensity, against your opponent's most vital vulnerability. By reacting with dignity, you earn the tacit respect of others in the room.

THE RIGHT ANSWER

Okay, you say. Now we know three pitfalls to avoid when personally attacked: Don't get defensive, don't go to pieces, and don't counterattack. But what's the right answer? What is the best way, specifically, to respond to a personal attack?

The ideal response will do two things: (1) shut off your insulter neatly and quickly, and (2) get you immediately back onto the topic of the talk.

To see how it's done, let's look at one proven example of the best way to handle this kind of sticky challenge:

INSULT: *"Ha! What's a woman know about a subject like this?"*

REPLY: *"I'm sorry, sir, but I can't consider that a serious question . . .*

[pause]

. . . but if you'd like to ask me a question on the topic I'm here to discuss, I'd be happy to answer it for you."

Say no more--you've said it all. Now just move on smoothly to the next questioner.

But note: it's very important *how* you speak this reply. You must sound firm but also calm, self-confident, and relaxed. If you snarl it from between clenched teeth, it fails to carry the same disarming impact.

Here, your best "tone of voice" for getting the upper hand conveys the light touch--even, if you can manage it, in a spirit of tolerant friendliness with a "knock-it-off" smile.

Instead of defensiveness, fear, or hostility, show that you have mastered the cool professionalism of self-control under pressure. This response is best because it allows you to "put them in their place" without joining them in their muddy ditch.

QUESTIONS, QUESTIONS

In summary, one of the most critical, valuable and magical moments of your entire presentation usually occurs when someone "out there" asks you a question.

It's a threat, but it's also an opportunity.

And if, in your next Q&A, you'll practice the techniques you've learned, like the "NO-BLUFF" Rule, the Ten Q&A Commandments, and the tactic of staying "firm but polite," you can say, *"I'm glad you asked me that question"* . . . and honestly mean it.

Chapter 17

RULE #7:

USE GOOD DELIVERY

"All the great speakers were bad speakers at first."
-- Ralph Waldo Emerson

THE "UH" SYNDROME

To repeat a key point, it's often not only *what* you say but *how* you say it.

Remember Ms. McGillicutty--your eighth-grade history teacher, wasn't she?--the one who said "Okay?" at the end of almost every sentence? At first it was just an annoying habit, but after a while (how could you resist?) you made a game of counting her total each period: "O-Kay?, O-Kay?, O-Kay?" Her all-time record was about 143 "okays" in 15 minutes, wasn't it? . . . but how much ancient history did you remember?

We (UH) have all (UH) attended presentations where (UH) the speaker (UH) talked in a way that (UH) called more (UH) attention to (UH) himself or (UH) herself than to the (UH) real (UH) topic. Sound familiar?

Under high-pressure, most untrained speakers display one or more nervous mannerisms--personal habits (verbal or visual) that transmit no meaning but spark plenty of interfering static.

Some people utter repetitive nonsense sounds, such as: "uh," "okay?," "like," "y'know?" Others rattle coins or keys in their pockets. Some like to fiddle with pens, pencils, notes, or pointers.

A few just drum their fingers on the table or caress the side of the lectern. The most frenetic types get their whole bodies involved--they rock, they sway, they roll their eyeballs, squirm their feet, fidget, and scratch.

These nervous habits are all big trouble because they add absolutely *no meaning* to your talk!

Worse, as a speaker you can exhibit some distracting, odd mannerism (y'know?) but be totally unaware of it--yet, if it exists, it still works against you secretly like an irresistible magnetic force that (y'know?) pulls your audience's mind off-center (y'know?).

The problem is: Once anyone becomes fascinated by *how* you speak--by that queer way you pronounce "nu-cu-ler" instead of "nuclear" or by the curious manner you constantly smack your lips--they are surely not hearing as much of *what* you say.

Your techniques of delivery, then, help you enhance or sabotage your overall message.

DEADLY DANGER #7 - **POOR DELIVERY**

SAY WHAT?

Habitual mannerisms in everyday speech (like punctuating "uh's") can be especially disastrous if they make you sound indecisive or unsure in public about matters of substance.

As a famous example: In late 1979, the signals were that Senator Edward Kennedy was planning to challenge his own party's incumbent, Jimmy Carter, for the 1980 Democratic nomination for President.

During the press coverage, Kennedy spoke with Roger Mudd of CBS News in an interview that was broadcast on national TV, with portions also printed in newspapers.

As aftermath, this one interview proved damaging to Kennedy's intended campaign--in particular, by the way he answered a single question.

Roger Mudd had asked the Senator: *"Mr. Kennedy, why do you think you should be President of the United States?"* and Kennedy's answer was punctuated by a good number of "uh's," "um's," and "er's."

In fairness, this habit of speech (the "uh" syndrome) seems to be a family trait, since both of Kennedy's other brothers in public life (John and Robert) also shared the same tendency, as do many others.

Nevertheless, Ted Kennedy's apparent on-camera "hemming and hawing" about his motives as a candidate had a negative impact on his image as a potential President. Based partly on what he said--but even more so on how he said it--some commentators felt his performance made him appear unfocused or ill-prepared.

HOW TO STOP MANNERISMS

Almost all speakers at one time or another display one or more of these mannerisms, so let's look at their root causes and their probable cures.

CAUSES:

Mannerisms usually appear in the speech of otherwise-articulate people as a result of three basic causes: (1) habit, (2) nervousness, and (3) incomplete preparation. Let's consider each . . .

1. *Habit.*

Some people learn mannerisms as a habit of speech that they utter, continuously and unknowingly, whether in a formal briefing or in everyday conversation.

Today, for example, it's common to hear locker-room interviews after the game, with athletes who sound like this: *"Well, like (y'know) we (y'know) did it together (y'know) and like (y'know) played as a team (y'know) and like (y'know) finally won the (like, y'know) big one."*

Like Ms. McGillicutty's "okay's" and Ted Kennedy's "er-uh-um's," these repetitious "y'know's" are simply a habit of speech. When you speak this way to a public audience, however, the ordinary mannerisms sound more prominent and do more harm.

2. *Nervousness.*

For most people, mannerisms are not habitual: They are hidden quirks that lie under the surface, waiting to pop up only when the culprit must speak under pressure. They are, in other words, byproducts of nervousness.

The extra tension of being in the spotlight, and thus on-the-spot, makes the speaker extraordinarily self-conscious and tense, so (against his or her will) the invasion of the "uh's" and the fiddling begins.

Such mannerisms will normally disappear when the speaker learns to relax and control the nervousness.

3. *Incomplete Preparation.*

We often spout nonsense sounds like "uh" and so forth as a pause filler, too.

We're not completely prepared, but suddenly we're standing there, thinking what to say next, and that moment of silence (which is only a second) feels like eternity, so we get the urgent need to fill the space--we must say *something!* but don't know what--so then we quickly temporize and say: "UHHHHHH!"

It's hard to resist the urge to "uh," but thoughtful silence is always better.

CURES:

Once you identify the cause, the cures for getting rid of any mannerism become clearer.

The cures for mannerisms are: (1) awareness, (2) practice, (3) relaxation, and (4) preparation.

1. *Awareness.*

Usually, the first step is to determine whether you *do*, in fact, have any distracting mannerisms, even if you're convinced you don't.

Start by soliciting feedback. Ask colleagues and friends: Do they know--but have never told you--of any mannerisms you have when you speak?

Also view a videotape of yourself speaking, perhaps in a dry-run rehearsal. If possible, obtain an in-depth critique of yourself by an experienced speaker or trainer.

2. *Practice.*

Awareness typically brings about a desire to change. Once you find the desire, attack the habit ruthlessly with daily practice.

You needn't get paranoid about it ("Oh, lord, I said *'uh'* again!"). Everyone slips mannerisms into their normal speech--it's common and natural.

Just keep seeing and hearing yourself as others see and hear you. Become more acutely aware of your mannerism and practice *not* doing it. When you feel a mannerism coming on, practice staying quiet instead.

3. *Relaxation.*

As already suggested, your mannerisms will often disappear effortlessly as your nervousness goes away.

To beat your mannerisms, use every technique you know to get comfortable and stay relaxed: deep breaths, positive visualization, mind games-- anything you find that works for you.

To exhibit less mannerisms, learn to stay alertly relaxed.

4. *Preparation.*

The key to a predictably effective presentation is total preparation. If you know where you're going and what you'll say next, you'll be more focused and less apt to derail yourself with distracting mannerisms.

So, prepare yourself with: (a) complete notes, (b) an adequate rehearsal, and (c) sufficient feedback (as in a videotaped dry-run).

NO MORE UH-OH'S

Getting rid of a mannerism may seem like only the absence of a negative, but the results are always a very positive step.

With practice and experience, you can eventually gain poise and develop polish as a speaker, while your mannerisms (and thus distractions) disappear.

Surely, factual substance--not merely smooth delivery--is of most importance.

However, if two people are both equally qualified and intelligent, and both express similar but competing ideas, the one who wins the game is often the one who *communicates* the idea best.

SPEAK THE SPEECH

Your main tool for speaking to groups--and the most flexible, dynamic instrument of communication--is the human voice. How's your own speaking voice? How's your total delivery system (gestures, eye contact, body language, etc.)?

As a speaker, would you say you are: (a) dynamic and exciting, (b) above average, (c) just so-so, or (d) pretty awful?

If you're not truly sure, it would pay you to get an objective assessment: to know your real strengths and learn what can be improved (and how) about your own techniques of delivery.

To help your assessment, here are seven possible sources where you might get valuable feedback for improvement:

(1) **MIRROR:** Rehearse your presentation while watching yourself in a mirror.

Advantage: You'll gain a glimpse of how you look when talking to people--especially your gestures, body language, and image.

Disadvantage: The perceptions are only your own (thus subjective and not fully reliable), plus you get no feedback on your voice.

(2) **AUDIO TAPE:** Record yourself on audio tape (for example, a home cassette), then study it.

Advantage: You'll hear yourself more as others hear you, and can thus analyze your speech "outside" yourself.

Disadvantage: Here, you get no visual feedback. Your perceptions of yourself--since they're also totally subjective--may again be incorrect: too harsh, too kind, or simply wrong.

(3) **OTHER PEOPLE:** Make your talk in front of others (family, friends, colleagues) and ask for their advice.

Advantage: Since this feedback comes from others, not yourself alone, it should be more useful, less subjective.

Disadvantage: If the audience is untrained, their feedback may be too vague, too critical, or just impossible to convert into action. Also, if they're too close to the speaker or subject, their feedback can still be overly subjective.

(4) **VIDEOTAPE:** Make a videotape of yourself talking, then study it.

Advantage: You will benefit from both hearing *and* seeing yourself. Once you get past the initial shock reaction ("Is THAT what I look/sound like?"), the opportunity for self-awareness and improvement is tremendous.

Disadvantage: Working alone, you may overlook deficiencies or strengths of yours that to others are obvious. Without guidance, you may also find it hard to convert your new self-awareness into positive changes.

(5) **SPEAKER'S CLUB:** Join a speaker's club or similar organization (such as Toastmasters International).

Advantage: You get to practice on a regular basis, with feedback from knowledgeable peers who share your problems. You may learn a well-tested sequence of practice speeches, with competition to help you stay motivated to improve.

Disadvantage: Meeting times or locations may be inconvenient, the feedback is not always from experienced professionals, and the styles may be geared more to "speechmaking" than for factual persuasion in on-the-job situations like briefings.

(6) **TRAINING COURSE:** Enroll in a class or workshop in "Speech," "Oral Presentations," or "Effective Briefing Techniques."

Advantage: Such training (especially if it employs videotape replay) can give you invaluable feedback from both the instructor and peers. It can motivate and guide you to improve better and quicker than by working alone or with untrained peers.

Disadvantage: Such training requires an investment of time and money, and--for long-lasting results-- must be conducted by a professional. If the training is poorly guided, is not well-designed, or is overly negative, your efforts might be wasted.

(7) **PRIVATE COACH:** Hire a personal coach, counselor, or consultant to work with you privately, one-to-one.

Advantage: You get an intensive, totally-focused, personalized program that is designed entirely to meet your own unique needs.

Disadvantage: You may find it hard to locate the right professional to help you and, in some cases, the cost may be prohibitive.

Most people will apply a combination of all or as many as possible of these sources for feedback and improvement. What's best for you depends on your own circumstances, personal desires, and professional requirements.

DELIVERY IS SPECIAL

Altogether, your delivery techniques consist of three major aspects: PLATFORM SKILLS, INTANGIBLES, and STYLE.[35]

The basic *PLATFORM SKILLS* are: (a) Voice, (b) Eye Contact, (c) Posture, and (d) Gestures.

The major *INTANGIBLES* are: (a) Enthusiasm, (b) Image, (c) Poise, and (d) Charisma.

STYLE is the result of all choices you make and all techniques you apply--the total impact of everything you do and say.

---

[35]For a Quick Checklist on Delivery Techniques (useful for critique and feedback), see Appendix B, page 321.

Chapter 18

THE VOICE OF AUTHORITY

*"Speech is a mirror of the soul:
as a man speaks, so is he."*

--Publilius Syrus

YOU ARE YOUR VOICE

As a speaker, your most basic tool is your voice. To put it simply: Good speakers have good voices. Moreover, it's an uphill challenge for you to be a "great," or even merely "effective," speaker if your voice fails you.

In the mind of others, your personality can be strongly shaped by the sound of your voice. Leaders, it's said, look and *sound* like leaders. Your voice should not only fit your personality, it can also *become* your personality.

Does your voice sound oh-so-fragile or squeak like a teensy mouse? Or does it rasp ultra-sexy with a throaty deep whisper? . . . Then how in either case can you command on-the-job authority?

Or does your voice boom mightily like sonic thunder? Or sharply attack the ears like a fingernail's chalkboard scrape? . . . How, then, can you be diplomatic or gently soothing?

Worse, how can you keep people awake if your voice drones on, on, and on, in solemn monotone--without variety, without zest, without real signs of life?

When you're speaking in a stand-up situation, your voice carries more impact than normal. Will it antagonize, amuse, or convince your audience? Will it bore, annoy, or inspire them?

The most effective voice for *you* does not necessarily sound professionally trained. In fact, people are often turned off by the flawlessly-correct "announcer's voice," which in everyday speech may sound too slick, synthetic, and insincere.

Your own best voice will almost invariably sound your most *natural*. If the plain-speaking Harry Truman had tried to talk using the bombastic eloquence of a Winston Churchill, he would surely have been less effective because, to his constituents, he would have sounded like--and been--a phony.

No speaking tool is more valuable to you than an effective voice, and in most cases a genuine, natural style is far superior.

To choose a "natural" style does not mean, however, that you're dooming your voice to sound, forever and unalterably, exactly as it does today. With personal desire, a systematic plan, useful feedback, and dedicated work, you can improve your voice significantly.

OFF THE RECORD

Anyone who's ever heard his/her recorded voice knows the shock. The first reaction is often: "Do I really sound like *that*?--no way!" Why the surprise?

Sound itself is only a wave of vibrating air. Human speech is air from the lungs being formed into sound by unique variations in the transmitter's body parts: mouth, nose, teeth, tongue, and throat (or, more precisely: larynx, vocal chords, glottis, diaphragm, etc.).

To you, your "normal" voice sounds much better because when you speak, you're inside your own head: You hear the added acoustical resonance of skull bone--as if you're always singing in a tiled shower or talking in an empty cathedral.

The bleak truth is: To everyone else, your voice sounds mostly like your recorded voice does to you.

So, mirrors, videotapes, and audio tapes can make you miserable: they strip away illusion; they confront you objectively with the reality of how you've always looked or sounded to everybody else.

Nevertheless, the discomfort of true feedback--from seeing or hearing yourself as others really do--can be invaluable as a motivator. Sometimes, the shock itself makes you relentlessly eager to change.

ELEMENTS OF VOICE ANALYSIS

You can evaluate your own voice, when it is recorded, by using four primary vocal characteristics:

(1) QUALITY,
(2) PITCH (including Range),
(3) LOUDNESS, and
(4) VARIETY (including Rate and Stress).

1. QUALITY

The first vocal characteristic is QUALITY. Usually, a voice's strongest first impression is made by its overall quality.

If a voice is so unusual that it's easily recognized, it often becomes an instant vocal "signature" for that person's whole personality. This fact is used skillfully by comedians and impressionists, who mimic famous people like Humphrey Bogart or Marilyn Monroe by imitating their voices and body language.

Since we all respond to expectations, it can be unsettling to hear a "wrong" voice that somehow fails to fit a speaker's image--for instance: a trembling squeal coming from a 250-pound linebacker or an earthy growl uttered by a 13-year-old nymphet.

On the other hand, a voice that sounds pleasing to an audience's ears can be a great asset--to help build rapport, or soothe the pain of bad news, or at least not inflame the angry opposition any worse.

If your voice were a musical instrument, we'd call this overall sound quality its *timbre*. Timbre is the "color" of a sound--the combined characteristics of frequency vibration and resonance that make, for example, a tuba sound different from a cello.

As an illustration: Imagine from memory the sound of a trombone playing a single tone. Can you hear it clearly?

Can you identify what makes this sound be a trombone instead of a piano or flute or trumpet playing the same note? The trombone's difference is its timbre. And like each instrument's different timbre, the raw difference in a voice's sound is its QUALITY.

Just as different virtuosos play the same instrument with personal styles that are remarkably unique and recognizable, so does everyone (even those with *similar* voice *quality*) speak differently.

No one has your exact voice. Each human voice is truly unique, so today you could be identified scientifically by an instrument called a sound spectrograph on the basis of your "voiceprint" alone.

On balance, the sound of your voice to others is very important. However, if you fear that your own voice quality is poor, remember three things:

(1) if your voice is now imperfect, you are not alone;

(2) with desire and effort, you can improve;[36] and,

(3) voice quality is not the only (nor most important) key to speaking success.

One man who proved this last point is now remembered for his great public speeches although he supposedly had a very poor speaking voice in person--namely, Abraham Lincoln.

---

[36] A number of helpful books are available on the topic of voice improvement. See, for example: Morton Cooper, *Change Your Voice Change Your Life* (New York: Macmillan, 1984); Dorothy Sarnoff, *Speech Can Change Your Life* (New York: Dell, 1970); and, Lilyan Wilder, *Professionally Speaking* (New York: Simon & Schuster, 1986).

Reportedly, Lincoln's voice sounded so unappealing and scratchy it would have handicapped him badly in the modern era of TV campaigning. Yet, today Lincoln is remembered as a great speaker: he offset the poor quality of his voice by his eloquence of expression and profundity of ideas.

So can you.

2. PITCH

The second vocal characteristic is PITCH. Pitch is comparable in musical terms to the individual note being played, sung, or spoken. For example:

Is it a *d-flat*? . . .   or a *g-sharp*? . . .

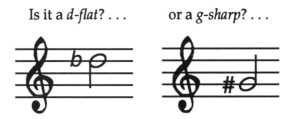

Although two different instruments (say, a trumpet and clarinet) sound different because of their distinct timbres (their QUALITY), they can both play the same note at exactly the same PITCH--for example, the note "concert A," which is produced at a frequency of 440 vibrations per second.

Like each note we sing or play, each word we speak also has its own frequency (its pitch). The greater the frequency of vibrations, the higher a note's pitch.

The pitch of your voice, therefore, is the "note" or cluster of notes on the musical scale where you habitually speak-- soprano, alto, baritone, bass, or otherwise. If you speak more in high notes, you have a *high*-pitched voice; more in low notes, you have a *low*-pitched one.

The customary sound of your voice, including its pitch, is formed by a combination of:

(a) *physiology* (with, for example, women being more likely than men to have higher-pitched voices);

(b) *past conditioning* (with family influences being the most formative: we hear, we copy); and,

(c) *personal choice* (with some speech habits modeled after the speech patterns of influential peers, as with teenagers or "in"-groups).

Pitch can also reveal something about the speaker at the specific moment. For example:

* Is your pitch creeping higher?--you may feel nervous, anxious, threatened, or uncertain.

* Is your pitch rising to the point of stridency?--you could be angry or extremely uptight.

* Is your pitch sinking lower, along with a slow breathy whisper?--you might be trying to sound seductive.

A change of pitch within a single note is called vocal **INFLECTION**:

We show differences in meaning between the same literal words by using inflection (substituted for in writing by punctuation). Compare:

a statement: "John came."   (*JOHN* came.)

a question: "John came?"   (John *CAME*?)

an assertion: "John came!"   (*JOHN CAME!*)

Vocal inflection is desirable. By introducing change, it adds variety and expressiveness to your speech and helps prevent a "monotone" voice.

RANGE

Whereas PITCH locates a limited group of musical notes (where you *are* speaking), RANGE is a measurement of the entire span of notes where your own pitch can possibly exist (where you *could be* speaking).

Your range encompasses all the tones that you personally are physically capable of producing, from the highest to the lowest:

RANGE:

Two corollaries therefore follow: (a) Your PITCH will always lie within, never beyond, your RANGE (unless you speak in an unnatural *falsetto*). (b) By varying your PITCH more--up or down towards the higher/lower limits of your RANGE--you get a more flexible, more interesting voice:

RANGE   Narrow PITCH   W i d e r PITCH

With effort, you may extend the normal limits of your vocal range. For instance, an accomplished opera singer may do constant practice to push his or her actual singing range wider, say, from two-and-a-half octaves towards three or even more.

If a speaker's entire range (and thus available pitch) is severely limited, he or she will always and inevitably talk in a near-monotone.

By varying your PITCH more widely within your given RANGE, you can become a more expressive speaker.

3. LOUDNESS

The third vocal characteristic is LOUDNESS. At times, some speakers talk too softly. Some talk too loudly. Some just talk the same all the time--never louder, never softer, without variety.

For any speaker a problem of loudness is critical . . . whether it's from too much (with listeners cringing in discomfort while you blast their ears off) or too little (with people straining just to hear you at all).

Although often equated with volume, LOUDNESS in speech is actually the result of two different factors working together . . . not only your **volume** (the total *amount* of air expelled) but also your **projection** (the *depth* and *force* of the air:

VOLUME
+   LOUDNESS
PROJECTION

Of the two, projection is more important to a speaker than volume, since good projection enables you to be heard clearly and distinctly at a distance, even at whisper levels or in the midst of background noise.

A person with small volume but good projection will be heard (and listened to) better than one with big volume but poor projection.

To get more volume, you basically just emit more air by opening up your throat wider--as you do, for instance, at a football game: to cheer for joy or to shout the unspeakable about the referee and his parents.

Projection, on the other hand, is determined by how well you use your entire vocal projection system while pushing the air you "speak" out from your lungs. *Poor projection* results if you push the air out shallowly, from the upper half of the lungs with chest tension only.

If you inhale the air fully and deeply to the bottom of your lungs, then exhale with sustained pressure from all the way down at your abdomen--that is, upwards from your diaphragm--the result is *good projection*.

You've probably heard it's important to "breathe from your diaphragm," so where and what is your "diaphragm"?

The diaphragm is an elastic, muscular wall between your chest cavity and abdomen, located slightly below your lowest rib at about the solar plexus:

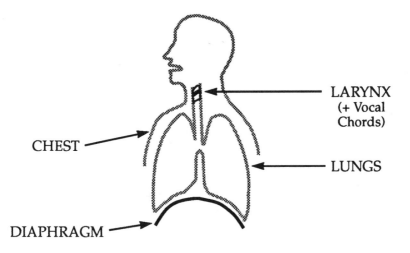

The Physiology of VOCAL PROJECTION

Speaking with excellent projection is, by analogy, like squeezing out your toothpaste firmly from the bottom of the tube--not just near the top, halfway up.

How can you truly judge whether your own projection is good or poor?

For personal assessment, you can begin by soliciting helpful feedback from others, or try making an audio- or video-tape of yourself.

If such helpful feedback isn't handy, though, here's a quick "projection test" you can do as a rough check:

PROJECTION TEST: Find a comfortable, private place where you won't be interrupted, and lie on your back on the floor. Place one hand on your abdomen, just below your navel.

Now, talk out loud for several minutes--saying anything that comes to mind (for example: slowly recite the alphabet) and, as you breathe and speak, pay attention to the hand on your stomach.

What happens when you inhale? Does your hand lift upward or does it more or less stay still? It's not a surefire test, but if your hand moves as you breathe and talk, it's likely your projection is good. On the other hand, if your hand just lies still or hardly moves, you're likely breathing at chest level: your projection is probably weak.

In experimenting by yourself for vocal projection, you may still wonder: "How will I know when my projection finally gets good? How does it *feel*?"

Good vocal projection begins with a full, deep, inhaling breath--followed by a firm, sustained inward and upper tension that you feel as a tightened support at the lower stomach area (slightly below your diaphragm, in and up from the abdomen).

You may, however, find it hard to catch the "feel" of good projection from words alone. If so, seek an in-person demonstration on "breathing from the diaphragm" from someone else--a good speech therapist, band director, drill instructor, or singing coach.

This powerful kind of breathing is commonly practiced by people who play brass instruments, perform martial arts, sing in concerts, practice yoga . . . or speak well.

One other point is that *relative* loudness, if controlled artistically, can itself add finer shadings to music or to speech. In other words, a different meaning is achieved when the same note is played more loudly or more softly:

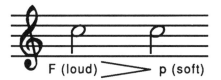

F (loud) ⟩ p (soft)

Likewise, the same *word* may carry a wholly different connotation if shouted versus whispered. In loudness, the best speakers do two things:

(a) they avoid extremes, by being neither too loud nor too soft; and,

(b) they use variety, avoiding not only mono-*tones* of pitch but also mono-*levels* of loudness.

4. VARIETY

The fourth vocal characteristic is VARIETY. Variety indicates *changes* within the other vocal characteristics of a speaking voice.

The average speaker (who lacks the vocal fluency of, say, a trained actor) can usually control only two vocal characteristics--PITCH and LOUDNESS. Vocal QUALITY is more complex, more inborn, and less easily modified by the untrained speaker.

A good speaker uses expressive variations in PITCH and LOUDNESS, plus variations of Rate (including pauses) and Stress, to hold people's interest. Variety helps you to avoid unleashing the four fatal dragons of speaker monotony:

    (a) monotone PITCH (always the same);
    (b) uniform LOUDNESS (always loud or soft);
    (c) constant RATE (always fast or slow); and,
    (d) unvarying STRESS (always equal).

RATE

RATE is simply the speed at which a person talks--slow, medium, or fast--and is thus comparable, in musical terms, to *tempo*.

Music, for instance, can be a slow *adagio* waltz in 3/4 time or a brisk *allegro* march in 2/4 time. Also, in a given tempo, the notes might vary from beat to beat, or could echo in repeated patterns of, say, half-notes, quarter-notes, or eighth-notes:

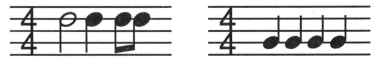

VARIED   REPETITIOUS

Your personal rate of talking is immediately apparent, easy to judge, and often habitual.

A fast or slow rate can influence how others react to you, since some habitual speaking rates are associated with regional stereotypes--like the caricatures of a "fast-talking" hustler from the urban North or a "slow-drawling" rustic from the South.

RATE, like PITCH, also tends to change in response to the psychological state of the speaker. For example, nervous people under time pressure tend to talk faster. Belligerent aggressors, when issuing a threat, frequently slow down and speak in taut, deliberate phrases: *"Now. Listen. YOU. And. Listen. Good . . .".*

To maintain audience interest, the lesson on rate is to avoid repetitious cadences except for impact: normally, keep your rate varied and never be reluctant to simply stop and insert a silent pause. A pause brings a nice change of pace and also gains attention by surprise.

The drone of a repetitious speech pattern is like the steady drip-drip-drip of a leaky faucet: the longer it piddles-- same tone, same loudness, same speed--the more it becomes an annoying snore-generator. The worst speakers never vary their ways of speaking; the best speakers always do.

STRESS

We add STRESS to our words by talking more loudly, more quickly, or at a higher pitch. (The most intense speakers do all three at once.)

STRESS is an *intensifier* of speech, and may determine the relative force (i.e., how much or how little) we hear of the other vocal characteristics.

Your goal is always to stay interesting through VARIETY. So, if you habitually talk with high STRESS, you might suddenly gain attention better--from the contrast--by talking more softly, more slowly, or at a lower pitch.

Is there a single, ideal intensity level for your voice, for every speaking situation? No, it varies: to be most effective, your delivery must be appropriate to the moment.

In some formal, top-level briefings, a quiet, casual ("laid-back") approach may seem to signal a low-key commitment to the work and thus be damaging.

In' other talks, an approach that's too highly charged ("gung-ho") or too confrontational could be equally wrong and counterproductive.

Remember that a speaker's intensity is felt by an audience as variations of tension and relaxation: The more tension they feel--in you or in themselves--the more you become (to them) "intense."

Typically, the best speakers keep stress well-modulated between the far limits (neither too tight nor too loose), so their listeners feel both invigorated but soothed, challenged but placated, alert but calm, all at once.

The best advice on stress, then, is to avoid extremes except at rare moments for emphasis or variety.

VARIETY IS MORE THAN SPICE

Most audiences have a low tolerance level for boredom, so it's a major, unforgivable error when a speaker inflicts ruthless monotony upon them. Plus, the longer you make people sit and listen, the more variety you'll need to keep everyone awake to your topic.

The best, most charismatic speakers are delightfully unpredictable. Even within a 5- or 10-minute talk, they change pace, create surprises, and express different ideas or new moods in fresh, scintillating ways.

Variety, in essence, is the capstone skill of speaking--the unifying culmination of all other vocal characteristics when used well. Bluntly: To be a dynamic, interesting professional (not an ineffectual, boring amateur), a speaker needs artistic variety.

ARTICULATION

Another speech process you should understand is ARTICULATION (or "enunciation"), which measures how clearly and correctly a speaker pronounces his or her words.

Articulation shapes the vibrating buzz of your vocal chords into a recognizable noise (making, for instance, the sound of a "p" different from a "b," or a "t" from a "d") and it's performed mainly by mouth, lips, teeth, and tongue.

Someone who mumbles unintelligibly is guilty of poor articulation. In severe cases, a person who speaks with faulty articulation might mutter a garbled phrase like *"Aw - AzwudCHOOzay!"* that sounds incomprehensible until deciphered plainly into: "Oh, that's what *you* say."

Articulation problems may occur: (a) for reasons that are purely physical (such as the formation of your palate or teeth); or, (b) as the result of learned speech behavior patterns that are careless, affected, or wrong.

How or why, in the latter case, do we "learn" patterns of poor articulation? We adopt almost *all* patterns of speech-- right and wrong--in copycat fashion from childhood on.

During our formative years, we learn to speak by imitating uncritically the speech heard around us, from family and social environment. Blame your parents or where you grew up, therefore, if you're told you sound Southern, New Yorker, blue-collar, Ivy League, or otherwise.

In most cases, unless we consciously re-learn to speak "standard" language, our adult speech (most notably, articulation) continues to betray our upbringing.

According to John T. Molloy, the speech patterns of socioeconomic groups (primarily, upper versus lower) are not only distinctly different but also, "Each group is annoyed by the vocal patterns of the other."[37]

So, successful speakers, trial lawyers, and salesmen learn to become mutable chameleons who freely adjust their speaking patterns slightly up or down, depending on the class of audience they're facing.

Molloy concludes that to succeed in corporate America, you'll have a decided advantage if your speaking pattern is "upper-middle class"--preferably with an overtone of New England or, even better, Great Britain.

These sobering, provocative, but probably true insights help to explain the emphasis upon speech in George Bernard Shaw's play, *Pygmalion* and the latter-derived musical by Lerner and Loewe. In that plot, you'll recall, Professor Henry Higgins orchestrates a total transformation of Liza Doolittle from an uncouth street waif into "My Fair Lady."

---

[37]John T. Molloy, *Live for Success* (New York: William Morrow, 1981), p. 56.

For Liza's makeover, Higgins focuses singlemindedly on her voice. From hours of elocution drills, she alters her everyday speech from Cockney vernacular into acceptable upper-crust English.

In the end, of course, Higgins actually succeeds beyond his own expectations--proving, satirically, that the primary difference between a London flower girl and a passable lady is in how she speaks.

Like Professor Higgins, you, too, should be aware that, of all characteristics of voice, none broadcasts more loudly a signal of your own personal background, education, and social stratum than your articulation.

Good articulation in speech is like clear legibility in handwriting: it helps your listeners grasp your points quickly and easily; it helps create a positive impression. Poor articulation, if chronic, makes you seem ignorant or indifferent.

If people frequently ask you to repeat yourself--but you're sure you talk loud enough to be heard--it's a warning: you might have an articulation problem.

To evaluate and improve your own articulation, you must seek professional help from a teacher, therapist, or pathologist qualified in the area of speech counselling.

A NOTE ON "ACCENTS"

Sometimes, what appears to be an articulation problem is in reality a national, regional, or social ACCENT. An accent shows up, as with Liza Doolittle, in mispronunciations or idiosyncratic, non-standard ways of saying things.

John F. Kennedy, for example, was readily satirized by comedians after the Cuban Missile Crisis for his habitual Bostonian pronunciation of "CUBE-R" for "Cuba." Likewise, in some localities, words like "these," "those," and "you" get translated when spoken into "deeze," "doze," and "yooze."

If you live in a country where the national language (for example, English) is to you a second language, you may also talk with a *foreign* "accent." For an English-speaking American in America, the burden is similar if he or she has a strong *regional* accent.

For instance, John T. Molloy suggests that an American with a certifiable rural accent (say, Alabama or Texas), who ventures into the Northeastern United States, is liable to be treated by city dwellers there as a mere "rube."[38]

Racial, ethnic, and *social* groups, too, have their own distinct speech idioms--with, for example, unique variations likely to be heard between the "English" of a Wall Street banker, a ghetto black, and a West Coast longshoreman.

If you yourself have any sort of noticeable accent, you might have personally wondered: "So what? Should I study the language harder to lose my accent or not? Is it worth it?"

How far should a person go to change his or her regular way of speaking? The answer is debatable: It depends.

Without question, everyone who attempts to speak any language should speak it as perfectly as possible, and never stop studying and improving.

Yet, at some point, by striving towards a more "homogenized" way of speaking, you may risk some negative tradeoffs, like feeling you've been untrue to your natural heritage; or the fear that, by changing your speech, you are also violating your own uniqueness.

The decisive question to ask yourself is this: "Does my accent damage my credibility or my everyday ability to communicate or succeed?" Also ask: "When I speak normally, do people in my audiences ever find me difficult to understand?"

If you can confidently answer: "No, my normal accent is harmless; they all understand me; my speech has no bad impact on my image or their expectations," then your accent may be disregarded.

If, however, you answer "Yes" or "Maybe," you might choose to work vigorously to soften your accent--since, to be understood, you must speak clearly and *correctly.*

You should realize that an accent (or any other unusual way of speaking) is not, per se, a shortcoming: it depends on your objectives, your audience, and yourself.

If the main decision makers in your world can really understand you, you should probably just speak in your own natural style, be yourself, and forget it.

---

[38]Molloy, *Live for Success,* p. 50.

It may be helpful, too, to keep in mind that there's an important difference between: (a) speaking unintelligibly or incorrectly, versus: (b) speaking only "differently."

TONES OF VOICE

To someone else, the sound of your voice can affect the way he or she will hear your words. As was once said: "How many arguments are started by a tone of voice?"

So, if you're ever startled by someone's reaction to your ideas, maybe it's because the words that person hears are not the words you say . . . even though they are (literally) the same words.

In the future, when you evaluate a human voice (your own or anyone else's), stay objective about how it sounds by remembering to focus upon the four primary vocal characteristics.[39]

---

[39]For practical application, you will find a detailed guide for doing your own Voice Analysis in Appendix C, page 322.

Chapter 19

PLATFORM SKILLS IN ACTION

"Eyes are more accurate witnesses than ears."
-- Heraclitus

PLATFORM SKILLS

The basic skills of a speaker are sometimes called "platform skills." These are skills used on the *platform* (wherever the speaker is located) to get points across in a clear and stimulating manner.

Platform skills are both verbal and nonverbal. While Voice is exclusively a *verbal* skill, good speakers also use the *nonverbal* platform skills of: (1) EYE CONTACT, (2) POSTURE, and (3) GESTURES.

Thankfully, all platform skills are just that--skills--so, with effort, they can be learned by anyone.

Eye Contact and Posture require you to know mainly what to do right. Gestures require you to avoid doing things wrong. Voice is more complex and, if problems exist, may require systematic, long-term practice before you improve.

We've already discussed VOICE (in chapter 18), so let's look now at the main nonverbal platform skills, with tips on how best to use each for dynamic speaking.

1. EYE CONTACT

Your most important *nonverbal* way to create quick, full communication with any audience (whether in a conversation, face-to-face interview, or stand-up talk) is by eye contact.

The eyes send a hidden message in an unspoken language. Someone else's eyes can tell you: "I agree," or: "I'm puzzled," or even: "I'm distracted and not listening to you at all."

To read other people's intentions, we often watch their eyes. Are the eyes shifty?--then we tend to distrust that person. Do they give a warm, clear gaze?--then that person seems more sincere, more trustworthy.

We can be wrong, of course, as any shrewd con artist or wily seducer knows: the eyes can lie, by design. Still, when it comes to power to grab attention and communicate without saying a word . . . the eyes have it!

For any speaker, then, good eye contact is a mandatory skill. Good eye contact helps establish a double link with the audience:

(a) THEY see *you* better: as you look intently at an audience, you build rapport with them, helping to hold their attention--but also:

(b) YOU see *them* better: when you watch them carefully, you'll see how they react, pro and con, to your ideas as you speak.

Speakers who avoid eye contact (even if only because of shyness) put an isolating distance between themselves and their audience. Undeniably, poor or no eye contact can be a serious barrier to successful communication.

So, to be most effective, you must learn to think and talk on your feet while you look at your audience squarely, eyeball to eyeball.

TIPS ON EYE CONTACT

Here are eleven practical tips to help you master the use of eye contact in your talks:

a. **BE SINCERE:** Dynamic eye contact is direct, one-to-one, and genuine. It's no gimmick--it's a real, shared communication with another human being and (even if you are a trained actor) most audiences can feel whether it's honest or faked.

b. **STAY FOCUSED:** Don't let your eyes flit around too quickly. Stop to really look at people in your audience long enough to register understanding with each one. (With a small group, especially, this kind of empathy is essential.)

c. **KEEP MOVING:** Look but don't stare them down. If you look at any one person for *too* long, you'll both start to feel uncomfortable, and (at some point) your target may get irritated or hostile.

d. **USE VARIETY:** Don't look them over in a mechanical "radar sweep" motion, either. Keep your eye contact random and natural. Be unpredictable as you gaze here, then there.

e. **STAY INVOLVED:** Ignore the disastrous advice to "look at a spot in the back of the room." No, look at the people--*they* are your decision makers. Don't look at the ceiling, floor, wall, or your notes (except briefly), nor anywhere else but at the audience.

f. **BUILD RAPPORT:** If you're shy or nervous, beware of a natural tendency to avoid eye contact. To other people, a total lack of eye contact by you--no matter why--is a signal to distrust your words.

g. **INCLUDE EVERYONE:** Learn to look at everyone in your audience. (If you are inexperienced, you may tend to talk only to friendlier faces or only to "bosses.") Force yourself, though, to include all listeners, even those at the outer edges of the audience.

h. **SEGMENT LARGE GROUPS:** With a large group (50 or more), divide the audience mentally into small, 5-to-10-person segments. First talk to one person in one slice (ideally someone smiling and nodding agreeably), then look at someone else, gradually "painting" all slices with eye contact.

i. **CONCEAL NOTES:** When you use notes--even if reading them verbatim--keep eye contact with your audience. As a help, write your text in *LARGE* letters, using only one side of paper, with plenty of space for readability, and practice the speech in advance several times for familiarity.

j. **KEEP VISUAL AIDS SECONDARY:** When using visual aids, be careful to keep eye contact primarily with the audience. Don't look hypnotically at your own chart or board or viewgraph instead of at the people.

k. **OPEN AND CLOSE WELL:** In particular, remember always to give your audience full eye contact at the *two most critical parts* of the presentation--the opening and closing. If it helps, write the words, "EYE CONTACT," into your notes as a reminder.

2. POSTURE

Posture is another way that, when you take the platform, you strongly but silently establish your relationship with an audience.

Your posture tells a story on two levels: not only your *physical* posture (how you actually stand and look), but also your *mental* posture (the unspoken attitudes that your body language implicitly projects).

As a rule, your audience will react, involuntarily, to your physical posture as if it truly reflects your mental attitude. Thus, both physical and mental posture are closely related.

Imagine, for example, two speakers . . .

(a) Speaker #1 walks in slowly, hesitantly. After a cautious glance, she approaches the lectern. She blinks rapidly, her hands fidget, and she slouches uncomfortably, unable to stand still or get settled.

(b) Speaker #2 storms in stiffly erect, tensely coiled, with hands on hips. He glares, his head is ramrod straight, and his every move is hard and quick. He stares out at everyone, smugly, with piercing eyes.

Think about your first impressions . . . (a) Before she says a word, will Speaker #1 inspire your confidence? (b) Before he says a word, will Speaker #2 make you feel relaxed or comfortable?

Probably, in both cases: not at all.

Clearly, whenever you enter a room or walk towards the platform--before you even speak--your apparent viewpoint is signaled, nonverbally, by your posture.

So what posture, in general, is most effective?

AUTHORITY POSTURE

For formal, stand-up speaking situations (like a press conference or briefing), there is one common, basic posture-- which we'll call the "Authority Posture"--that works best for asserting control and projecting authority.

If you study the platform skills of top leaders who are experienced public speakers (Presidents, members of Congress, corporate CEO's), you'll notice they almost always use this same Authority Posture, whether by instinct or practice.

Here is a description of the basic Authority Posture:

(1) **BODY** - Follow the ageless advice of mothers and drill instructors: "Stand up straight; don't slouch." You are not at military "attention," however--simply stand erect and upright, with shoulders back, alert but relaxed.

(2) **FEET** - Keep your feet flat on the floor and avoid any unnecessary, random movements: Don't dance; don't shift balance from leg to leg. Keep equal weight on each foot, with a slight space between them.

(3) **EYES** - Keep good eye contact (as already explained), looking straight ahead--not up, down, nor anywhere else primarily but at the audience.

(4) **HANDS** - The most frequent (and often most perplexing) question about posture is: Where should you put your hands?

First, here's where *not* to put your hands, for the formal style required in the Authority Posture:

- *not* behind your back, in the "handcuffed" position (it lacks authority), nor in the "parade rest" stance (unless you are a military instructor);
- *not* in your pocket (that's for a less formal, more casual style);
- *not* loosely dangling behind the lectern (it leaves a void between you and the audience).

So where, then, is the recommended "best" location for putting your hands?

Normally, it's best to rest them lightly on the outer, back corners of the lectern. This (with the other elements of Authority Posture) projects the best overall impression of professional authority.

Note: your hands only *rest on* the lectern, not *clutch* . You must not become an immobile wooden statue--you merely wish to look formal, professional, and authoritative.

The Authority Posture is thus a holding-pattern position only--to be used especially in the OPENING and CLOSING of your talk. To be dynamic, you'll gesture and move around.

The complete Authority Posture looks like this:

AUTHORITY POSTURE

What about Authority Posture without a lectern?

For the Authority Posture *without* a lectern, the basic pattern would remain exactly the same except for the hands, where you have two preferred choices: (a) to hang your hands comfortably at your sides, or (b) to clasp them together naturally, in front of your lower body (in what some jokingly call the "fig leaf" position).

It's best to try both options, checking yourself in a full-length mirror, then choose the one that feels most natural to you and gives the best image. (That position, once found and used, quickly becomes habitual.)

You should use the **AUTHORITY POSTURE** when:

* You feel that your subject, audience, or situation requires an atmosphere that is *formal*.

* You expect your audience to be intimidating or hostile, and wish to *neutralize* them. (For example, you are young or inexperienced and your audience is a bunch of testy higher-up's; or you are a woman and must face a skeptical group that's all male.)

* You aren't certain of the appropriate style, so you want to stay conservative and play it *safe*.

* You have a *practical need* or *necessity* for that kind of arrangement. (As examples: The room set-up demands it; the audience will be large and unruly; you'll use lots of visuals and need a lectern for your notes; etc.)

CASUAL POSTURE

Some authorities recommend that--to get closer to your audience and build better rapport--you should come out from behind the lectern, move around, and be less formal.

Certainly, for a more informal topic or setting (such as a training workshop, "chalk talk," sales pitch, or unplanned quick-response), the Authority Posture could seem too stiff, too distant.

Sometimes, then, you'll want to relax the elements of posture and use what we'll call "Casual Posture." Typically, the Casual Posture looks like this:

CASUAL POSTURE

The main differences and similarities between Authority Posture and Casual Posture are these:

	AUTHORITY Posture:	CASUAL Posture:
BODY:	Remains erect; does not sit nor lean on things. Mostly static.	More likely to sit lightly on a table or lean against the lectern. Mostly mobile.
FEET:	Relatively stable; stay fixed in place, except when you move to show visual aids.	More likely to come out from behind lectern; walk around. Often no lectern is used at all.
EYES:	Good eye contact with everyone in audience.	Good eye contact with everyone in audience.
HANDS:	Use selective gestures; basic resting spot is on back, outer edges of the lectern, not in pocket nor behind back nor in limbo.	More frequent gestures; less controlled. Hands may occasionally be put in pocket, behind back, or in motion.

You should use the **CASUAL POSTURE** when:

* You feel that your subject, audience, or situation requires an atmosphere that is *informal.*

* You expect your audience to be uncooperative or timid, and wish to *relax* them. (For example, you are the boss, addressing a gathering of junior employees; or you're an auditor, who must overcome local resistance to "outsiders.")

* You're willing to gamble with a less conservative style because, even though it's risky, for you it's more *natural.*

* You have a forced *necessity* to be casual. (As examples: You are speaking out-of-doors, with no public-address system; no lectern is available; you will speak while walking through a building; etc.)

The factors that dictate the right posture are complex and seldom absolute. Some speakers, for example, can convey authority even from a loose Casual stance; others can relax a roomful of people even in the upright Authority posture.

Your best line of attack is to learn and practice both Authority Posture and Casual Posture, then (based on your topic and situation) apply the one that seems preferable for each specific talk.

3. GESTURES

What makes one speaker dynamic and exciting while another one seems static and oh-so boring?

One reason is often simple: The dynamic speaker uses gestures to add motion and variety--literally, he/she moves--while the static speaker uses very few gestures: he/she just stands there, unmoving, predictable, and monotonous. Talk, talk, talk.

By adding gestures, you vividly (and visually) reinforce the words you say. However, for the unwary speaker, trying to get more dynamic by simply adding more gestures can be a trap, too.

To work well, gestures must be *natural*, not mechanical nor rehearsed. President Richard Nixon had trouble as a public communicator because his words and actions seemed contrived. His gestures looked wrong, not spontaneous: he never quite appeared to be comfortably natural.

In the pivotal 2nd Presidential debate of 1988, Michael Dukakis had trouble communicating well: he seemed "wooden" and appeared to lack warmth. George Bush, by comparison, projected himself better as a speaker, using dynamic gestures and relaxed intensity to show emotion.

Here is the most useful advice for you about Gestures:

(1) *Do* have gestures. Loosen up those hands and arms and add some visual (body language) communication when you talk. *Don't* just stand there without any gestures at all. It's boring.

(2) *Do* use gestures carefully. People who "talk with their hands" constantly like a windmill are not being dynamic: they often annoy and distract many listeners. *Don't* overdo your gestures.

(3) *Do* stay spontaneous. Instead of calculating your moves step by step, relax and let them happen naturally. *Don't* rehearse or plan specific gestures-- they'll just look awkward and phony when used. Just be sure every movement has a motivation.

To judge your ability as a "gesturer," have yourself videotaped and view your own communication habits. (With a videotape, you can freeze-frame, replay, and study yourself fully and objectively.)

For comparison, you might also study the gestures and body language of some other good speaker whom you respect, either in-person or by videotape recording.

Remember that any speaker--even one who talks in an interesting way--can lose or bore people if he or she stands up there frozen, like some lifeless artifact.

In particular, if you often make presentations that last 15 minutes or more, learn to be dynamic; come alive; loosen up; and add natural, unprogrammed gestures to your talks . . . you'll keep more people awake.

BODY LANGUAGE

The nonverbal skills ("body language") speak louder than words. When your nonverbal signals contradict your verbal message, people usually trust what they see and feel more than what you say.

Try, for example, telling people, "I'm very happy to be here today," or, "I'm glad you asked me that question," when you don't mean it at all--when, inside, you really hate the whole mess and wish you could scram.

Most times, they'll guess the truth; they'll "read" you well: Never mind *what* you say; they'll react to how you say it.

For audiences, then, a speaker's body language is (at least subliminally) a kind of nonverbal lie detector--to confirm or deny the words--and their instincts for deception are often remarkably on-target.

In recent years, attention has rightfully been paid to the importance of nonverbal communications.[40]   It's even been suggested that from body language, you can learn to "read a person like a book." You will know what someone is thinking by where he rests his arms or how she tilts her head.

Maybe, but speakers beware: Body language can give insights and clues, but it's also sometimes unreliable. In particular, to read an audience, the true test isn't how they look, nonverbally--it's what they finally say and do. To put it simply, do they say "yes" or "no"?

So, yes, watch the people in your audience, but don't overreact to their body language. For example, do you see that angry-looking guy in the back row?--the one there, with the mean, intimidating scowl, propping his chin on a fist and frowning? Looks like an Absolute No, right?

Well, don't jump to conclusions: he may not disagree with your ideas at all--he may be suffering from a bad day or a toothache. You won't be absolutely sure what he thinks until he speaks his mind out loud.

---

[40]For more on body language, see: Julius Fast, *Body Language* (New York: Pocket Books, 1970); Gerard I. Nierenberg and Henry H. Calero, *How to Read a Person Like a Book* (New York: Pocket Books, 1971); Nierenberg and Calero, *Meta-Talk* (New York: Cornerstone Library, 1973); Allan Pease, *Signals* (Toronto: Bantam Books, 1984).

In summary, for good person-to-person communications, remember that nonverbals relate to the verbal in these ways:

1. Normally, when you speak, the most important element is clearly the *verbal*--which gives your message's content, the substance of your talk. The *nonverbal* merely helps reinforce the ideas more memorably.

2. However, when the nonverbal message *contradicts* the verbal (if, say, your actions make your words look insincere or untruthful), then the nonverbal is "heard" more loudly and believed more strongly.

3. For good communication, therefore, your goal is to be sure your nonverbal messages stay in *harmony* with your verbal ones; be sure all your "language" (spoken and body) conveys the same message, not mixed signals.

Yet, what is the best defense against using the "wrong" body language and thus transmitting a bad message? Your solution is *not* to start trying to orchestrate and control all your body movements. (That is always a mistake because it makes you act unnatural and look phony.)

Instead, recognize that sooner or later your real attitude is usually tipped off by your body language. To paraphrase Joe Louis again: "You can run but you can't hide." Almost always, involuntarily, your nonverbal actions support or betray your innermost feelings.

So, never mind the nonverbals . . . WATCH YOUR ATTITUDE. Check your thoughts: if you think hostile, it will show; if you relax and think positive, your body will fall in line.

Chapter 20

PROJECTING THE INTANGIBLES

"Speech is the image of actions."

-- Solon

THE INTANGIBLES

For speakers, the platform skills (Voice, Eye Contact, Posture, and Gestures) are the fundamentals: they do for an oral presentation what a bat, ball, and glove do for baseball.

Besides the platform skills, though, a truly effective speaker needs other, more *intangible* powers, which are harder to learn and practice.

The four intangibles that a good speaker commands are: (1) ENTHUSIASM, (2) IMAGE, (3) POISE, and (4) CHARISMA.

1. ENTHUSIASM

Consider this viewpoint . . .

THERE IS NO SUCH THING AS A "BORING" TOPIC.

No topic is automatically and inevitably boring-- although we all hear plenty of presentations that end up tedious and dull. Why?

Have you ever attended a talk eagerly, on a topic you really cared about (something with built-in appeal, like: "How to Get Richer, Live Longer, and Love Better"), and yet where, amazingly, the speaker disappointed and bored you into daydreams?

On the other hand, haven't you also (to your surprise) felt excitement over another, seemingly lifeless topic, by the entertaining way some speaker told it to you? Why?

Most times, the difference is not in the topic itself; it's intangible: it's the enthusiasm (or apathy) projected by the speaker (the Boomerang Effect at work again). As usual, the speaker's attitude infects the audience.

Anyone can build a presentation to excite people on any topic (even "How to Use Dental Floss") if you'll do two things: (a) always show the topic's impact on your audience personally; and, (b) be sure to add a fresh *enthusiasm* that's genuine, not faked.

DIGGING FOR ENTHUSIASM

Ralph Waldo Emerson once observed that "nothing great was ever achieved without enthusiasm." Okay, sure, right. Hooray for enthusiasm . . . when it exists.

But where's the enthusiasm when a topic is certifiably dull and deadly? What's so scintillating about paperwork control? Or engineering change proposals? Or (that all-time favorite) personnel policies and procedures?

As a help, here are four ways to unearth your enthusiasm in future talks, when you don't naturally feel enthusiasm for a given topic:

1. **SKIP THE NEGATIVITY.** If your topic looks boring, why not focus on the "half-full" glass, anyway? Choose to be positive (stop moaning it's a dull topic) and take action. Find *something* in this subject that does interest or excite you, and build your talk around that. In other words, start with the "good parts."

2. **CONSIDER THE AUDIENCE.** Maybe *you* find the topic boring, but will your audience, too? Ask yourself: What's in it for them? Why are they coming to listen? You may then see a way (despite yourself) to make this talk useful for *others*. (And, if absolutely nothing at all in the talk seems relevant to them?--call off the talk!)

3. **PLAY "EXCITEMENT."** If the topic still leaves you cold (all you can think of is: "B-O-R-I-N-G"), try pretending it's a *game*, a personal challenge, whose main rule is: "Your mission, should you choose to accept it, is to find some interesting angle for this horrendous topic." Then, don't quit; keep playing until you win.

4. **"BRAINSTORM" YOUR TALK.** Maybe this topic is so old, so familiar to you that it's simply gone stale. If so, try exploring your *creative* mind with Brainstorming, to unlock fresh approaches and restore some old fun.[41] For example, list the "Ten Most Unusual Ways to Present this Topic," then pick and use the best one.

"THE THINKING WAS . . ."

Normally, few of us (besides con artists or chronic liars) are very good at convincing people to believe things we don't personally believe. Ideally, to be an effective seller of a product, service, or idea, you should be an enthusiastic "true believer."

The reality of modern organizations, however, is that things are not always ideal. You'll sometimes find yourself in tough corners, arguing hard-to-defend positions. For example, what if you must defend a controversial decision you don't personally agree with--maybe even one you fought *against*--but now it's your job to go out and persuade others to accept your organization's new "party line"?

What do you say to the skeptics?

How do you answer, especially, if some disgruntled colleague reacts like this?:

"That's crazy! How can you feed us such a dumb-fool idea? Listen, it's those headquarters clowns thinking this one up, isn't it? Come on, tell the truth--you don't buy this yourself, do you?"

---

[41]To review Brainstorming, see chapter 14, pp. 128-144.

Make a hundred warning lights flash "DANGER!" in
your brain, and firmly resist all temptations to go off-the-
record or grind your own, suppressed axe. For example, do
not reply:

> *"Yes, you're absolutely right. It's really a dumb-fool
> idea! But did those bozos on top listen to me?--No! So
> now we're stuck with it, like it or not."*

In its naked candor, this answer may be true, but it's a
terribly poor choice: it makes you sound disloyal and look
unprofessional; it stirs up fires of discontent. Normally, the
role of a spokesperson is to be a team player: you must
support the chosen policy and do your best job of explaining
it, tactfully.

If you can't defend your leadership's decision, it's better
to send someone else to speak. Or, at least--before you go
into the field to face the troops--you must understand exactly
why a decision was made, and be ready to defend it, in its
own terms.

(The only exception, of course, would be a matter of
conscience--where, to you, a proposed action seems unethical
or illegal. In such cases, you would decline to defend the
action and might choose to resign from the organization, as
well.)

Most times, however, you won't face a major struggle of
personal conviction, but only a minor internal difference of
opinion.

So, again, how can you handle this situation best? How
can you defend the decision, while gracefully sidestepping
arguments over whether you personally agree with it or not?

As a solution, try using the helpful key phrase: *"The
thinking was . . . ."* Specifically, when the question comes, first
say, "Well, the thinking was . . .," and then explain (factually
and objectively) why and how the decision itself was
reached, and do not voice judgment on it.

In essence, you're avoiding the temptation to state your
own opinion, for the record; instead, you refocus attention on
the decision itself. And, if the incorrigible reply comes back?:

> *"Sure, that was their thinking--but it's not yours, is it?
> Don't you really think it's a stupid idea?"*

Again, take a deep breath, stay professional, don't take the bait, and say something like:

"This decision has been made. It's what we're going to do and I intend to give 100% effort to make it work. Will you help, too, and give it a fair try?"

This phrase, "the thinking was" (or similar ones), thus helps you escape from a compromising dilemma. No longer must you choose between being: (a) disloyal to your organization, or: (b) dishonest about your own inner convictions.

By putting the argument at half-arm's length, you should now feel more confident (if not totally enthusiastic) about defending a decision, policy, or action you may not privately agree with.

2. IMAGE

Ideally, when talking to a new group, you'd like them to pay attention to what you say, think, and feel--in sum, to what's in your heart and mind, no matter how you happen to look, physically.

In reality, however, it's no secret that before you speak a word, people are already judging you, subconsciously, by factors that are both intangible and superficial: in a nutshell, by your personal *image*.

Your image is the total impact you make (especially visually) when you face a group: How do you look? Do you breed confidence or send "bad vibes"? Are you disheveled and ill at ease? Are you handsome, beautiful?

To others, your personal "image" is how you *appear* to be; however, it may or may *not* be what you also really are. Someone may quickly react to you with prejudice (*pre*-judgment) and jump to a generalized, mistaken view of you, based on superficial aspects like your skin color, age, or sex.

It is the reality of our world. Wrongly or not, other people *do* react this way: they form strong first impressions of you based on secondary factors (your looks, manners, or sound of voice), and these impressions influence how you get treated, in every way.

Moreover, psychologists have shown that a definite "halo effect" exists, by which people who are taller and better-looking, for instance, tend to be more influential than those who are shorter or less attractive.[42]

At the extreme, John T. Molloy has implied that your odds for success are best in 20th-century America if you are a tall, youngish, dark-haired, handsome, healthy-looking, white male, with upper-middle-class social skills and speech patterns (preferably a New England accent).[43]

In general, therefore, human communication is easiest between people who are the most "alike," although, as time passes, our "differences" can become less important.

Your image is most potent, then, as a first impression; later, its effects may wear off. Often, however, the impact of a first impression (good or bad) can never be fully undone; it remains long-lasting and irreversible.[44]

DRESS FOR SUCCESS?

In recent years, much attention has rightfully been paid to the importance of IMAGE and the need for ambitious people to look good--namely, to "dress for success." [45]

Does how you dress make any real difference? Yes, dressing well--or especially dressing *correctly*--can be very important. If nothing else, it assures you of the absence of a negative--that is, it keeps you from dressing wrong, looking silly, feeling embarrassed, being discounted.

---

[42]Another common example of the "halo effect"--according to the *Oxford Companion to the Mind* (Oxford: Oxford University Press, 1987, p. 300)--would be that "we may regard people wearing spectacles as especially intelligent."

[43]John T. Molloy, *Live for Success* (New York: William Morrow, 1981), passim.

[44]For a detailed look at the power of first impressions, see: Leonard Zunin, with Natalie Zunin, *Contact: The First Four Minutes* (New York: Ballantine Books, 1973). Also see: Janet G. Elsea, *The Four-Minute Sell* (New York: Simon and Schuster, 1984).

[45]The term, "Dress for Success," was originally derived from John T. Molloy's popular book, *Dress for Success* (New York: Warner Books, 1975). Numerous other books have by now been written on the subject for both men and women.

Numerous books, articles, workshops, and consultations offer you detailed guidance on how to choose, buy, and wear clothes to look your best. Some even guide you in dressing yourself by well-chosen colors to match your personality and "season."[46]

How you look is not something to get careless about. On the other hand, an obsession with image (to the detriment of performance) can be overdone, too--as the famous image consultant, John T. Molloy himself, finally suggested.[47]

Another thoughtful writer, Srully Blotnick, has also argued against trying too hard to "dress for success." His own research suggests that in top U.S. corporations today, to look "high-fashion or excessively neat" is to convey the wrong image: that of someone more concerned with style than substance.

A better image (says Blotnick) turns out to be "the slightly rumpled look," which suggests you're someone willing to roll up your sleeves and dig into the job.[48]

At the rough-edged extreme, apocryphal tales sometimes get told, like: "Remember old so-and-so, who strolled into that Wall Street showdown in a cowboy hat and boots? Yeah, and how 'bout that gal who held a labor negotiation while wearing a see-through blouse? Mercy!"

Such tales extol alleged victories of legendary folks who supposedly dressed, on purpose, against the expectations of the crowd, and succeeded. But stop and think. Maybe, occasionally, some rare genius does follow his or her own drummer and dress outlandishly. But should you?

When you dress for eccentricity--even if you calculate exactly what you're doing--you run a big, unnecessary risk. (At a minimum, if you knowingly break the rules, be sure you really *are* a genius, not just someone trying to look eccentric.)

---

[46]For an interesting approach to image, based on color, see: [for women] Carole Jackson, *Color Me Beautiful* (New York: Ballantine Books, 1984); and, [for men] Carole Jackson, with Kalia Lulow, *Color for Men* (New York: Ballantine Books, 1984).

[47]Robert Masello, "Mr. Dress for Success Fights Back," *Success*, April 1984, pp. 18-22.

[48]Srully Blotnick, "Loosen that Tie," *Forbes* (December 29, 1986), p. 124.

Usually, isn't it smarter and safer to go *with*, not *against*, expectations?

YOUR IMAGE: GUIDELINES

For your best image, then, here are a few traditional guidelines likely in most business settings to stay true:

(1) Always look neat and professional. Be clean and well-groomed. Avoid wrinkled clothes, dirty shoes, unkempt hair.

(2) Be subtle, not brash. Avoid clothes that visually "shout" (e.g., polka dots against stripes). Also, don't wear noisy jewelry.

(3) Get a sense of color and harmony. Learn to pick clothes and accessories that blend together well. Look well-coordinated (but not prefabricated).

(4) If in doubt, stay traditional. Shun most trendy fashions: no outrageous hairstyles, no bizarre accessories.

(5) Add, however, a personal touch for personality: a splash of color, a fine watch, a leather belt, a top-quality briefcase, etc.

(6) For serious business, wear your best "power" suit (normally, dark blue or black, with a white shirt or blouse), to look dignified and feel most powerful.

(7) Improve the body inside the clothes, too. To look good, get fit and stay healthy with enough rest, proper diet, and regular exercise.

(8) Always act (as well as look) like a professional: be courteous and friendly, never arrogant nor aloof. Actions speak louder than expensive suits.

(9) On balance, simply know and meet the expectations of the moment--in other words, follow decorum and dress appropriately.

IMAGE IS ALL THINGS

The sanest approach to IMAGE, then, is to accept those qualities you cannot change (your age, race, sex), and focus solely on what you *can* control: your dress, posture, neatness, attitude.

Everything you do (not just your appearance) will affect your image. So, be careful to treat everyone with attentive respect off-stage, too (in other words, *before* and *after* as well as *during* your great performance).

As a last word on IMAGE, remember: The right image is only a way to *enhance* your message--it's not an end in itself nor a replacement for real substance. The main thing is simply to look your best and dress appropriately for the situation.

Be aware of IMAGE, and learn to use its power to your advantage, but also don't over-rely upon it. Even in the finest clothes money can buy, a fool is still only a well-dressed fool.

3. POISE

A facetious statement goes: "If you can keep your head, while all about are losing theirs, it's just possible you haven't grasped the situation."[49]

Likewise, it's been said: "It's hard to think of draining the swamp when you're up to your eyeballs in alligators."

The point is, of course, that when tension gets high and things go wrong, it's hard not to panic. One true test of a solid professional, then, is how well he or she maintains *poise* after being clobbered by the unexpected.

POISE is the ability to think on your feet, clearly and quickly, in midst of a crisis, and act with the kind of guts that Ernest Hemingway called "grace under pressure."

---

[49]Jean Kerr, *Please Don't Eat the Daisies* (1957).

To have poise is to project (at least outwardly) a sense of staying calm and being in control.

In real life, furthermore, the question is seldom: "What will you do *if* things go wrong?" but rather: ". . . *when* things go wrong." No matter how ready you feel before a talk, Reality can usually find some new, freakish surprise to spring on you. A real professional learns always to expect--and plan for--the unexpected.

"But I assumed . . ."

In self-defense, however, you cannot just play everything safe. To gain success, you usually have to risk failure. In other words, your plan must *not* simply be "to avoid the threat itself" (to skip the talk and sidestep all errors).

Take football, for example. Is the winning team always the one with the least fumbles or fewest interceptions? No, while winning, most winners make some mistakes: they fumble, get penalized, have interceptions.

The winner, though, is the one who (when the final whistle blows) has scored the most points. In baseball, too, the greatest home-run hitters (Babe Ruth, Hank Aaron, Reggie Jackson) often have the most strikeouts.

The difference between winners and losers usually is what happens *after* a mistake is made: Do they crumble or dig in harder? Do they minimize the damage? Do they learn from each mistake and avoid it next time?

Before you walk into a major presentation, anticipate the most likely things that could go wrong. Then, protect yourself: make a set of "what-if" contingency plans (Plan B, even Plans C or D, if needed), and know what you'll do if this-or-that occurs.

As a few examples:

A. *WHAT IF* ....they ask an unanswerable question?

> BEST: Anticipate the question, and know how
> you'll handle it, beforehand.
> PLAN B: Admit you can't answer and promise to
> get the answer promptly (NO-BLUFF).

B. *WHAT IF*........they ask you, on the spot, to cut
> your 30-minute pitch down to only
> 5 minutes?

> PLAN B: (1) Have a short, capsule version of the
> talk ready, going in; or, (2) be prepared to
> explain why you need the whole 30 minutes.

C. *WHAT IF* ....your projector breaks down?

> PLAN B: Have an extra projector on hand.
> PLAN C: Carry a set of back-up handouts (to use
> as substitute visuals).
> PLAN D: Know whom to call for help.

KEEPING YOUR HEAD

Your list of "what-if" contingencies can get infinite, so it's sensible to just figure out (and get ready for) only the most likely "Murphies."

For future encounters, here are five other suggestions on how to keep your poise when things go wrong:

1. **EXPECT TO BE "MURPHIED."** Murphy's Law
   is inescapable; it's a universal law of reality. So,
   realize--at that bitterest moment when chaos
   strikes--that it's rotten but normal: If anything can
   go wrong, it often does. Try to prevent it, but
   when it happens, don't be overcome with
   innocent surprise ("Why me, Lord?").

2. **STAY CALM.** When things go wrong, don't choke: stay calm. Don't react emotionally; *think* your way out. Teach yourself (by will power, if necessary) to relax quickly in a crisis. Make it a habit. (A good place to start practicing is the dentist's chair--keep telling yourself to relax, and learn to do so.)

3. **KEEP PERSPECTIVE.** When it's a true disaster (everything really *is* falling apart), you might just laugh and tell the truth. Humor beats anger. For example, you can (in an honest, unapologetic way) just say the obvious: "I'm sorry, but this won't work without a projector. Let's stop now, and I'll fix it, then call you back later."

4. **DON'T PASS THE BUCK.** If things go wrong, *you* take the responsibility. Never publicly chastise others (absent or present) for foul-ups. You'll only harm yourself by blaming someone else ("It's that stupid secretary who screwed this up!"). As far as your audience is concerned, if it's your show, *you* take the rap.

5. **ACT QUICKLY.** The best way to handle a snafu is to be decisive. Don't hesitate: act! Correct the problem at once, then get right back onto your original track. By taking action, you'll shift their attention off your mistake and return it to your ideas. Make your motto: "Panic later--but right now: adjust and cope."

Finally, your own attitude of high (or low) confidence will trigger how your audience reacts. They'll literally take cues from you, and be provoked by your fear, soothed by your poise.

So, don't be overly self-conscious or apologetic: "I'm not ready to talk, but I could try, I guess." Don't deliver an ongoing self-critique of your mistakes: "Oops, I dropped my pointer, again, didn't I?" Don't sound sarcastic: "You were holding your breath for this, right?"

Instead, just do the job. Tell your story positively, with the facts you know, and, if you drop something, either leave it alone or quietly pick it up and keep talking.

Overall, don't fear mistakes. To paraphrase Alexander Pope: if you're human, you'll make some mistakes ("To err is human"). However, handle those mistakes--when they do come--with tact, wit, and aplomb. With such poise, you'll earn respect from your audience quickly. They'll recognize you as a cool, calm pro.

4. CHARISMA

The ultimate power for a speaker is that magical quality called "charisma"--a unique intangible that sets one person widely apart from ordinary human beings.

Yet, what is charisma? Who has it, and why? Charisma is hard to define. Try describing it, and it sounds almost supernatural: Charisma is a mysterious force. It acts in unknown ways. It's like a hypnotic attraction. Someone with charisma can fascinate individuals and mesmerize whole crowds. It's akin to "star quality."[50]

Rasputin, Hitler, Churchill, and Elvis Presley all had charisma. So did Marilyn Monroe and James Dean. Many TV evangelists have had charisma, as well as some modern politicians (John F. Kennedy, Jesse Jackson).

Charisma is the power of personality. By its intensity, and high-pitch excitement, it makes a speaker extraordinary. Does this mean you have to be a mad monk, a rock star, or someone else in the limelight to have charisma?

No, in essence, to have charisma, you must simply dare to be yourself--completely. Follow your best instincts, all the way, and you'll probably show the most charisma--your peak intangible skill. To add excitement and charisma to your own performances, there are some specific things you can do.

------

[50]For other views on charisma, see: Doe Lang, *The Secret of Charisma* (New Choices Press, 1980); Ronald E. Riggio, *The Charisma Quotient* (New York: Dodd, Mead & Co., 1987); Roger Ailes, with Jon Kraushar, *You Are the Message* (Homewood, Ill.: Dow Jones-Irwin, 1988; chapter 9).

HOW TO HAVE CHARISMA

1. **STAY YOURSELF.** Don't pretend. Charisma is real-person power; it's acting *natural* in a high-pressure situation (i.e., speaking to groups) where most people flounder.

2. **BE DRAMATIC.** Charismatic people are not boring. They are mysterious. They generate strong emotions. Learn to *dramatize* the situation, yourself, and the topic.

3. **KEEP MOVING.** Hardly anyone can hope to be charismatic by being frozen and static. Use dynamic *body motion*: walk around, point, gesture, show visuals--move!

4. **PROJECT ENERGY.** Charisma is a positive force: it's a sense of vitality; it's *high-energy* joy. Dull, lifeless performances bring apathy, not charisma.

5. **USE VARIETY.** To have charisma, do the unexpected. Keep them interested and guessing. Use suspense, change of pace, pauses, etc. Be daring. Be *unpredictable.*

6. **KEEP CONFIDENT.** A charismatic person inspires faith and communicates pure *confidence.* To have charisma, then, overcome your self-doubts. Believe in yourself, fully.

7. **ANALYZE THE GREATS.** To know charisma better, study the exciting speakers you'd call *"spellbinders"*: Why do they have charisma? What can you learn from them?

BE THYSELF

Still, are you convinced you're just a normal, regular person? You seldom (if ever) expect *yourself* to have strong personal charisma? That's a sane, realistic expectation.

Few speakers *are*, at first, truly "charismatic." To speak effectively, most people must first improve their basic delivery techniques--their Voice, Eye Contact, Posture, and Gestures. Only afterwards, once your delivery gets solid, should you expect to display Charisma.[51]

Yet, all the intangibles--including charisma--are tools that you, too, can master. Without a doubt, your ability to speak well is often an essential part of your ability to persuade others.

Also keep in mind, though, that the most impressive-sounding speaker is not necessarily the best person.

For you, the power of Charisma itself--like the other intangibles of Enthusiasm, Image, and Poise--should only be an enhancement of (not a substitute for) good ideas, quick wits, and a kind heart.

When you speak, then, the most successful (and most charismatic) person *you* can be is still . . . your natural self!

---

[51]For more on how to develop your Charisma, see: "Secrets of the Spellbinders" in chapter 4, pp. 45-51.

Chapter 21

SPEAKING WITH STYLE

"Style is the dress of thoughts."
-- Lord Chesterfield

HOW TO BE HEARD

Perhaps a nagging question still remains . . . who cares if your charisma can't move mountains? Isn't the real goal to know *what* you're talking about, not *how* you say it? In other words, how important--really--is STYLE?

In the long run, there's no substitute for solid knowledge. Any victories won by crafty communication alone, without substance, usually bring a glory that's shallow and fleeting.

Haven't plenty of successful men and women won recognition without being orators of the first degree? What about Harry Truman? If you compare Truman against a bombastic speaker like Winston Churchill, you'd label Truman's own oratorical ability as plain-spoken and ordinary.

Still, Truman got the job done--so well, in fact, that many now rate him as one of the greatest leaders the United States has known. So, isn't *substance* superior to "style"?

Of course. Substance comes first. Yet, it is *style*, when used well, that gives substance its best chance for success.

A DIAMOND IN MACARONI

Imagine a finely-carved diamond. By itself, the stone is lovely, awesome, priceless. To showcase a diamond's beauty, however, a shrewd jeweler adds enhancers: a background of black velvet, a setting of gold, a well-aimed light.

If the same diamond is displayed carelessly (plopped atop a bowl of macaroni salad?), it loses allure. Yet, objectively--whether on velvet or macaroni--that diamond is still that diamond: it's the same substance, just in a different environment.

In everyday reality, many *ideas* get presented like diamonds in macaroni ("here's an idea"--plop!). Fortunately, some ideas survive by selling themselves. As ideas, they are so good without enhancement that they get heard *in spite of* the ineffectual ways they get presented.

Few ideas sell themselves automatically, however. Plus, a person with good ideas (like yourself) can be even *more* successful by communicating those good ideas to others in the right style.

What determines the right STYLE for a speaker?

A SPECTRUM OF STYLE

The overall "style" for any presentation can be analyzed as the sum of many separate, personal choices.

In practical terms, these choices are *not* made from absolute extremes. A speaking style that is "formal," for instance, is not simply the exact opposite of a style that is "informal."

Instead, a certain *style* is a complex "mix" of elements from along a continuum (i.e., a range) of many possibilities. Thus, the stylistic mix symbolized at point A below is very formal; Style B would be relatively informal:

FORMAL / /\/ / / / / / / /\/ / / / INFORMAL

     ↑   ↑

   Style A   *Style B*

Every other "mix" point (possible styles C, D, etc.) is likewise relative, not absolute. So, every style is best understood by comparing it to other possible choices.

Normally, you make such stylistic choices instinctively-- nobody really thinks about it; he/she just does it subconsciously.

When unsure, however, a speaker can stop and think about the choices. To select the right STYLE for a presentation, you need to ask yourself six questions, which cover all elements in a SPECTRUM of style:

A SPECTRUM OF STYLE

FORMAL .... INFORMAL
DIRECT .... INDIRECT
LOGICAL .... EMOTIONAL
OBJECTIVE .... SUBJECTIVE
IMPERSONAL .... PERSONAL
SERIOUS .... HUMOROUS

Question #1: Should the overall style for this talk be **FORMAL or INFORMAL?**

Your first, most basic choice about style is whether to be formal or informal. How do you choose?

Like appropriate styles of dress (tuxedo or gym shorts) or eating (at a picnic vs. dinner party), the correct style of speaking is often dictated by the situation itself. It depends: Sometimes, a formal style should be used; in other situations, a more informal style is best.

To help you choose between a formal or informal style, consider three things about the situation:

(a) the topic . . . what seems most appropriate?;
(b) the audience . . . what do they expect?; and,
(c) your own tendencies . . . what feels most natural?

FORMAL

FORMAL style follows the strictest standards of a most conventional approach. It has clearly-defined expectations, so it allows the speaker less flexibility.

The speaker projects a "businesslike" image. He or she normally speaks from a stand-up position behind a lectern, using the Authority Posture. If seated, the speaker still keeps erect body posture.

The appropriate dress is traditional business attire (i.e., for men: a coat and tie; for women: a tailored dress or suit).

The speaker's word choice is businesslike and precise, too. Slang is avoided (except for business jargon); profanity is out-of-bounds; humor is acceptable but rare. The speaker's gestures are natural yet also well-controlled. Everything looks crisply professional.

From start to finish, the talk is tightly-focused on a single topic. The structure has a clear pattern; it develops the key ideas within a definite framework.

Some visuals are expected, and those used are neat, sharp, and meaningful. Overall, the talk is well-planned and (whenever possible) well-rehearsed.

Typical situations requiring a **FORMAL** style are: an Entry/Exit Briefing; a City Council Presentation; a Press Conference; a Paper at a Technical Symposium.

INFORMAL

The INFORMAL style has looser standards and less rigid expectations. It allows the individual speaker more room for personal expression.

The image projected is less deliberate, more casual. The speaker may stand (probably using Casual Posture) or sit. Even if a lectern is used, the speaker is likely to roam out from behind it.

The stricter code of attire is also relaxed, depending on the audience and situation (you might, for example, take off your coat or roll up your sleeves).

The speaker's language remains clear and precise, but more leeway is possible. Words can be more colloquial, more down-to-earth. Idiomatic slang is more permissible; profanity may occasionally appear; humor is more likely. The speaker's gestures are freer, less controlled. Usually, the audience is more tolerant towards personal idiosyncrasies in expression or dress.

The structure can also be looser and less obvious, with no definite framework. The focus stays on a single topic, but the scope may range broadly. The speaker may stray off onto sidetracks. The standards for visuals are usually relaxed, too, to accept last-minute additions.

Nevertheless, an informal talk may actually be as well-planned and well-rehearsed as a formal one--it's more often just the style of presentation that changes.

Typical situations requiring an **INFORMAL** style are: a Late-Notice Briefing; a Club Talk; Classroom Instruction; an After-Dinner Speech.

> Question #2:   Should your approach be **DIRECT** or
>   **INDIRECT**?

DIRECT

In the DIRECT approach, you simply "come to the point" immediately, as in the AGENDA opening (chapter 9). Tell the audience exactly what the topic is, why you're talking about it, and (when so) that a decision is being sought from them.

You'll recall that if your talks convey factual information, for neutral-to-receptive audiences, you should prefer this *direct* approach at least 95 percent of the time.

DIRECT OPENING: If you ever wonder--"To be direct, or not to be?"--then check your audience. Can you realistically expect that: (a) your credibility is high (i.e., they already like you and trust your expertise); or, (b) that your message is neutral, or even good news? Then, in either case, your OPENING should normally be direct.

DIRECT CLOSING: Also, consider the CLOSING based on audience. Do you believe that your decision maker: (a) is habitually indecisive, (b) often makes snap judgments, or (c) hates to make tough choices? In such cases, you should end *directly*, by giving them a specific request or one definite recommendation (not a "laundry list" of possibilities).

For example (Direct Closing):

"So, as you've seen, the Treetop Project is now on schedule, under budget, and technically feasible. We welcome your agreement to move into production phase."

INDIRECT

The INDIRECT approach, on the other hand, occurs when you do *not* immediately reveal things like the topic, your motives, or the desired outcome. The indirect opening relies for its effect upon mystery, suspense, and even deception.

However, you'll also recall that, from the audience's standpoint, an indirect approach is normally dangerous. By concealing your real purpose, you may create confusion, misunderstanding, or audience "tune-out."

So, for factual talks (like information briefings, in particular), you should avoid the Indirect approach. Use it, at most, no more than about 5 percent of the time.

INDIRECT OPENING: When *should* you be Indirect? As always, first check your audience. You might consider an Indirect OPENING if you expect that: (a) your credibility is low (i.e., they already dislike or distrust you); (b) they'll walk in hostile, ready to counterattack any argument you make; (c) they are skeptics who (wrongly) consider themselves to be experts in your own field, too; or, (d) you're bringing very bad news.

INDIRECT CLOSING: Consider the audience, again, for an Indirect CLOSING. Do you expect that your decision maker: (a) is habitually decisive, (b) seldom jumps to conclusions, and (c) prefers to consider all aspects of a problem. In such cases, you might rather end a talk less directly, by laying out two or more alternatives from which to make a choice.

For example (Indirect Closing):

"So, at the moment, we can go one of three ways: We can do nothing, we can keep studying the problem, or we can move ahead into market testing."

Note that even with closings that indirectly list alternatives, you can still reasonably state your own ideas for the record, too--for instance: "Personally, I would recommend that it's time to test the market."

Of course, in a pure *sales* situation, the selling job is usually more complex, less predictable than most briefings. So, a slower, more indirect approach--when selling products or services--will get better results than a quick leap to the bottom line: "How-do-you-do. So-glad-to-meet-you. Wanna-buy-a-truck? Sign here!"

Again, understand: Your actual decisions about style are more complicated and more difficult than simply choosing from between opposites like "direct" or "indirect."

```
┌─────────────────────────────────────────────┐
│ Question #3:  Should your argument be LOGICAL or │
│               EMOTIONAL?                      │
└─────────────────────────────────────────────┘
```

LOGICAL

A LOGICAL argument is built upon a systematic weighing of the facts. It is analytical, well-reasoned, comparative; it avoids appeals to emotion. It requires the audience to *think*.

Logic is fine, as a tool--it's just not the way most human beings really operate. The main pitfall is that what appears "obvious" or "logical" to you may not look the same to someone else.

Here's an extreme example of "Logical" Argument:

"The solution for this problem is obvious . . . you should fire six people from your staff, reorganize the whole operation, and then quit yourself. It's logical."

The trap, of course, is to assume that *your* logic is theirs. Sometimes, a brilliant solution that is so totally logical (to you) will unexpectedly provoke an angry response that's highly emotional.

Therefore, when you choose what appears to be the most logical solution, be sure to avoid your own blind spots. Beware of dangerous assumptions lurking hidden inside comments like these:

> "I *assume* my logic will be overwhelming."
> "There is *no way* they can say 'No.'"
> "We must do this . . . it's *obvious!*"

Are you an engineer or scientist? Perhaps you intend to propose a technical solution to a research problem? Surely, here, the appropriate argument must be logical? Surely, here, emotion is the wrong basis for a decision.

Even in technical-scientific areas, be prepared to face hidden resistance (at gut-feel level) if your proposal somehow contradicts other people's deeply cherished beliefs, or competes for their money, or just causes them extra work.

A critical peek out your window, at the chaotic planet we live on, gives daily evidence that people do *not* always behave themselves on the basis of logic. As Pascal said: "The heart has its reasons which reason knows nothing of." Today, a skeptical observer might say: "Human beings are illogical creatures who use *logic* to rationalize their emotional decisions."

EMOTIONAL

An EMOTIONAL argument is based on an appeal to deeper passions, with less concern for facts. It's instinctive, simplistic, one-sided; it tries to short-circuit critical thought. It requires the audience to *feel.*

However, an appeal to pure emotion--without any application of logic--is often no argument at all; it's manipulation of the sort we brand "demagoguery." Moreover, if your argument relies mainly upon emotion, it can be weak and ineffectual unless your target crowd already agrees with you fully, so you are already "preaching to the choir":

> *"You want more money, right? YEAH! Let's go on strike! YEAH! We'll show Them, right? YEAH! Are you with me, then? YEAH! Okay, let's do it!"*

Sometimes an argument that pretends to be logical is actually false: it's built on a foundation of underlying emotional assumptions so well-entrenched that its believer is blinded to other viewpoints. Fanatics, for example, feel their premises are self-evident and totally unquestionable. In a sense, their emotions become their logic.

For centuries, amused philosophers have noticed how people tend to argue in repetitious patterns of false logic, called logical "FALLACIES" (such as: begging the question, using invalid syllogisms, arguing in a circle, over-generalizing, and more). It's human nature.

Finally, to answer the question: Should your argument be logical or emotional? Most times, you'll want a balance--namely, an argument that fits together logically yet also moves the audience emotionally. Here are a few guidelines:

1. In general, the more that your audience is intelligent, well-educated, and self-confident, the more a straight emotional pitch towards them will likely be a flop (usually).

2. Almost always avoid making an argument that's purely emotional. You may earn cheers and applause, but the disbelievers will stay unconvinced. Instead, to turn opponents into converts, make your key points appeal to *their* reason and logic.

3. Pure logic alone--like pure emotion--also ends up unconvincing. Logic, minus the human touch, comes across as cold, clinical, and heartless. Whenever possible, go beyond abstract logic; try to stimulate your audience's deeper emotions in a powerful, positive way.

4. Often, the best way to stir your listeners' emotions is to express, sincerely and dynamically, your own emotions--in particular, your *belief* in what you're saying, revealed with genuine enthusiasm.

```
┌─────────────────────────────────────────────┐
│  Question #4:  Should  your  overall  approach  be  │
│                OBJECTIVE or SUBJECTIVE?             │
│                                                     │
└─────────────────────────────────────────────┘
```

OBJECTIVE

The evidence in an OBJECTIVE approach is indisputably provable. The facts are either true or not, and their proof can be shown using tools of the scientific method (such as research, testing, or experimentation).

For example, these points can be proved objectively:

(a) that the boiling point for water at sea level is 100° Centigrade;

(b) that the gross sales made by a business during its third quarter were $34 million;

(c) that the airline distance from Vancouver to Cairo is 6,725 statute miles.

In reality, information that is totally "objective" is rare. Typically, for an objective approach to be possible, the issue must be narrow and deal with mathematics, physical phenomena, or past events. Once you cross the barrier into *future* events or *social* phenomena, your approach becomes inescapably more subjective and less provable.

SUBJECTIVE

The evidence in a SUBJECTIVE approach is not absolutely provable beyond a possible doubt. The facts may be true or not, depending on factors that are perhaps unavailable or unknowable. Subjective proof, therefore, is more a matter of opinion.

Indeed, few things in life are absolutely, positively, "objectively" provable. This realization gave birth to Anderson's Law:

> ## ANDERSON'S LAW
>
> *"You never really know what you're getting into . . .*
> *until after you're already in it."*

Most human decisions are, in truth, subjective. Using past experience, probabilities, inner voices, or whatever, we choose to take a job, buy a house, hire an employee, etc. But how do you know, really, if that's the correct decision?

You may not know if a decision is good until you make *some* decision and try it. Only afterwards can you look over your shoulder and test its validity with 20-20 hindsight.

What is the relevance of "subjectivity" to your style in a briefing? In essence, recognize how little of the information we get each day is truly objective. Strive to uncover those "unshakable facts." Much of what we think or say (even in presentations) is often personal opinion, masquerading as objective fact.

Most audiences expect you to filter blatant subjectivity from your talk. Others (for example, in scientific or business communities) will expect more--that your talk is thoroughly and rigorously objective. *Prove it!*, they'll demand.

Question #5:   Should you stay **IMPERSONAL** or add **PERSONAL** elements?

IMPERSONAL

Basically, an impersonal approach is one that avoids all personal references. Instead of talking about specific people in first-person, active voice ("Nancy felt the best solution was . . ."), you tell of neutral operations and procedures, of processes and outcomes, using a third-person, passive voice ("It should be noted that the value was determined to be . . .").

Generally, an impersonal approach is safest with unknown audiences or in unpredictable situations, and often the impersonal is expected for on-the-job, stand-up, business style. The impersonal approach is also preferred in most scientific and technical arenas.

The impersonal style has a significant drawback, though. Because it avoids the human dimension, it can sound antiseptic, mechanical, bloodless, and dull.

PERSONAL

The personal approach does not cast decisions in terms of vague and impersonal processes. Instead, situations are depicted as vital accomplishments of specific women and men. Outcomes are treated as the result of real people, thinking and acting.

Personal style thus focuses your talk upon the human element. You might cite key persons by name, allude to earlier group milestones, or spotlight this moment in the context of history.

Normally, personal style keeps better "human interest"; impersonal style breeds more yawns and snores.

Compare:

IMPERSONAL: *"CRP, Limited, was founded in 1969 by a consortium of investors with the goal of providing a nexus of skills on micro scale in response to the service needs of certain macro, multi-faceted client bases."*

PERSONAL: *"CRP started in 1969 in Joel Finster's basement when he, Helena Bass, and Willy Ornot decided the world was ready for a small, flexible company to serve larger, multi-faceted clients."*

As a rule, you ought to personalize each talk for each specific audience. You can add life to even the most impersonal talk with a personal touch or two.

Exactly how "personal" should you get? In most situations, it's good to explain your own involvement in the topic, to answer the frequent (though unspoken) audience question: "Why are *you* talking about this?"

Avoid gratuitous self-promotion, of course--don't start handing out a flood of business cards. Mention your own authority and personal experience without fanfare. Your willingness (and ability) to tell an audience, "Look, I've been there," is the best credibility-builder.

```
┌─────────────────────────────────────────┐
│                                         │
│  Question #6:  Should  you  stay  SERIOUS  or  be  │
│               HUMOROUS?                 │
│                                         │
└─────────────────────────────────────────┘
```

SERIOUS

In some offices, feeble humor seems almost expected in a talk. It's an unwritten tradition, compelling each speaker to follow the habitual routine: first, stand up and tell a dumb joke to "warm up" the audience before shifting onto the real subject.

Certainly, neither life nor oral presentations should stay purely solemn, deadly serious all the time. But while there's a time for laughs, there's also a time to be serious, and good speakers can tell the difference.

In most cases, the SERIOUS approach, which avoids any attempt at humor or frivolity, is actually best.

Situation may also demand that your style be strictly-business and highly serious. For example, keep your style serious when:

(a) the audience has a major fear (e.g., loss of jobs, survival of bankruptcy, risk to life and limb);

(b) the audience is known to be "stuffed shirts," who are ultra-pompous, imperial, and humorless;

(c) the topic clearly demands a special reverence (e.g., it deals with someone's basic values, religion, or family);

(d) the topic is sensitive, inflammatory, and provokes strong feelings on all sides (e.g., homosexuality, capital punishment, abortion);

(e) the overall mood of the situation is very serious (e.g., a national or professional crisis).

HUMOROUS

The tone of your talk is usually dictated by three factors: (1) the audience, (2) the topic, and (3) the situation.

Comedians make things comic by *reversing* normal expectations--by treating a reverential subject or person (the President) with silly disrespect (in satire), or by handling a trivial matter (the death of a flea) with mock seriousness (in burlesque or farce).

Humor is difficult to pull off because everyone's sense of humor is personal and idiosyncratic--what one person finds totally hilarious may just cause someone else to frown, look puzzled, or groan.

Humor can also be a swift, memorable way to get your point across. A few leaders (notably, John F. Kennedy and Ronald Reagan) have made quick wit their ally and used it admirably well. A good chuckle can bring insight to your talk, neutralize opposition, and humanize yourself as a speaker.

When applied poorly, however--as many speakers do--humor is a fast highway to embarrassing oblivion. Like a jalapeno pepper, humor adds a dash of spice; but also like high-potency flavorings, a little goes a long way. Use it with caution. Of all elements of style, humor (when it backfires) can be the most harmful.

In particular, avoid making flippant remarks or ad-lib put-downs you think are funny. Public attacks against others are easily misinterpreted, and also--by offering the media its most colorful "quote of the day"--are most likely to be broadcast and re-heard.

Speak kindly. All your earthly, good deeds may be quickly forgotten if a single, juicy, vicious wisecrack immortalizes you instantly and eternally as a flaming so-and-so.

As a final word on humor, just remember that it can be treacherous. Never use any joke unless you're fully convinced it is: (a) relevant to the topic, (b) appropriate for the audience, and (c) reliably funny.

When you pick a STYLE for your next talk, you'll be deciding (consciously or subconsciously) whether it's better to lean towards one or another extreme:

FORMAL	- or -	INFORMAL
DIRECT	- or -	INDIRECT
LOGICAL	- or -	EMOTIONAL
OBJECTIVE	- or -	SUBJECTIVE
IMPERSONAL	- or -	PERSONAL
SERIOUS	- or -	HUMOROUS

If in doubt, *play it safe*. Choose each element of your style from the left-hand column. For a professional stand-up briefing, the normal expected style would be FORMAL using a DIRECT approach, with LOGICAL and OBJECTIVE arguments, staying generally IMPERSONAL in a SERIOUS tone. (This may also be a recipe for chronic boredom.)

By adding right-hand column components (the INFORMAL, INDIRECT, etc.), you'll add color and excitement to your style. They should be used in talks, too; otherwise, your speech will be bland. Keep in mind, however, that these elements are less conventional and are riskier. Therefore, since they add new dangers, use them sparingly and artfully--or not at all.

SAY IT WITH STYLE

"Style," as we've seen, is really the unique combination of all choices you make for a given talk--your dress (formal or casual), words (slang or technical), structure (tight or free-flowing), and everything else--all of which add up to a total impression made upon your audience (i.e., your overall style).

Your style must also reflect your own personality and natural tendencies. Two different speakers might use two opposite styles, yet each could be equally effective. Churchill and Truman as speakers were very unalike, but both were highly effective--largely because each chose a style that allowed him to stay true to himself.

In choosing an appropriate STYLE for any talk, ask yourself this critical question:

"Is this the most effective style for speaking to *this* audience on *this* topic at *this* time . . . and is this style naturally comfortable for me?"

Chapter 22

RULE #8:

ADD IMPACT WITH VISUALS

"One showing is worth a hundred sayings."
                     -- Chinese proverb

INFORMATION, PLEASE

Suppose, in talk after talk, you tell facts that are true and startling . . . yet still audiences with undue disrespect keep falling asleep and sometimes even rudely insist on saying "No" to you.

What's the problem? Could it be that your talk was built only from what Hamlet called "words, words, words"?

Many people create a talk, without thinking much about it, in three straight steps: (1) do the research, (2) outline the findings, and (3) face the audience to report the facts. They concentrate only upon the talk's verbal content--as if facts are facts and truth is truth, no matter how you say it.

The unforgiving reality, however, is that words are very seldom neutral or impartial. Words can carry high-intensity charges (connotations and associations) that have power to soothe or inflame.

Consider how differently the same words, "You really look great," would sound when spoken with honest appreciation versus biting sarcasm.

Unlike mathematics, words can be hopelessly sloppy and imprecise. Words can be ambiguous and confuse us. Words can seem overly abstract, cold and empty, almost meaningless. Or words can be intensely personal, immediate and emotional, full of hidden meaning.

Although the information in your talk is usually "verbal," those words and numbers seldom tell the whole story. (Any speaker who thinks, "Facts are facts and that's that," implies that there's no difference between saying you're "having a steak" or you're "eating dead cow meat.")

Normally, you communicate orally with people in three modes at once: verbal, nonverbal, and audio-visual, each of which helps determine how well you do or don't get your message across.

The **VERBAL** is, of course, the basic "content" of the message itself: it's *what* you say.

The **NONVERBAL** is the body language (tone of voice, eye contact, facial expression, and so forth) which gives real, personal meaning to your words: it's *how* you say it.

The **AUDIO-VISUAL** is any extra aid or equipment outside yourself that your audience sees or hears (such as a chart, handout, photo, or model), which helps them understand your ideas better: it *amplifies* or *vivifies* your message.

Audio-visual (AV) aids are important to you because most people remember what they *see* much longer and better than what they *hear*. (The usual estimate is that what you show an audience carries about THREE TIMES more impact than what you tell them.)

So, long after they've forgotten your spoken words, they'll typically remember your visuals. Yet, this most powerful communication tool--the visual sense--is also the one that many speakers often use most ineptly.

DEADLY DANGER #8 - **BAD VISUALS**

BLINDED BY LIGHT

Anyone who attends enough oral presentations can compile a full catalogue of horrors on the use and abuse of audio-visual (AV) equipment. For instance, pity the poor audience who must watch the first public encounter between a nervous, ill-prepared novice and an overhead projector.

Sometimes it's the beginning of a major briefing for a high-level audience with an important decision at stake. Yet, amazingly, the speaker acts as if he is discovering AV equipment for the first time in his life. Astonished, the audience watches as he fumbles and moans: "How do you turn this thing on, anyway?"

With AV aids, even experienced speakers can be awkward and amateurish beyond common sense--by showing visuals that are too small for anyone to see without binoculars, or too busy and complex to highlight their key points, or simply inappropriate for a professional setting. The examples are endless.

However, a good audio-visual, well-used, is a tremendous aid (in every sense) to a presentation. It can dramatize an idea, make it memorable, and add clarity. The right graph can show your audience a picture--simply and directly--that ambiguous words and scattered numbers could never capture.

Nevertheless, many speakers seem reluctant to add audio-visuals to their talks. Their presentations stay just talk, talk, talk, without visual clarity. Why?

Some are reluctant because they're unfamiliar with the equipment. It's always awkward to handle an intimidating technology (even a slide projector) until its use becomes second nature.

The main blame, however, most likely goes to all those maladroit mishaps we've endured as frustrated victims of someone else's audio-visuals, which were designed badly and used poorly. Visual aids have been so misused so frequently by so many that by now many presenters and audiences have gotten "turned off" to visuals altogether.

BASIC AV PRINCIPLES

Visuals can be valuable, though, and need not be used poorly. Here are a dozen-and-one principles (with practical tips) for the successful use of audio-visuals:[52]

---

[52]For more guidance on audio-visuals, see also chapter 23, "Facts into Visuals"; chapter 24, "AV Murphies and Gremlins"; and appendix D, "Audio-Visual Aids and Technology Selector."

```
┌─────────────────────────────────────────────┐
│   PRINCIPLE #1 - *KEEP IT SIMPLE*             │
└─────────────────────────────────────────────┘
```

PRINCIPLE #1 - *KEEP IT SIMPLE*

The worst and most common mistake made when people use AV aids is over-complication. Typically, the speaker tries to cram far too much complex, detailed information onto one visual and all the audience gets is confused.

To assure yourself of good visuals, then, always follow the K.I.S. principle: KEEP IT SIMPLE. In every visual aid you use (including handouts), plan for and demand simplicity!

Show only one basic idea or image per visual. Don't piggyback additional information onto the same slide or chart.

With a detailed photo or complex drawing, ease your audience in: First, show them a simple line drawing that explains the item as a model before you spring "the real thing."

In general, with audio-visuals *less* is usually *best*.

```
┌─────────────────────────────────────────────┐
│   PRINCIPLE #2 - *MAKE IT BIG ENOUGH FOR*     │
│              *EVERYONE TO SEE*                │
└─────────────────────────────────────────────┘
```

PRINCIPLE #2 - *MAKE IT BIG ENOUGH FOR EVERYONE TO SEE*

Another common and unforgivable error is to show an audience visuals that are so tiny they are impossible to read or understand.

Occasionally, speakers who show illegible visuals boldly attempt to gloss over their misdeed by intoning: "I *know* you can't read this--but . . . ." But this excuse can never salvage the fact that the visual is too small. ("So why *show* it?" wonders the bewildered audience.)

Never show an audience a visual that is too small to be read or understood easily by the person who is seated or standing farthest away from it.

If you must use a visual whose detail is impossible to see fully, explain why. For example: "I'm showing this just to give you a rough idea of what this form looks like--I don't expect you to read all the fine print."

Don't forget that the size factor applies equally to models, components, photographs, or other things that you might hold up and show--not just projected visuals or charts.

```
┌─────────────────────────────────────────────┐
│                                             │
│  PRINCIPLE #3 - KEEP AUDIENCE INVOLVEMENT   │
│                                             │
└─────────────────────────────────────────────┘
```

Visual aids can become seductive traps. Many times an otherwise-competent speaker falls into rapt conversation with his visual aid, totally ignoring the people in his audience. It's a frequent mistake.

Don't make this error yourself. Make a special effort at all times to stay fully involved with your audience when you use visual aids.

Talk to the audience, not the visual aid. Keep eye contact at least 85 percent of the time with people; look no more than 15 percent of the time at visuals and notes.

Also avoid blocking your audience's view by unforeseen obstructions--i.e., lectern, overhead projector, other attendees, or yourself (standing in front of the screen). Consider suggesting, as people arrive, that they sit where their view of the screen is clear.

If your visuals are projected onto a screen behind you, walk back next to the screen and talk from there. Be a conduit of information between the visual and your audience (not a "disembodied voice," narrating from afar, while pictures flash by, on the horizon).

```
┌─────────────────────────────────────────────┐
│                                             │
│  PRINCIPLE #4 - USE COLOR WHEN POSSIBLE     │
│                  FOR EMPHASIS               │
└─────────────────────────────────────────────┘
```

Normally, a visual that's monochrome (all black and white) is less exciting than one with color. With detailed pictures or drawings, also, a one-color visual can look like a complicated jumble.

Continued on Page 243

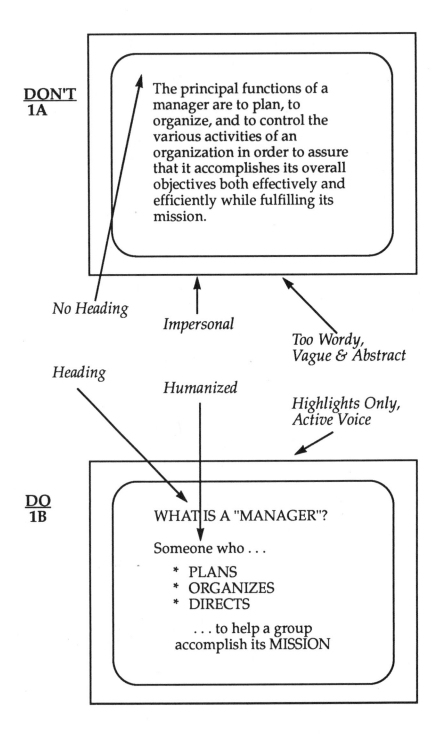

DON'T
1A

The principal functions of a manager are to plan, to organize, and to control the various activities of an organization in order to assure that it accomplishes its overall objectives both effectively and efficiently while fulfilling its mission.

No Heading

Impersonal

Too Wordy,
Vague & Abstract

Heading

Humanized

Highlights Only,
Active Voice

DO
1B

WHAT IS A "MANAGER"?

Someone who . . .

* PLANS
* ORGANIZES
* DIRECTS

. . . to help a group
accomplish its MISSION

Continued from Page 241

So, to help simplify complex visuals and make different parts stand out, it's often essential to add color to your visuals.

When adding color, keep your visuals functional, not "artsy." Be sure they do the job they're intended for, without going overboard. Choose colors that contrast and complement each other well. (If you aren't sure, get advice from a graphic artist.)

When using colors, consider their psychological impact, too. For example, when asking for money, avoid RED (it suggests negatives like danger, blood, stop signs, and literally "red ink"). Normally, BLUE and GREEN are better, more soothing colors for positive effects. BLACK is generally strong but neutral.

Before you build your whole pitch around color in your visuals, do some research on the tastes and limitations of your audience. (Remember: some people are color-blind.)

Finally, despite its virtues, expect the addition of color to add more time, complexity, and cost to your preparation, too.

```
┌───────────────────────────────────────────────┐
│ PRINCIPLE #5 - ALLOW ENOUGH ABSORPTION TIME    │
└───────────────────────────────────────────────┘
```

You are guaranteed to lose your audience if you hit them with a rapid-fire machine-gun attack of flashing slides or viewgraphs--especially: (a) in a darkened room, (b) with poor ventilation, (c) right after lunch.

Too many visuals, delivered too quickly, are certain to numb your audience's brains into a daze of distraction. It frustrates people to watch slides click on and then, too-fast, disappear--gone before their minds could grasp or study them properly.

Take long enough for each visual to be savored and fully appreciated. As a good rule of thumb, plan for a maximum of two minutes' viewing time (on average) per visual. You'll thus have no more than 2-3 visuals for every five minutes' worth of talk.

Continued on Page 245

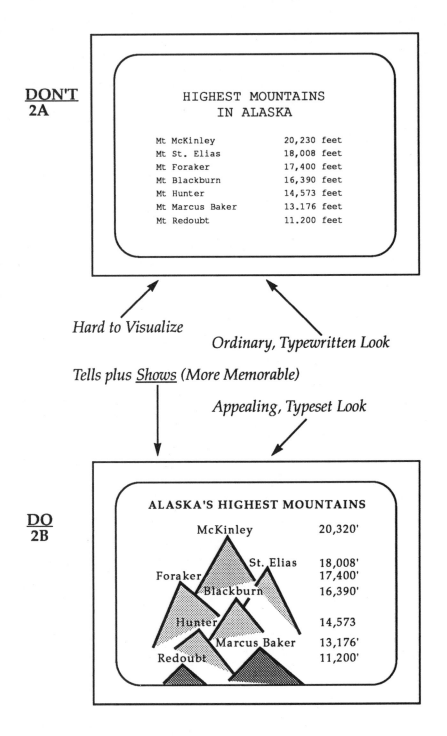

Continued from Page 243

It's a judgment call, of course. Visuals that simply show a key word or phrase (e.g., "ILS") can be on-and-off quickly. Ones that are detailed and comprehensive (e.g., a flow chart of an entire process) should remain in view the entire time.

PRINCIPLE #6 - *ONCE USED, GET IT OUT OF SIGHT*

Visual aids are meant to call attention to themselves, insistently. However, if visuals stay in view after being used, they can change from *aids* to *distractions*.

A leftover aid distracts your audience in two ways: (1) visually--because it lures them, by design, to keep looking at it; and, (2) conceptually--because they assume it's still relevant, so they keep looking to make a connection.

A basic principle for the effective use of visuals is . . . once you've used it, get rid of it.

If you've written or drawn on the board, erase it. If it's on a flipchart, turn the page. If it's a viewgraph, go on to the next one or darken the screen with a solid slide.

Also, make it a habit at the end of presentations to use an overall "summary" slide or chart. You'll then avoid the common mistake of delivering a closing with your last sub-point left showing.

PRINCIPLE #7 - *FAMILIARIZE YOURSELF WITH
THE EQUIPMENT BEFOREHAND*

Never try to use audio-visual equipment that you can't operate comfortably. Invest the time beforehand to learn how to use it. It's awkward for everyone when a talk gets disrupted in mid-stream because the speaker has neglected to do his/her basic homework.

Continued on Page 247

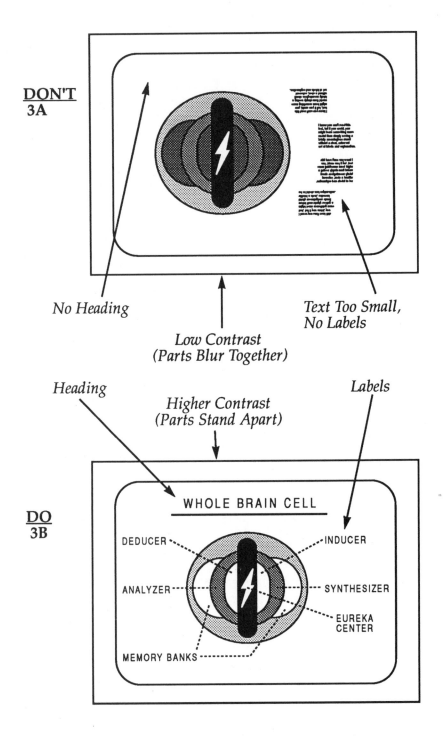

DON'T
3A

No Heading

Low Contrast
(Parts Blur Together)

Text Too Small,
No Labels

Heading

Higher Contrast
(Parts Stand Apart)

Labels

DO
3B

WHOLE BRAIN CELL

DEDUCER

INDUCER

ANALYZER

SYNTHESIZER

EUREKA
CENTER

MEMORY BANKS

Continued from Page 245

For any AV equipment used, know how to do first-line troubleshooting, specifically: (a) what to do if something goes wrong; (b) who to call for help; or, (c) where to locate backup equipment quickly.

For a major presentation, go to the meeting room early (as much as an hour in advance) to take control of the room. Get familiar with the surroundings. Have all AV equipment set up, tested, and ready to operate before the first audience member arrives.

```
┌─────────────────────────────────────────────┐
│  PRINCIPLE #8 - PREARRANGE THE COMPLEX       │
└─────────────────────────────────────────────┘
```

Despite their value, AV aids also add complication to a talk, especially if more than one is used at the same time. As usual, you'll avoid disaster best by prearrangement.

If you plan to use more than one aid (even some simple combination like chalkboard and flipchart, or viewgraphs plus handouts), plan additional preparation time to make sure everything goes off well.

```
┌─────────────────────────────────────────────┐
│  PRINCIPLE #9 - USE AN ASSISTANT             │
└─────────────────────────────────────────────┘
```

Some AV aids can be used very effectively by one person alone. For best results, however, many aids require the help of an assistant.

Having an assistant gives you one less thing to worry about and allows you to stay focused on the audience and keep your Authority Posture. Otherwise, you'll be tempted to whirl around, checking and straightening the slide, turning back to the audience, looking back over your shoulder at the visual--it's a back-and-forth nuisance.

Who'll be your assistant? You probably don't have a full-time chart-flipper on your team.

Continued on Page 249

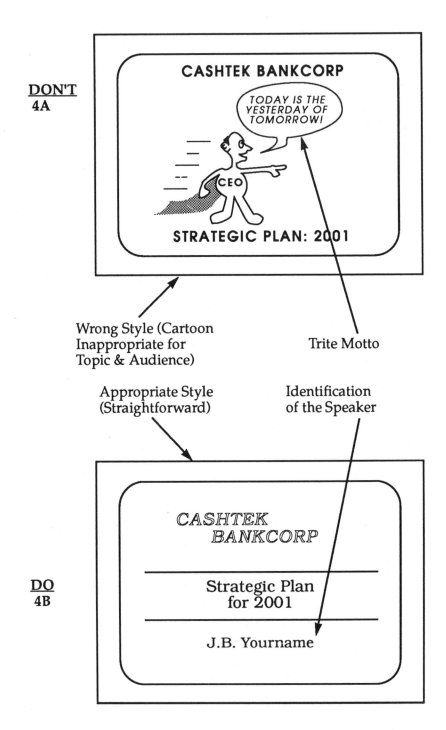

Continued from Page 247

Answer: *Anybody* can be an assistant . . . a secretary, key aide, friend, colleague. (In some organizations, it's not unusual for the assistant to be the boss, helping to make the pitch go right.) People who do a lot of talks from the same office can also use the "buddy system," and take turns being each other's assistant.

If the visuals in your talk must be changed by hand (in particular, viewgraphs), use an assistant whenever you have more than four visuals.

Choose your assistant carefully. Don't just pull somebody out of the audience. Also, take time to coordinate and rehearse the signals between you two, in advance. Make sure all signals are clear and mutually understood. (Often, a simple nod is fine.)

Also, be sure the assistant knows how to avoid causing distractions, by staying unobtrusive.

```
┌─────────────────────────────────────────────┐
│         PRINCIPLE #10 - REHEARSE            │
└─────────────────────────────────────────────┘
```

By now, you realize that the effective use of AV aids requires advance preparation. You cannot just walk in cold with AV equipment in tow and expect to have everything go well.

You must rehearse--to get familiar with the equipment, to orchestrate the complex, to coordinate the talk with your assistant, to time the running length, and to pinpoint weak spots for improvement.

When you rehearse, conduct a full-scale dress rehearsal; don't just do a spoken talk-through. Do a real *hands-on* simulation, using any and all audio-visual equipment, aids, charts, etc., that you expect to use, exactly as you'll actually use them.

```
┌─────────────────────────────────────────────┐
│    PRINCIPLE #11 - RECHECK EVERYTHING       │
└─────────────────────────────────────────────┘
```

When using AV aids and equipment, it's smart to get almost paranoid in rechecking things--such as the operation of equipment, instructions to assistants, condition of the room, and any other last-minute essentials (like a projection screen, pointer, table, lectern, etc.).

Check the sequence of your visuals one last time, to be sure they're in the right order--even when you're *sure* they are (somebody may have borrowed one and accidentally put it back in the wrong place).

```
┌─────────────────────────────────────────────────────┐
│                                                       │
│     PRINCIPLE #12 - EXPECT THE UNEXPECTED            │
│                                                       │
└─────────────────────────────────────────────────────┘
```

Still, the question will be . . . not *if*, but *when* things go wrong. Remember Murphy's Law (and O'Toole's Commentary). Even with the best-laid plans, something will go wrong. So, expect it, and be ready as much as you can. Just keep your POISE when it happens.

If total chaos with the equipment *does* erupt, take a break or adjourn the meeting. Don't make your audience sit and watch you struggle. Solve problems with your equipment while they relax someplace else.

```
┌─────────────────────────────────────────────────────┐
│                                                       │
│     PRINCIPLE #13 - MAKE IT MEANINGFUL               │
│                     (OR DON'T USE IT)                 │
│                                                       │
└─────────────────────────────────────────────────────┘
```

Despite all the positive virtues of visual aids (and there are many), they can also be positively disastrous if: (1) they are inappropriate, (2) the speaker doesn't use them effectively, or (3) there isn't enough time to prepare them properly.

So, when you put audio-visual aids into your talks, be sure they *add* something . . . make them meaningful or don't use them at all.

Chapter 23

FACTS INTO VISUALS

"Things seen are mightier than things heard."
-- Alfred, Lord Tennyson

TELL AND SHOW

After deciding to show a fact as a visual, you must still choose the best *format* for converting your point into a meaningful picture.

Let's look at the twelve basic visual formats, and see when each should be applied . . .

1. **PIE CHART** - to show the *parts* of a whole:

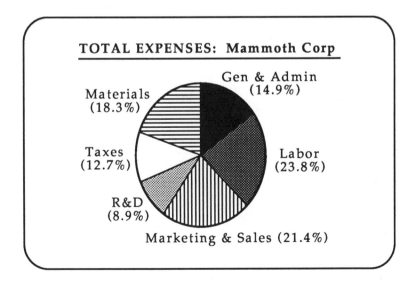

2. **BOX CHART** (or **TREE CHART**) - to show the *relationship* of parts within a system or organization:

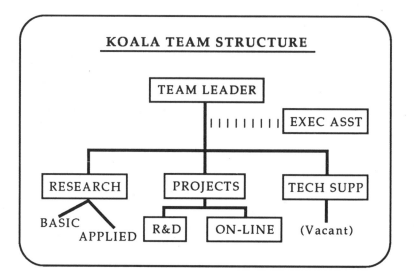

3. **STACKED-BAR CHART** - to show the parts of a whole *varying* over time:

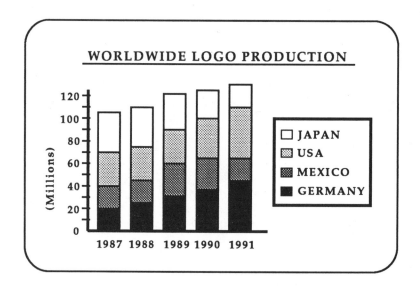

4. **STACKED-LINE GRAPH** (or **AREA GRAPH**) - to
    show the *distribution* of parts in a dynamic whole
    changing over time.

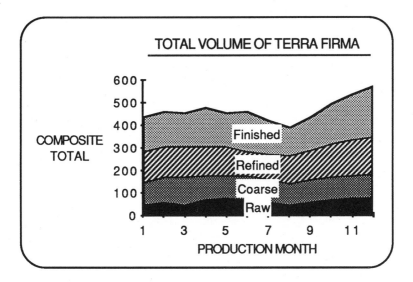

5. **LINE   GRAPH**   (or **XY GRAPH**) - to show the
    mutual relationship between *two variables*:

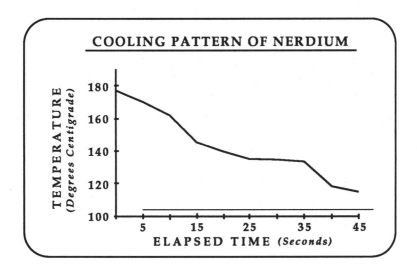

6. **MULTI-LINE GRAPH** - to show the changing mutual relationships between *two or more variable sets*:

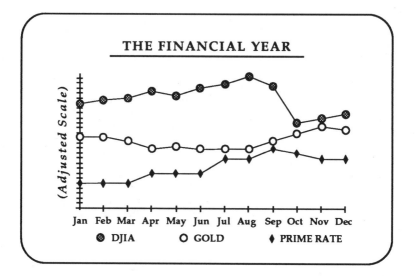

7. **BAR CHART** (or **COLUMN CHART**) - to show: (A) a *side-by-side* look at certain characteristics of different items:

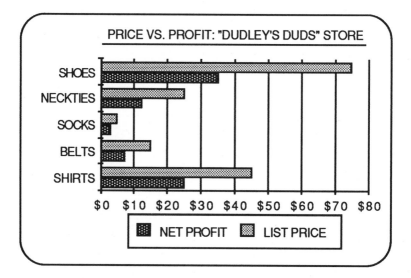

BAR CHART (or **COLUMN CHART**) *[Continued]* - to show: (B) a *side-by-side* comparison of one or more items varying over time:

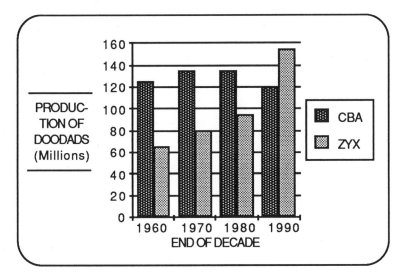

8. **DOT GRAPH** (or **SCATTER GRAPH**) - to show *individual events* plotted separately to reveal an overall pattern or relationship:

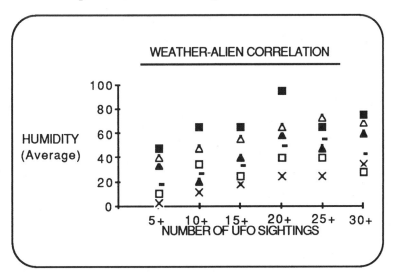

9. **MATRIX** (or **TABLE**) - to show a head-to-head comparison of two or more items on the basis of their *shared characteristics*:

CHOOSING YOUR NEXT CAR

FACTOR:	ALPHA	BRAVO	ZORRO
Cost	$20,499	$18,369	$38,650
Wheelbase	95.7	114.3	110.2
Curb Weight	2,750	3,741	3,220
Displacement	1.3/80	5.0/302	3.0/181
Fuel Capacity	16.6	18.0	18.5
Repair Record	Good	Average	Good
Warranty	36/36	12/12	48/50

10. **FLOW CHART** - to show the *logical order* of actions or decisions within a complex process:

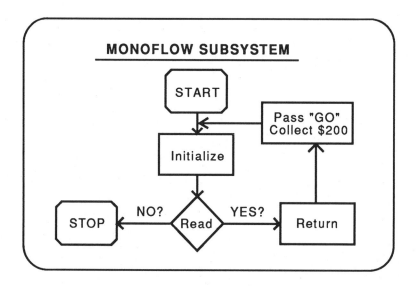

11. **TIME CHART** - to show the *milestones or sub-tasks* required to complete a larger task in a schedule--or the *"critical path"* of such events.

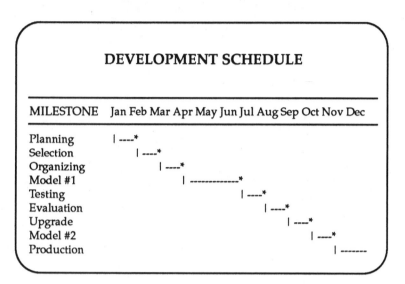

12. **LINE DRAWING** - to show a *simplified pictorial view* of an object, frozen in time.

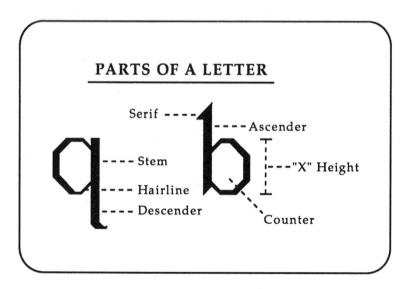

THE GOOD, BAD, AND UGLY

You'll use the preceding twelve visual formats primarily for static, *two-dimensional* views in simple media such as a Board, Chart, Handout, or Overhead transparency.

If, however, you need *sound, motion,* or *very accurate detail,* you'll choose more complex media like a Photograph, Slide, Audiotape, Movie, Videotape, Demonstration, or Computer Simulation.

Even with simple media, though, you can find creative ways to make static visuals more dynamic: You can draw your visuals, step by step, while you talk. You can build and highlight key parts of a visual with color markers. You can use special techniques like "cover-up," "reveal," or "add-on."

For your benefit, here's a summary of the various formats and when each should be used:

Chapter 24

AV MURPHIES AND GREMLINS

"The medium is the message."
-- Marshall McLuhan

A TRIO OF PH.D.'S

How many Ph.D.'s does it take to use an overhead projector correctly?

At a national conference, a disastrous presentation was made by three Ph.D.'s, each a recognized authority in his field.

Their talk was well-promoted and eagerly awaited. The audience (who had paid substantially to attend) arrived with a keen interest in the topic, so the atmosphere was friendly and receptive at first.

However, *what* those speakers said that day was lost forever, overshadowed by their inept handling of an overhead projector.

In a classic demonstration of "How Not To Use A Visual Aid," the presenters showed an array of viewgraphs that were totally befuddling, with words too small and pictures too complicated to follow. Worse, all three proved to be totally unfamiliar with using the equipment.

The Ph.D.'s had chosen to flip their own viewgraphs, but had never bothered to figure out in advance how to position them (16 in all) correctly on the screen. The result was a comical yet frustrating game of high audience participation, with attendees crying out: "Turn the slide around. No, the other way. Wait, stop. Go back. You had it. No, the other way," and on, and on.

Unfortunately, by appearing to be awkward fools that day, these highly competent people lost their audience (many of whom walked out while the speakers fumbled along) and, in the process, lost even more: they damaged their professional credibility. They were masters of the topic . . . but they were novices at using visual aids.

To help *you* avoid the most common audio-visual mistakes, here are 23 practical tips:

IF YOUR VISUAL CONTAINS WORDS . . .

TIP 1:   Do *not* write complete sentences.

TIP 2:   Be telegraphic. Write the least words necessary: key words and highlights only.

TIP 3:   Do *not* read the visual aloud word-for-word to the audience.

TIP 4:   Build the visual from short "bullet" phrases that you *amplify* (not repeat) in your spoken words.

TIP 5:   Follow the **"RULE of 6-by-6(9)."** Based on orientation, a rectangular visual (e.g., 35mm slide or overhead transparency) has either a "horizontal" or "vertical" aspect ratio. The visual will be longer either horizontally (*landscape*) or vertically (*portrait*):

HORIZONTAL   **VERTICAL**
Aspect Ratio   **Aspect Ratio**

The Rule of "6-by-6(9)" is your practical guideline on how many words--at most--to use per visual. This rule of thumb is that:

(a) in a list, no *item* should contain more than 6 *words* maximum; and,

(b) no *list* in horizontal aspect ratio should contain more than 6 *items* (nor 9 *items* in vertical aspect ratio).

[The "6-by-6(9)" is a rule of thumb *only*, of course. Good judgment would obviously put a list of ten items all onto a single vertical visual.]

IF YOUR VISUAL CONTAINS PICTURES ...

TIP 6:   Explain what you're showing and why. Assume that nothing "speaks for itself."

TIP 7:   Label every major element, boldly and clearly.

TIP 8:   Use color to accent/separate an object's components.

TIP 9:   Eliminate extraneous details. Cover up distracting parts of the visual that will not be discussed.

TIP 10:   To show increased detail as you talk, use "overlay" (add-on) or "reveal" (uncover) techniques.

TIP 11:   For a complex visual, use a pointer to "walk" the viewer through and focus attention on the key items.

IF YOUR VISUAL WILL BE PROJECTED ...

TIP 12: To make projection visuals that are easiest, cheapest, and quickest:
　　　　(a) If most of your visuals contain *words*, use overhead transparencies ("viewgraphs").
　　　　(b) If most of your visuals contain *pictures*, use 35mm slides.

TIP 13: Number all slides and viewgraphs, in the same way in the same place--normally, on the upper-right corner of the outer frame, not on the transparency itself.

TIP 14: Make a *cue sheet*, listing each transparency (by number and identifying phrase) so you can find one quickly and smoothly, if asked to go back.

TIP 15: Avoid adding organizational 'logo' symbols to your visuals. Logos work as subliminal advertising, but they also disrupt a clean, simple look.

TIP 16: Be sure you have a spare projector bulb, correct for that projector model. (A burnt-out bulb is a projector's weakest link.)

TIP 17: For any AV equipment (like a projector) that requires electricity, bring along an extension cord (3-prong, grounded) plus a 3-to-2 adapter plug (for older 2-hole wall sockets).

TIP 18: If you use the same transparencies over and over, inspect them regularly for wear and tear. Keep them clean and unbent.

FOR AUDIO-VISUALS **in general** ...

TIP 19: When using a pointer, don't reach across your body, in front of yourself. Point with the hand closest to the screen: If you're *right*-handed, stand (as seen by your audience) on the right side of the screen; if *left*-handed, on the left side.

TIP 20: Keep things moving. Never make an audience sit and wait, watching you write on a pad or board, for more than a few seconds. Instead, *write* a little, *talk* a little; *write* a little, *talk* a little . . . and so on, back-and-forth.

TIP 21: Avoid making an AV presentation in someone else's private office. Instead, ask to meet in a nearby conference room where you can go beforehand and get set up.

TIP 22: If you use audio-visuals often, assemble a standard emergency kit--including masking tape, a penlight, marker pens, scissors, and anything else you might need on the spot.

TIP 23: Be sure you choose the right AV aid or technology for the task. Audio-visual tools are not interchangeable: each has its own advantages and disadvantages.[53]

---

[53]For a detailed comparison of the various AV aids and technology, see the "Audio-Visual Aids and Technology Selector" in Appendix D, pp. 329-356.

Chapter 25

SELL THEM WITH PERSUASION

"It is terrible to speak well and be wrong."

-- Sophocles

THE BETTER MOUSETRAP

Some issues are predictably controversial. They always provoke lively debate because no final proof, to everyone's satisfaction, has yet been found. For example: What are UFO's? Should you take vitamin C supplements? Who shot John F. Kennedy? Is there life after death?

Every day on Earth, human beings argue such questions. They argue religion and politics, philosophy and baseball.

Yet, they often lack an absolute, objective standard by which to measure "the Truth." Many of our very cherished, deeply-felt beliefs are subjective: they get repeated and accepted on faith, yet can't be proved by any scientific method.

Once we choose up sides, an idea can start to look so clearly true, wise, justifiable, and desirable that it's hard to see how *any* thinking person could ever disagree with it . . . how could anyone say "No" to your absolute Truth?

Plus, if your idea is really good enough, won't it sell itself automatically? Won't the world "beat a path to your door," eager to jump onto your bandwagon?

No, not necessarily--that's the Better Mousetrap fallacy. No matter how "obvious" or "logical" a conclusion seems to *you*, your audience can sit silently unconvinced until they have a will to believe--regardless of all evidence to the contrary!

So, if you're trying to persuade others, stay cautious. Keep reminding yourself: there is no necessity for anyone to believe anything. To believe or not to believe--yes, even to disagree with what you feel is obviously the certain truth--is always an option for an obstinate audience.

DEADLY DANGER #9 - WEAK EVIDENCE

THE PITFALLS OF EVIDENCE

Evidence by itself is neither strong nor weak; its value is relative, depending on how it is accepted by the audience. Proof is like beauty--in the mind of the beholder.

To find the best strategy for arguing your case, then, first understand the situation from the viewpoint of your audience. An in-depth Audience Analysis is essential [see chapter 6, especially pp. 64-65].

Since the way you communicate an idea can determine whether it's accepted or rejected, remember there are stronger and weaker ways to state the same evidence.

WEAK EVIDENCE. Evidence is likely to come across as *weak* if it:

* is vague, general, or abstract (not supported by specific, concrete examples);

* is extremely one-sided or obviously slanted (i.e., ignores legitimate concerns or realistic obstacles, such as costs involved);

* appeals solely to the emotions (demagoguery) or solely to cold logic (insensitivity);

* is poorly delivered in any way (verbal, non-verbal, or graphic);

* is neither understood nor truly explained from the viewpoint of the audience (i.e., with emphasis on "I/WE" instead of "YOU").

STRONG EVIDENCE. Conversely, evidence is likely to come across as *strong* if it:

* backs up general conclusions by hard specifics and apt examples;

* gives a balanced look, which anticipates (as well as answers) the main objections of opposition;

* uses credible sources (or justifies the reliance upon a questionable source);

* appeals to commonsense logic, but also stimulates the positive emotions (by means of the speaker's enthusiasm, intensity, or sincerity);

* is effectively delivered--in both verbal and non-verbal ways, plus reinforced with strong graphics;

* is directly on-target from the perspective of the audience (with emphasis on the "YOU").

RESISTANCE CHECKLIST: *Avoid the mistake of weak evidence.* Be sure you're not just talking to yourself. Challenge all your sources and evidence through the eyes of your audience. And do a "resistance check" with questions like these:

(1) Are any of your sources questionable, compromised, or otherwise subject to challenge?

(2) Have you relied upon any procedures or tests that are new, untried, controversial, or non-standard?

(3) Is there any reason to expect that someone may seek to discredit this idea by discrediting you, the presenter?

(4) Are there any signs of a personality clash between yourself (or anyone else in your organization) and your key decision makers?

(5) In the past, has any idea similar to yours already been tried by your decision maker(s)--and failed?

(6) Is there any sign of prejudice, prejudgment, or built-in resistance on the part of your audience?

(7) Do your suggestions step on any toes, by stumbling into someone else's "bailiwick" (i.e., his or her personal agenda)?

(8) Does anything in your argument appear, at first, to contradict the logic of everyday common sense?

RELIABILITY VS. CREDIBILITY

At the heart of persuasion is the need for RELIABILITY. To have "Reliability" means simply that you have the facts straight. You are telling the truth; your information is accurate and complete.

To persuade others, however, you'll need more than an unquestionable Reliability--you must also have a legitimized CREDIBILITY. "Credibility" means your audience *believes* your facts are straight. They *believe* you're telling the truth and your information is accurate and complete. So, you become credible if your audience trusts that you are reliable.

Of course, in the mind of your audience, you could still have either Reliability or Credibility without the other--that is: (a) you can be believed, even though you are lying (like a con artist); or, (b) you can be correct and truthful, even if no one believes you (like a Cassandra).

HIT OR MYTH

Cassandra, you may recall, lived in the city-state of Troy, during its war against Athens. According to ancient myth, Cassandra was given both the gift of prophecy and a curse: She could foretell the future accurately . . . but no one believed her.

Thus, although she warned her fellow citizens to "beware of Greeks bearing gifts," they ignored her--disastrously. They neglected to look the wooden gift horse in the mouth and opened their gates to the fall of Troy.

Clearly, then, telling the truth is not always enough. To succeed, you must also be *believed* to be telling the truth. (Cassandra's problem is obvious: She had terrific reliability but lousy credibility.)

Do you sometimes feel cursed, like Cassandra? Do you think you're right, but somehow feel that omnipotent and ubiquitous overlords (often called "They") keep failing to believe you?

In future battles, then, keep the lesson of Troy in mind. Don't assume--just because you think your information is *reliable*--that your audience will find it *credible*.

Your goal as a persuader must be: to attain authentic Credibility, built on a foundation of true Reliability. Then, your decision-makers can comfortably rally from "No" to "Yes," to the side of your superior ideas.

ABSOLUTE *"NO"* AND "YES"

Have you heard apocryphal stories about sharp-witted, silver-tongued salesmen who can talk anyone into anything? These heroes are so slick, they could sell refrigerators at the North Pole, right?

Don't take such tales too seriously, however. Nobody wins them all.

Sometimes, even before you walk into a room to speak, some audiences will already have a totally closed mind. No matter what you say, they will resolutely sit and stare and stay at Absolute "NO"! That's reality.

A highly-motivated person might complain that to take "No" for an answer, ever, is just a sign of weak "negative" or "defeatist" thinking. A never-say-die salesman will argue that--if you just keep on pushing the sale long enough, with enough dogged persistence--sooner or later, every prospect will eventually come around, give in, and get "sold."

Does your prospect think he can't afford it? Does she say it doesn't meet her company's requirements? Never mind--whenever they voice any objection, just translate it mentally into something else: To you, it's really only a plea, begging: "Tell me more." So, talk on, relentlessly!

(Obviously, this formula ignores one fact: that, after a while, if you just keep repeating a sales proposition, stubbornly refusing to take "No" for an answer, you are *not* acting nobly persistent . . . you're just nagging.)

This kind of narrow, self-serving attitude about "selling" is what makes a lot of people wish that ideas *could* sell themselves. Conscientious people dislike (and reject) high-pressure sales tactics. To them, the ultimate goal of the transaction is *not* simply "to make the sale," seeing other people as "marks" on which to "score," no matter how the outcome affects them or their organizations. Instead, they want to build long-lasting relationships.

Correctly applied, persuasion is not a one-shot contest. It's good communication; it's the search for an outcome where all parties benefit, in a WIN-WIN way.[54]

Today, enlightened sales people--whether of computers, refrigerators, municipal bonds, hair spray, or ideas--all learn this same lesson: Any approach that is manipulative or one-sided is not only ineffective and self-destructive but also (to be blunt) stupid.

If you can't sell an idea, that's a signal itself that something is wrong . . . maybe the idea is really bad, or your approach is off-target, or it's just timing. Step back, think, and find out, before you plunge full-speed onward.

Suppose your prospect is already an Absolute "YES"?--that is, they trust you fully. Today, you could sell them something that would bring you fast recognition and big bucks. (Let's assume you need both.)

The only thing is, you secretly suspect that it's probably a bad idea for them. Still, on faith, they are ready and willing to buy it. It's a judgment call . . . what should you do?

---

[54]For more views on WIN-WIN selling, see: Jim Cathcart, *Relationship Selling* (Costa Mesa, Ca.: HDL Publishing, 1988); Robert E. Miller and Stephen E. Heiman, with Tad Tuleja, *Strategic Selling* (New York: William Morrow, 1985); and Ron Willingham, *Integrity Selling* (Garden City, N.Y.: Doubleday, 1987).

Before you go for the jugular (rationalizing to yourself: "If they're willing to do it, that's their choice, isn't it?"), please stop and consider these "Bad Idea" Axioms:

THE "BAD IDEA" AXIOMS

1. A bad idea--even if "sold" skillfully--is still a bad idea.

2. Anyone who knowingly sells someone else a bad idea will regret it, sooner or later.

3. Axioms #1 and #2 are universally true in all situations: for bad ideas, bad products, or bad services. Always, badness will surface.

Resist the temptation to sell that bad idea, even if it brings you a momentary victory. To be successful as a persuader, you must know when not to sell, too.

Let's acknowledge not only that "you can't win them all," but that--in your world--you should not even *try* always to win.

Consider, each time, whether an idea is truly in the best interest of the person being sold. Seek and find that WIN-WIN outcome--or walk away from the deal. If the outcome is WIN (for you) and LOSE (for them), then in the long run, you're guaranteed to lose, too.

PERSUASION IN ACTION

What is "persuasion" and what is it *not*? . . .

Good persuasion is good communication. It respects the other party as an equal participant. It is not coercion but seduction.

In a nutshell, **PERSUASION**:

IS *NOT* ... talking people into doing things against their own self-interest.

IS .... finding mutually-beneficial outcomes, which you communicate to others in ways that are clear, positive, and compelling.

Now, with persuasion defined, let's look at ten basic principles of persuasion (with ten practical Checkpoints) for turning your ideas into action:

1. KNOW YOUR SUBJECT.

Since reliability breeds credibility, you must know your subject thoroughly. (It won't matter how well you talk, if you don't know what you're talking about.)

Study your idea, service, product. Know it from all angles--especially from the viewpoint of your target group. Do your homework, so you're ready to answer any tough, unexpected questions.

There are no exceptions: If you don't know your subject, postpone the talk--or send somebody else.

CHECKPOINT #1: *Do you know your SUBJECT thoroughly?*

2. BELIEVE.

Strong belief alone is, of course, no substitute for knowing the subject's details: knowledge comes first. Nevertheless, real enthusiasm helps to sell things, too, just as phoniness or apathy can "un-sell" them. Often, a person with sincere belief (even with less knowledge) is more persuasive than someone who fakes it.

The best seller, therefore, is the person who truly believes in the product or idea.

CHECKPOINT #2: *Do you sincerely BELIEVE in what you are selling?*

3. BE PREPARED.

By now, you know that "Be Prepared" is more than an echo of the Scout motto. It's also a watchword for all your presentations, so you'll pay attention to details, large (like knowing your product) and small (like having enough copies of your handouts).

Naturally, you can't pre-program everything. You must stay flexible, ready to respond to opportunities and defend yourself against the unexpected.

But always have a game plan and follow it, until you see a reason to shift gears. Consistent success in your talks is no accident: it's the result of painstaking forethought and homework.

CHECKPOINT #3: *Are you now fully PREPARED,*
in every detail, to make this talk?

4. KNOW YOUR AUDIENCE.

Before a difficult selling situation, if you do only one thing to get ready, this is it . . . study the customer; know your audience! Know their perceived needs, so you can speak their language and build rapport.

Persuasive communication starts with rapport--with a comfortable feeling that you and your prospect are both "in sync" together. Rapport (which leads to trust) is influenced by everything: your reputation, your actions, even your personality.[55]

RAPPORT BUILDERS: To help foster this sense of shared empathy, you can use these proven rapport builders in your communication with others:

(a) find common ground immediately;
(b) spotlight your "likeness" with them (by mutual
      interests, appropriate dress, etc.);

---

[55]For more on how selling anything starts by selling yourself, see two books by Joe Girard: *How to Sell Anything to Anybody* (New York: Warner Books, 1977), and *How to Sell Yourself* (New York: Warner Books, 1979).

(c) be fully responsive to their problems/needs;

(d) stay courteous towards everyone;

(e) emphasize the positives;

(f) don't whitewash the negatives;

(g) listen (and feed back) reflectively;

(h) avoid pointless arguments;

(i) be a problem-solver, not a "salesman";

(j) call people respectfully by name (i.e., by title
and last name, until told otherwise);

(k) use gentle humor, when appropriate;

(l) work for a WIN-WIN outcome (and be willing to
lose the sale if necessary);

(m)exhibit total competency in all things.

While seeking rapport, however, do not become a honey-mouthed chameleon--don't fawn blatantly over your audience's every mood or whim, nor look too hungry, passive, wishy-washy, or too eager to please.

Sharp people (even if they disagree with your proposal) will respect firmness based on a deeply-held principle; they will detest weak opportunism.

CHECKPOINT #4: *Do you know the problems and understand the needs of your AUDIENCE--really?*

5. ACCENT THE BENEFITS.

In general, human beings prefer "the way it is." We cling to the status quo because any change--even life changes that look positive (like a birth, promotion, or sweepstakes win)--can cause psychological distress. Since change can bring stress, people cleverly avoid stress by avoiding change and resisting new ideas.[56]

What could make the threat of change worthwhile to your audience? . . . Clearly, they must expect to gain some overriding benefits.

---

[56]The relative impact of various stress events was quantified in the famous "Social Readjustment Rating Scale" devised by Thomas H. Holmes and R.H. Rahe. See also: Hans Selye, *Stress without Distress* (New York: Signet, 1974).

These benefits may be *tangible* (e.g., a cost savings) or *intangible* (e.g., an increase in morale), but they must be absolutely real, meaningful, and probable in the mind of your target audience.

To find a winning argument, ask yourself this basic question: "What does this idea do for (or to) the decision-maker(s)?"   Pinpoint the strongest likely payoffs, and accent these benefits vividly in your talk.

CHECKPOINT #5: *Can you show definite BENEFITS to your audience if they do what you propose?*

6. PAINT THE CONSEQUENCES.

Suppose you propose something and get a reply like this: "That's a good idea, and we really ought to do it . . . *someday*, not now." How can you create a sense of urgency--a desire by your audience to DO IT NOW and not wait?

The benefits are an appealing carrot but sometimes you may also need to wave a gentle stick. Answer this difficult, important question: "What would happen if they did *not* do what you propose?"

What are the consequences (the likely losses and probable dangers) of choosing a different action, or of doing nothing? . . . Realistically, if your idea is rejected, could the job still get done? Can the mission still be performed? How would things change? These provocative (sometimes unpleasant) questions can help you sort the "nice-to-do's" from the "must-do's."

Remember that painting the consequences does not mean using scare tactics (which seldom work). Instead, you point out the likely outcome--factually--and let the audience decide for themselves. Examples of reasonable consequences might be:

ARGUMENT: *"Why should our company spend $50,000 to buy new production equipment now?"*

CONSEQUENCE: *"Because if we just keep renting the same equipment for $500 a month, it will cost us much more."*

ARGUMENT: *"Why should I close this deal now and not wait until later?"*

CONSEQUENCE: *"Because the price will soon increase and, for this weekend only, you'll get a special discount of 20 percent off."*

CHECKPOINT #6: *Can you show your audience CONSEQUENCES they may suffer by not acting now?*

7. MEET THE OBJECTIONS.

No matter what the idea, some people are likely to have objections to doing it. For example, someone might argue that your idea:

-- is "too experimental," "revolutionary," "blue sky," "off-the-wall," "beyond the state of the art";

-- has already been tried (and failed) in the past;

-- is too early, too late, or takes too long;

-- costs too much . . . or doesn't, but "there's just no money available right now";

-- is impractical and simply can't be done!

There are fifty-plus negative ways to kill ideas. Yet, never treat any such objection lightly, even if it seems ridiculous. If an objection belongs to someone whom you must convince, consider it as valid--then, get ready to meet it head-on with counter-arguments that are sincere, reasonable, and positive.

Before the talk, "smoke out" the likely objections. Ask yourself: "Why might a person *not* agree with me? What possible arguments could be made *against* my position--by a sincere person of good faith (or, for that matter, by an insincere person of bad faith)?"

You are not, of course, building a hostile case against yourself: Your pitch is assumed to be slanted in favor of your own views. However, for a stronger talk that's more credible, your argument should be fair, seem well-balanced, and show that you can see both sides.

CHECKPOINT #7: *Do you see the most likely OBJECTIONS to your own viewpoint--and their rebuttals?*

8. FOCUS ON THE KEY POINT(S).

For persuasion, it's better to be "deep with a few" than "shallow with many." Don't tell every good reason for doing something. Too many points only dilute your argument.

Instead, apply the "Rule of 1-2-3" . . . Find the one, two, or (at most) three best arguments for your idea and focus on them fully and single-mindedly.

Each lesser point is only ammunition for your opposition (since your 11th, 12th, and 13th reasons are probably weaker than the top three). You might end up sidetracked, locked in a defense of your own weakest argument that *you* brought up!

You shouldn't ignore all arguments except the top three. Be ready to cover any other points that might come up. But always focus on the few key points, and keep emphasizing them.

And what if--after you've analyzed the topic--you still can't see the three best arguments? . . . Then, back up to CHECKPOINT #4: You don't really know your audience yet.

CHECKPOINT #8: *Can you identify the three best KEY POINTS in favor of your idea?*

9. TALK IN SPECIFICS.

For a crash course in applied persuasion, look carefully at advertising in newspapers, magazines, and TV. In general, such ads use two methods for selling:

(a) to sell by creating an image or mood, or
(b) to sell with factual specifics.

A generic product (like soap or toothpaste) is hard to differentiate, so its ads often create an image or mood by association with something else. You'll see ecstatic young couples, cavorting together joyfully on a beach, while a voice-over singer moans: "Want love? Use CLOSE-UP!"

However, if the product is easier to differentiate by specifics (like a desktop computer), its ads may be more factual, using statistics, testimonials, or head-to-head comparisons.

A generic product can try a factual approach. For example, you might see a solemn, bearded man in a white, clinical lab-coat, intoning: "Nine out of ten dentists now say you'll get 14 percent fewer cavities with CREST."

Which approach is best?--perhaps a little of both: the image plus the facts.

In everyday life, however, your best bet almost always is to talk in specifics. (Review the earlier example in Tip #6 on consequences, where the specifics are: "Invest $50,000 now to avoid paying $500 extra every month after the first ten.")

You should forget about Madison Avenue's "image" approaches. Be sure you build *upon* (and not *around*) the facts. It's seldom good to rely upon generalities or abstractions. Back them up with concrete details. Show the numbers; make them real; and give relevant, well-chosen examples.

> CHECKPOINT #9: *Can you support each of your general conclusions with good SPECIFIC EXAMPLES?*

10. ASK FOR ACTION.

Sometimes, what seems like a persuasive talk ends up with no clear outcome, no decision. "Okay," say your decision-makers, "we'll think it over and get back to you."

It's disappointing, frustrating. . . but maybe you're partly to blame. Maybe (to them) the desired action wasn't so obvious, after all.

Frequently, to get action, you need to spell out for your target group--unmistakably--that an action is required or being sought. (Don't assume they already see it.)

If you want it, you may need to ask for it in explicit language, such as: "We therefore recommend that--"; or: "In summary, our request is--"; or something similar. To be convincing, don't be shy about talking straight.

Simply express your suggestion or request in a lucid and purposeful way and do everything possible to make it easy for them to say "Yes." Never overlook this powerful (yet less obvious) tool of persuasion . . . namely, *clarity*. How can they agree to take action, if they don't realize you're asking for it?

CHECKPOINT #10: *Have you identified an ACTION step you will ask your audience to take?*

WHAT'S IN IT FOR ME?

Two people, seeking approval to move ahead on a new project, once gave a "GO/NO GO" presentation to their boss. About halfway through, the boss interrupted, saying, "Hold it! What's all this have to do with *me*?"

They stopped to explain that the project would help his organization do a better job, save money, and thus reflect favorably on him as a leader.

"Never mind all that," he retorted impatiently. "What's this have to do with *me*? What's it do *to* me, or *for* me, personally?"

Again, they repeated the same benefits. The project would obviously be good for everyone.

At the end, the boss gave his answer: "Disapproved!" The idea was a good one, and should have been approved, but it was two years later before the idea was finally sold and implemented.

Was this boss short-sighted and self-centered? How much blame should the two presenters share for their failure, by not anticipating the boss's reaction? Did they really know their audience and plan accordingly?

It's a common, unspoken assumption: that since *you* are firmly convinced by the evidence, your target audience will be unavoidably convinced, too. As we've seen, this assumption can be self-defeating--but it's often hard to detect when you yourself are already a "true believer" in the idea.

Chapter 26

RULE #10:

KEEP A POSITIVE ATTITUDE

"They can do all because they think they can."

-- Virgil

IT'S ALL IN YOUR ATTITUDE

You'll recall that one of the three main Keystones for any oral presentation is ATTITUDE (see Chapter 3).

Unfortunately, many worthwhile ideas about attitude and positive thinking have been reduced to simple slogans:

- YOU CAN IF YOU THINK YOU CAN.
- WINNERS NEVER QUIT,
  QUITTERS NEVER WIN.
- WHEN THE GOING GETS TOUGH,
  THE TOUGH GET GOING.   [And so forth.]

Maybe these slogans still motivate and inspire you. Or maybe they seem like rah-rah nonsense. You've grown so sophisticated or jaded that such slogans are just clichés: you've stopped listening.

Yet, what is a cliche? Often, it's the truth: it's just been said so many times, you're tired of hearing it. It's lost the original freshness and become a stale truism.

Truism or not, your attitude has tremendous power. For instance, the strong negative attitude most people feel about speaking to groups can become predictably self-fulfilling. As a result, if you expect a talk to go poorly, you'll often get exactly what you dreaded most--a presentation that's both painful and bad.

DEADLY DANGER #10 - **NEGATIVE ATTITUDE**

INVASION OF THE BUTTERFLIES

On the whole, the greatest enemy of human beings who struggle to speak well before groups is *themselves*.

The speaker feels so nervous, so overly self-conscious, that he can't think, and (he believes) if he could think, he wouldn't find the right words, anyway.

Call it "stage fright" or "butterflies" or just plain "nervous panic"--it's that hungry fear that stabs us, turning our minds into a jumble and our stomachs into jelly. The dreaded butterflies strike again!

Beware! Angry butterflies lie in wait, invading the planet, ready to ambush you, too, whenever you speak in a new situation or on an unfamiliar topic.

No one is safe from attack by the evil butterflies--not even highly experienced actors, lecturers, TV newscasters, or other public speakers, for whom stage fright is a real and common occupational hazard.

The truth is, of course, that these "butterflies" are beasts of fear, arising only in imagination from within ourselves, and they can be conquered.[57]

RELAX AND WIN

Let's say you're facing a tough challenge . . . a major speech on a new, difficult topic to a large, unpredictable audience. For personal success, how should you try to feel inside?

---

[57]The powerful influence of our own inner self-talk upon our personal success has been re-emphasized lately by such authors as Shad Helmstetter in: *What to Say When You Talk to Your Self* (New York: Pocket Books, 1986) and *The Self-Talk Solution* (New York: William Morrow, 1987). For a wonderful book on conquering our inner "chatterbox" of fear--and much more--see: Susan Jeffers, *Feel the Fear and Do It Anyway* (New York: Fawcett Columbine, 1987).

Specifically, in tight situations, which inner state will most likely lead to your peak performance: (a) extreme fear, (b) total relaxation, or (c) moderate tension?

Let's consider each alternative . . .

(a) *EXTREME FEAR?*

Some people actually claim their best motivator is fear. Fear psychs them up and gets them moving. Without fear, they feel lazy and "go slow"; they need that extra adrenaline boost, caused by fear, to perform at all.

However, you'll usually find that fear--especially extreme fear--is unreliable and destructive. After its first jolt, fear can either drain off your energy (the fuel for charisma), or just leave you feeling so "hyper" that you'll overreact and make foolish mistakes.

At best, fear is a negative motivator. For peak performance, you need a more positive inner state, one that is better and more reliable than fear.

(b) *TOTAL RELAXATION?*

If fear is not best, how about total relaxation? To anyone who often feels fearful, it probably sounds ideal (though impossible) to be totally relaxed in front of groups.

Yes, it is better to be loose than uptight; however, *total* relaxation is an extreme, too--one that people normally reach only after falling asleep. You want to be relaxed, but not so happily low-key that you aren't awake to intricacies or nuances.

Thus, neither of the extremes (being too fearful nor too relaxed) works best. Extreme fear makes you too edgy; total relaxation makes you sluggish.

(c) *MODERATE TENSION?*

Moderate tension must be best, right? Yes, and no: The ideal answer to our hypothetical three choices may really be: "None of the above"--not extreme fear, nor total relaxation, nor moderate tension, either.

For you to do what is (and is not) best for peak performance, you must understand the difference between being "alert" and feeling "tense."

As an exercise, do the following: Take a deep breath and hold it; without exhaling, make very tight fists with both hands; then, with your whole face, frown deeply. Before you exhale, the feeling you'll get is a sample of tension.

Next, take a full, deep breath and exhale it slowly; shrug your shoulders and let them drop; then, moving only your head, focus your eyes quickly on a single object. The feeling you'll get now is alertness. See the difference?

RELAXED ALERTNESS

Tension can sabotage your ability to perform well: it can make you "choke." Alertness helps you perform best and keeps you aware of everything that happens.

The best inner state for peak performance is "relaxed alertness." You should be alert but not necessarily "tense," relaxed but not really "dormant."

This state of "relaxed alertness" is what any champion seeks when he or she enters an athletic event. It is what brings success to the martial artist. It is comparable to the highest stage of meditation for a Zen Buddhist. It is what some reportedly attain through the practice of transcendental meditation (T.M.).

Learn to attain this inner state yourself. Walk into your next briefing with a sense of relaxed alertness (or, if you prefer: alert relaxation). It will make you emotionally calm yet keep you mentally sharp. Then, with such a focused awareness, you'll easily do your best.

SEVEN WAYS TO KILL BUTTERFLIES

You can stop being a helpless victim of nervousness. If you find it hard to stay relaxed when speaking to groups, here are seven sure ways to help you kill your "butterflies":

1. **GAIN GOOD EXPERIENCE.** To get rid of butterflies, chase them away, head-on. Go speak more and you'll fear it less--especially if you get feedback that is non-threatening and encouraging (such as in friendly run-throughs or a good training class).

2. **PLAN IN DETAIL.** A big part of nervousness is fear of the unexpected, so butterfly-prevention starts with planning. Don't go in cold. Know your stuff; do your homework; anticipate the questions; have the answers. In short, to *feel* ready, *be* ready!

3. **HAVE A DRY RUN.** To strengthen your defenses against butterflies in advance, test your pitch in a "dry-run" rehearsal. With a good dry-run, you'll spot weaknesses, practice handling tough questions, and eliminate many ugly surprises. You'll then be more relaxed, going in.

4. **USE FAMILIARIZATION.** Butterflies thrive on uncertainty, so defeat them with familiarity. Convert the unknown into the known--for example, visit the room where your talk will be, beforehand, and imagine the event in your mind's eye. Familiarity reduces fear.

5. **LEARN TO RELAX.** If butterflies haunt you regularly, you need a reliable method to attain relaxation *physically*. Mind and body are complexly related: if you can relax the body, you'll also relax the mind. (For a set of proven RELAXATION TECHNIQUES, see the next section.)

6. **BE OTHER-CONSCIOUS.** Butterflies often disappear if you ignore them. How? Try focusing your attention outward, off yourself, towards the other people in the room. Start by chatting with those who arrive before your talk. As you become less *self*-conscious (by being more *other*-conscious), you'll get more relaxed.

7. **EXPECT SUCCESS.** Why be a defeatist? Why think: "Oh, no, I'll probably screw it up"? Instead, visualize a mental game plan with a positive outcome. Expect victory. No army of butterflies can win against a brave human being, armed with the right attitude.

RELAXATION TECHNIQUES

For anyone who needs a regular method for attaining physical relaxation, here are six well-proven possibilities you could try . . .

1. *Three Deep Breaths.*

The best, most powerful relaxation technique is also the simplest and easiest . . . right before your talk, take three deep breaths (in through the nose, out through the mouth). They should be full and slow, all the way down, filling the lungs, then all the way back out. Concentrate on breathing; think of nothing else.

Just three good, deep breaths are enough. They add oxygen to the system, distract your attention from fear, and help clear the mind. Three deep breaths are a superior way to relax.[58]

2. *Perspective.*

Since fear will exaggerate any imagined threat, many speakers learn to relax by putting the whole situation in proper perspective. For example, ask yourself: "How important will this moment be to me in 300 years?" (In another variation, Winston Churchill supposedly coped with difficult audiences by imagining that everyone was naked.) Shrink the threat, and your fear melts.

---

[58]For a comprehensive set of breathing exercises, see: Nancy Zi, *The Art of Breathing* (Toronto: Bantam Books, 1986). Also pertinent and valuable is: Richard Hittleman, *Yoga: 28 Day Exercise Plan* (Toronto: Bantam Books, 1969).

3. *Progressive Relaxation.*

Progressive relaxation is a way of systematically relaxing the body, part by part: for example, you first relax the toes, then the feet, then ankles, and so on. For best results, you might add more tension (the opposite of relaxation) to each area, on purpose, before fully relaxing it.

This method (which you've probably used if you've ever had trouble falling asleep) was developed by Edmund Jacobson, M.D., and has been adapted by others as a valuable tool for everyday stress management.[59]

4. *Mental Imagery.*

Another tool for relaxation is mental imagery. In a quiet place of privacy before the talk, you find a past experience or place that was pleasant and calming (say, a successful talk or a mountain scene). Then, you relax and visualize that moment, with all its feelings of comfort. As you do so, you "anchor" that memory with some signal (like: crossing your fingers) so that later, with the same signal, you can quickly trigger the memory later, and put yourself back in the same peaceful state again.

This form of relaxation combines aspects of meditation and self-hypnosis, and (though it may sound unusual) it works very well for many people.[60]

---

[59] See: Edmund Jacobson, *You Must Relax* (New York: McGraw-Hill, 1957); Herbert Benson, *The Relaxation Response* (New York: Avon Books, 1975); and Herbert Benson, with William Proctor, *Beyond the Relaxation Response* (New York: Times Books, 1984).

[60] For instructions on how to use mental imagery techniques, see: Charles Garfield, *Peak Performance* (Los Angeles: Jeremy P. Tarcher, 1984); and Bernie Zilbergeld and Arnold A. Lazurus, *Mind Power* (Boston: Little, Brown & Co., 1987). For a powerful self-help approach built upon similar principles, see the audiocassette program, *The Neuropsychology of Achievement* (San Leandro, Ca.: Sybervision Systems, 1982).

5. *Paradoxical Intention.*

Ironically, our fears often bring about the very thing we fear--for example, we spill things when trying hardest not to. By reversing this insight, however, the great psychiatrist, Viktor Frankl, developed "paradoxical intention" as a useful therapy. Frankl learned of a man with a severe case of stuttering, who remembered only one time when he could *not* stutter. Once, to win sympathy, he had *tried* to stutter, yet (paradoxically) no matter how hard he tried at that moment, he failed to stutter.

If you can't relax no matter what, then try going all the way: use paradoxical intention and try *not* to relax. Try to get yourself as nervous as possible--scared out of your wits: Imagine the audience will boo you, and throw tomatoes and rotten eggs; maybe you'll get fired; maybe they'll lynch you on the spot.

Most times, the harder you try to get tense, the more you will perversely get tickled and *not* be scared. This is a last-resort approach, but it helps some people to relax, finally, despite themselves.[61]

6. *Prayer.*

If your religious faith is strong, why not ask God (your higher power or divine spirit) for inner comfort through prayer? On the night before a talk, pray for success. Also, right before you stand up to speak, say a short silent prayer or repeat to yourself a calming Biblical verse (such as the 23rd Psalm: "The Lord is my shepherd").[62]

Many people know that prayer can be a powerful, practical source of spiritual strength at tense moments in their everyday lives.

------

[61]Viktor E. Frankl, *Man's Search for Meaning* (New York: Pocket Books, 1939/1963), pp. 198-199.

[62]See, for example: Norman Vincent Peale, *The Power of Positive Thinking* (Greenwich, Conn.: Fawcett Crest, 1952); and Robert H. Schuller, *Discover Your Possibilities* (New York: Ballantine Books, 1978). Any scripture or book of inspiration that you find personally meaningful can be used to bring you strength.

SMILE, YOU'RE ON . . .

It's not headline news that, for many people, speaking to a group can provoke fear and foster an unhealthy negative attitude.

The fear can result from habitual nervousness, from a memory of past failures, or from lack of experience. The fear may be normal and legitimate--if, for example, a major project (or even your entire career) seems to be riding on the outcome of a critical briefing.

As an antidote, here's another healthy formula to help ease (if not cure) your negative attitude about speaking to groups:

POSITIVE ATTITUDE FORMULA

$$PA = P_1 + P_2 + R_1 + R_2$$

As explanation: To derive "**PA**" (your Positive Attitude), you need the sum of four variables:

P_1 = **PREPARE**: Be ready for anything. Script the talk; rehearse it; carry good notes and back-ups.

P_2 = **PRACTICE**: Do a rehearsal. Get feedback and a critique. Time it. De-bug the approach.

R_1 = **RELAX**: Use relaxation techniques. Learn daily mental fitness habits. Build a positive attitude.

R_2 = **REWARD**: Avoid the perfectionistic tendency to always suffer: "I could've done better." If your talk is a success, celebrate. Reward yourself.

THE DANGER OF POSITIVE THINKING

A positive attitude results from a positive expectancy: you know you are ready and you expect positive results.

We customarily think of a "negative" attitude, on the other hand, as a lack of confidence, as the expectation of failure.

Yet, among those who speak to groups, a different kind of negative attitude lurks, too--the cocksure expectation of undoubted success.

Here's where your positive attitude can actually become a *danger*. Confidence (positive thinking) can be negative if it turns into *over*-confidence.

Overconfidence is particularly destructive because it causes foolish mistakes. For example, a speaker may talk too long, spawned by the thought, "I could talk about that subject *all day*"--without wondering whether the audience wants to *listen* all day.

Another overconfident speaker fails to "tune in" to the special needs of the audience. Or, someone else projects an arrogant, take-it-or-leave-it attitude.

So, yes, keep a positive attitude all right . . . but don't overdo it. Don't build up your self-confidence so high that your attitude gets positively negative.

DOPEY RELAXATION

Finally, sadly, some people--out of weakness, ignorance, or desperation--look in the wrong places to get relaxed or boost their courage.

The smartest pathway to find relaxation is by careful planning, hard work, and mental rehearsal. To seek inner calm or courage by using artificial substances is a foolish road towards a losing solution.

You'll painfully learn that neither alcohol nor drugs do anything as crutches but harm you. As a professional, doing on-the-job presentations, habitual drugs soon deaden your sharpness. They prolong your dependency. They are unpredictable, unreliable, wrong for your health, and totally bad news.

If you now feel trapped in a chemical dependency, find someone you trust and seek help immediately. The sooner the better. It's never too late.

Natural relaxation is not only more healthy, it's more long-lasting and it's free. The techniques of natural relaxation (including prayer) are a high-powered arsenal of weapons and they are enough. With them alone, you can fight your own butterflies and win.

Chapter 27

BE TOTALLY PREPARED

"Better three hours too soon than a minute too late."
-- William Shakespeare

ARE YOU READY?

Success in speaking to groups comes, not from natural talent alone, not from magic, stealth, nor Dame Fortune, but as a result of systematic preparation.

Yet, surely--realistically--not every successful speaker in the world can always be "prepared, prepared, prepared." Plus, some people just naturally seem able to think on their feet and talk well, without preparation? How about them?

How about those gifted characters who really can just stand up and ad lib impressively, on a moment's notice? They don't need any systematic preparation, do they?

The fact is: Any good "extemporaneous" speaker has probably done careful practice, but in less-obvious ways. The impromptu speaker draws upon the accumulated store of all past efforts.

Specifically, he or she probably has: (a) a self-confident attitude; (b) a working knowledge of the subject; (c) experience in speaking to groups; (d) the habit of thinking fast; and, (e) a bit of personal luck.

Even then, the most gifted speaker can still slip and fall by being over-confident or lazy. If you get careless when it counts, the eternal truth always waits to reassert itself:

"Consistent success in presentations is no accident; there is no substitute for good preparation."

DEADLY DANGER #11 - **SLIPSHOD PREPARATION**

GOAL-LINE DEFENSE

Truly, the riskiest and most fundamental mistake you can make is to do slipshod preparation. Some hardcore people might, in fact, define any preparation as "slipshod" if it fails to accomplish the outcome you seek, when something that you value is at stake.

Of course, for Monday's friendly chat at the office about the weekend sports, you won't carry along a detailed script. To write scripts for everyday conversations would be silly and weird.

You should, on the other hand, feel totally terrified about making a major, once-in-a-lifetime talk, on-the-job, without doing meticulous preparation. At such times, you need the control and guidance of a preplanned script.

For badly prepared talks, the faults take many forms--for example: the opening is boring or pointless; the idea flow is weak and hard to follow; the body wanders off the main topic; the ending is abrupt, with no firm conclusion. Some problems (such as: room conditions, visual aids, handouts, etc.) reveal a lack of attention to detail.

Some speakers give the impression, in general, that they're just not on top of things: they mishandle questions and get flustered by the unexpected. (The list could go on.)

In essence, each of the other eleven "Deadly Dangers" comes back to this one . . . each mistake is a symptom of inadequate PREPARATION.

So, don't neglect total preparation--it's a necessity--and don't worry that you'll lose your spontaneity. Instead, with good preparation, you'll only gain more clarity and better persuasion.

SCRUBBED

How important is systematic preparation for briefings? Here's a true-life example . . .

Once, a dynamic, highly competitive corporation began holding a series of mandatory weekly briefings by its key managers, to help monitor a series of critical management actions.

One Friday morning, during a session of what everyone was by now calling, unaffectionately, "The Briefing-of-the-Week Club," a certain manager named (let's say) Griswald was giving his briefing in a very disorganized, apathetic way.

The company's chief executive officer (who was known for his quick mind, impatient questions, and acerbic wit) asked a few pointed questions.

Griswald responded with answers that were vague and unresponsive. He seemed disorganized, unenthusiastic, and ill-prepared.

Finally, with obvious dissatisfaction, the CEO shouted at Griswald: "You haven't done your homework, have you?"

Griswald stood there frowning, stunned into silence.

"That's it! You're scrubbed!" said the CEO, abruptly. "Get out! I never want to see you again."

The man had been fired on the spot and was never heard of again by anyone inside the organization.

WHY HAVE A SYSTEM?

What are the personal benefits of using a systematic approach to prepare your major presentations?:

1. A system helps you *save time.*
2. A system *reduces* the *unpredictables.*
3. A system makes things *more automatic* when you're under pressure.
4. A system fosters better *quality control.*
5. A system *prevents* many common *mistakes.*
6. A system allows for more (not less) *spontaneous creativity.*

Following is a proven **SYSTEMATIC APPROACH TO ORAL PRESENTATIONS**: a step-by-step sequence to help you plan, organize, deliver, and follow-up any major oral presentation from start to finish (keyed to chapters in this book).

A SYSTEMATIC APPROACH TO ORAL PRESENTATIONS

A. ESTABLISH DIRECTION:

Step 1: **PURPOSE**.........................Define the stated reason for this presentation. [p. 56]

Step 2: **ACTION OBJECTIVE**...Identify your desired outcome. [p. 56]

B. PLAN A STRATEGY:

Step 3: **AUDIENCE**..................Do a full Audience Analysis (in writing). [pp. 64-65]

Step 4: **SCOPE** ....Define the limits and orientation of the topic. [p. 76]

Step 5: **APPROACH** ....Choose the appropriate style and best approach. [pp. 224-36]

C. ANALYZE THE TOPIC:

Step 6: **BASIC QUESTION**.......Identify the general question to be answered. [pp. 96-97]

Step 7: **KEY POINT(S)** ....State the answer(s) to the basic question. [pp. 94-95]

Step 8: **EVIDENCE**................Assemble facts and examples to prove your key points. *[pp. 265-66]*

Step 9: **OPPOSITION**..............Anticipate all possible objections and counter-arguments. *[pp. 275-76]*

Step 10: **FOCUS POINT**..............Summarize the main idea in one quick nutshell. *[p. 79]*

D. <u>ORGANIZE THE PRESENTATION</u>:

Step 11: **CLOSING**..................Build the closing first (from the focus point). *[p. 82]*

Step 12: **OPENING**....................Next, build the opening (with an audience link). *[pp. 85-89]*

Step 13: **BODY**...........................Structure the key points into a logical/persuasive sequence. *[pp. 109-13]*

Step 14: **OUTLINE**..................Create a total design: Opening-Body-Closing, Q&A, and Last Word. *[pp. 133-44, 153-57]*

Step 15: **NOTES**.........................Convert the outline into a set of good notes. *[pp. 102-04]*

E. <u>DO FINAL PREPARATIONS</u>:

Step 16: **AV AIDS**....................Have all aids finished and all AV equipment checked. *[pp. 239-50, 260-63, & 329-56]*

Step 17: **REHEARSAL** ....Do a dry run (in front of an audience, if possible). *[pp. 174-77]*

Step 18: **FINAL LOGISTICS**........Check all arrangements and last-minute details. *[pp. 247, 250]*

F. MAKE THE PRESENTATION:

Step 19: **ATTITUDE** ....Relax, and develop a positive expectation of success. *[pp. 284-86]*

Step 20: **DELIVERY**.................Make the talk, using good delivery skills. *[p. 321]*

Step 21: **FEEDBACK** ....Get meaningful feedback (both during and after the talk). *[pp. 161-62 & p. 308]*

G. FOLLOW UP:

Step 22: **FOLLOW-UP**.................Monitor the results; keep your promises. *[pp. 307-08]*

Chapter 28

THE LAST-MINUTE QUICKIE

*"When calamity strikes, sit down and think
things through before taking action."*
-- Tom Brown, Jr.

FIRE DRILL!

By now, you've probably heard enough wisdom on the joys of systematic preparation. Sure, you'd always like to be super-prepared--who wouldn't? But realistically, that's not always possible. The problem in the real world is time-- there's never enough of it.

Often, a talk may be thundering towards you, but you won't see it until the frantic last minute. Then, in midst of a crisis, your "presentation" becomes a fast-thinking explanation, under-the-gun, whose goal is survival.

Sometimes in a meeting you're caught off-guard, not ready to speak brilliantly. Who seriously has time to stop, sit, and ponder when a roomful of people turns to you, unexpectedly after someone asks: "And what do *you* think?"

Or maybe you feel your full-time job is to be a manager, not a professional speechmaker. You've got plenty of extra work, without all this infernal homework for all these flaming presentations! If any of these scenarios sound like you, here's what may be a typical situation:

Suppose, on a perfectly normal day, you're working quietly in your office when suddenly the phone rings and it's your boss, who says, *"Please drop down to my office in ten minutes, to talk to someone here about the PDQ Project."*

What's your next move? . . .

(a) Panic, choke, or faint?

(b) Say "Sure," and immediately start walking?

(c) Start research to get up-to-speed on the PDQ in a hurry: pull the file, make a phone call, gather the latest info?

(d) Do the first few steps of the Systematic Approach (find your purpose, know your objective, and analyze your audience)?

Think about it . . . which response is normally your own? Let's consider each possibility:

(a) *Panic-choke-faint?* - This response is human, and at times understandable, but obviously self-defeating. Control yourself: Why assume the worst? You can't stand up and wow them if you're lying senseless on the floor.

(b) *Start walking?* - You might do okay if you're expert enough on your topic to answer anything anyone asks, and if, as a speaker, you think quickly on your feet, handling the unexpected smoothly under pressure. (Even then, if you walk in blind, you're gambling.)

(c) *Do hurry-up research?* - Good, you want up-to-the-minute information. But what (in only ten minutes) will you now research? . . . all of PDQ?; or, if not all, what portion? Do you have any idea what they might ask, or even who's asking? (To be most efficient, don't jump into research until you know the talk's depth.)

(d) *Find the purpose, objective, and audience?* - Yes, most times--even for a quick-response--the best starting step is to find out: *whom* will you be talking to, *what* about, and *why*? Then, you'll know when you touch that doorknob, what will be waiting--friend or foe?

You may feel there's no time to plan. But it takes only a quick mental check--like: "Okay, why are they asking about the PDQ? Who's asking, and what do I hope to accomplish?" Better still, don't hang up the phone until you get a few good answers: "Sure, I'll be glad to come, but tell me, please: What part of PDQ are you really interested in, and who will be there?" (These are not unreasonable requests, and if you're asked why you ask, explain: "So I can get the latest facts and bring the right backup data.")

FIRE ESCAPE

Suppose you are unexpectedly asked to give a talk. You obviously do *not* have time to follow all 22 steps of the entire Systematic Approach in full sequence. You need some short-cuts.

As a help for future impromptu talks, here is a six-step formula for a QUICK-RESPONSE that works:

 **Know *WHO?*** *WHAT?* *WHY?*

For a QUICK-RESPONSE, don't start with fact-gathering nor by organizing verbal and numerical content.

Instead, first define *WHO* (your audience), *WHAT* (your purpose), and *WHY* (your objective). This initial step helps you focus all other preparation, saving you time for making the most of each remaining minute.

The "WHO-WHAT-WHY" lets you anticipate areas of the topic that your audience probably will (and will not) want to discuss or question.

You can do more efficient research, and organize the content better, by seeing: where to concentrate, what issues are hot, and what aspects can be downplayed or ignored.

| STEP 2 | ⟶ *SCOPE* the Topic. |

Based on the suspected agenda, crosscheck against your knowledge of the topic. Do you feel ready--right now--to handle this topic easily? Or, at the moment, does its likely scope look too broad or too narrow for you?

------------ BROAD SCOPE

------- NARROW SCOPE

For instance, you may be a research scientist. However, you suspect the key argument will not concern research, but rather the engineering feasibility of the total design (which is someone else's responsibility). Since you expect to be asked questions outside your own area of cognizance, or beyond your expertise, the discussion's scope may get *too broad*.

On the other hand, suppose you're the same research scientist, but this time you expect the visibility to center on an esoteric subdivision of your own field, where you yourself are not fully knowledgeable. This discussion may get onto a greater level of fine detail than you're comfortable at, so the anticipated scope may be *too narrow*.

Although you might conclude that managers often pose the right questions--but towards the wrong people--you'll nevertheless need a way to handle such situations when they inevitably occur.

What's the solution?

As self-defense, when you expect a discussion's SCOPE might be out-of-whack (too broad, too narrow), here are nine good tactics:

1. First and most important--<u>anticipate</u>. Always think ahead; try never to walk into a room without a good idea of what will be the real agenda.

2. If the scope looks too broad, <u>focus down</u>. Pull the discussion back to your own decision level, or into your area of personal expertise.

   EXAMPLE: *"Since my own expertise is in the area of research, I can't give very authoritative answers on matters of engineering."* If pressed, stay conditional: *"The answer could be [so-and-so], but, as I said, I'm not an expert in that field."*

3. On the other hand, if the scope is too narrow, <u>focus up</u>. Push the discussion level up to where you feel comfortable and competent.

   EXAMPLE: *"That question is on a level of detail I'm not able to answer right now. I can get back to you later or--if you prefer--make a phone call right now for those facts."* Then, re-focus: *"But I do have some definite ideas on the total research funding."*

4. Always be prepared, of course, to <u>admit gaps</u>: *" I don't know, but I'll find out."*

5. For "soft spots" on the topic (where your memory may be insufficient), carry along any possible <u>backup materials</u> (reports, books, charts, printouts, etc.) for on-the-spot reference.

6. If appropriate, take <u>someone else</u> (the true expert) along with you to field tough questions outside your own subject area.

7. Never be reluctant to <u>refer elsewhere</u> (without seeming to pass the buck nor point the finger) if some other person, not you, is really the right one to answer a given question.

8. Consider asking for <u>a delay</u>, to win time for covering your gaps. For example, on the phone, you might ask: "Could we get together in thirty minutes instead of ten?" (Then, during the postponement, you do a fast cramming job to brush up on the topic.)

9. Remember, you can still anticipate wrongly, or even get sandbagged--if you're told the agenda is one thing, and discover it's something else altogether as you walk in the room. Be cautious and <u>stay ready for surprises</u>.

Most quick-response inquiries pop up rudely, without warning: BOOM! Suddenly the heat's on and you are summoned to come explain something, now!

As a result, people tend unfortunately to simply *react* to a quick-response in a too-passive mode: They march in, hoping only to answer the worst questions and survive.

In any organization, you must be responsive to questions from your boss and others. There's no doubt that's a top priority.

But since they're listening (while you're talking), why not also exploit this serendipitous opportunity to plant some seeds of your own?

In other words, during your "ten minutes or less" of quick preparation, why not plot an *active* approach and consider your own agenda, too. Do you, for example, know questions that your leaders will *not*--but *should*--be asking?

By Step 3, you've already spent a few moments thinking over the situation. Now, ask yourself: Is there any specific message you would like to get across to *them*?--for example: to alert them to a hidden danger, or urge a budget increase, or request some vital new purchase?

Often, the best opportunity to sell an idea occurs when the "iron is hot," with people urgently aware of an alarming problem that demands an instant solution. To stay effective, however, tread softly and be sure your own private agenda is kept in the background, clearly subordinate to the main one your chiefs have in mind.

THE SILVER BULLET

Whether you have an overt message or not, take time to capture your own viewpoint in a strong "silver bullet"--a capsule message (25 words or less), that shoots right to the heart of the issue, summarizing things as you see them. (In radio and television, this capsule is often called a "sound bite.")

Your "silver bullet" is equivalent to what we've called the FOCUS POINT of your talk: It's the bottom-line wrap-up you'll be talking towards. In message sequence, it's usually your CLOSING.

Knowing your focus point is your ultimate rescue for an on-the-spot quick-response where you have no time to think but must reply instantly. With no prep time at all, your quick-response formula (in *one* easy step) is to speak your SILVER BULLET. Quickly choose a focus point, talk towards that, and (once you've said it) stop talking.

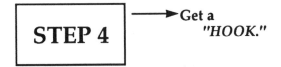

In most quick-response encounters, you'll be there to answer somebody else's questions. As you walk in, wisely listen before you talk. Let *them* lead, you follow.

Nevertheless, you should avoid being too defensive or too passive in a quick-response situation. See yourself as a mutual participant, not a sideshow target.

As you quickly plan beforehand, therefore, you can get ready (if needed) with a well-chosen "HOOK."

The HOOK is an attention-grabber, which links your viewpoint with the interests of the other people in the room.

To find the hook, ask yourself: "Why--in *their* terms, from *their* point of view--will these people care about this idea?" Your reply is the hook.

The hook answers, in advance, the vital question: "So what?" In your message structure, therefore, it also serves the function of a good OPENING.

To grab everyone's attention from the beginning, then, plan a HOOK. [For examples, review chapter 9, pp. 85-89.]

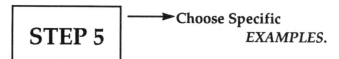

STEP 5 ⟶ **Choose Specific** *EXAMPLES.*

To flesh out the remainder of your talk (the BODY), you need mainly a few well-chosen SPECIFIC EXAMPLES. To get your examples, you can rely on brainstorming.

Concentrate again for a moment on your SILVER BULLET. Got it in mind? Then jot down (or think up) specific ideas, quickly and uncritically. (You may not have a full-fledged "brainstorm"--maybe just a "brain flurry"--but it's still a fast way for rooting up evidence to support your main theme.)

Now, choose the 1, 2, or (at most) 3 strongest examples to back up your viewpoint, and you're almost ready to walk down into the tiger's den.

By now, as you see, the basic HOURGLASS structure of a message has once again begun to form. The "focus point" or "silver bullet" (Step 3) will be your closing, the "hook" (Step 4) can be your opening, and the specific examples (Step 5) fill in and reinforce the theme. The whole pattern is thus:

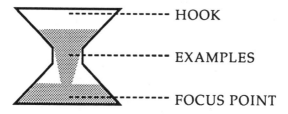

-------- HOOK

-------- EXAMPLES

-------- FOCUS POINT

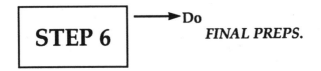

STEP 6 ———► Do *FINAL PREPS.*

Finally, do any last-minute preps needed to be sure all your quick thinking is worthwhile. For instance, you can do these things if any time is left:

(1) Jot down a few <u>notes</u>, to capture your ideas on paper so you don't forget them.

(2) Check on any <u>back-ups</u> you need (people, info, references, etc.).

(3) Locate any available <u>visuals</u>, which you might take along and use successfully.

(4) Do any other last-minute <u>logistics</u>, to be sure you and all you need are ready to go. (For instance, viewgraphs are useless without an overhead projector.)

As the last step: Assume a positive, can-do attitude . . . and go for it!

THE LAST-MINUTE ADVISOR

The spotlight can catch you unexpectedly in many ways, where suddenly you're called upon to make an impromptu talk. For instance:

* In a meeting, the leader turns to you and asks, "What do *you* think we should do?"
* In a briefing, delivered by someone else, you are unexpectedly called upon to defend a decision.
* You attend a conference as an attendee, then get "drafted" to sit on the panel as a major speaker.
* A news reporter holds a microphone in your face and, as cameras and recorders whirr, asks you for your comment.

These are realistic scenarios for many people. So, it's important for you to know--despite all the emphasis in this book on preparation--that you can also speak for success with very short notice. You can survive a talk that is a last-minute quickie. The secret is to stay calm and be methodical.

Finally, if you are regularly hit with such short-fuse briefings or quick-response talks, then face reality . . . realize that you'll have more in the future. Begin now to compile a "Fire Drill" file or briefing book, with backup and notes on likely hot topics. Then, each new time, you won't get caught cold.

Chapter 29

RULE #12:

FOLLOW UP FOR SUCCESS

"Do not turn back when you are just at the goal."
-- Publilius Syrus

THE EXTRA MILE

At last, the big event is over . . . you've finished speaking before a group. Thankfully, the presentation went according to plan.

You did great! You grabbed their attention instantly, kept everyone focused on the key points, backed up your facts with vivid examples and crisp visuals, finessed the tough questions, and neatly wrapped up the main idea in the climax. A big success--right?

Well, remember that every presentation is only a means to an end. Usually, your ultimate success is measured by your actual results. Yogi Berra once spoke the immortal words, "It ain't over 'til it's over." For you, if it's an oral presentation, it may not be over even when it *is* over.

Don't drop your guard now! The real "moment of decision" may occur after your presentation--often apart and away from you--as your audiences silently make their real choices ("GO" or "NO GO") by which you'll succeed or fail.

If you've pinpointed your Action Objective in advance (Rule #1, chapter 5), you already know what outcome you seek. You want approval to budget another $25,000; or a commitment to revamp the forward-wing design; or agreement to subcontract with Résumé Associates; or whatever.

But even if you get told, "Yes, we'll do it," there's no absolute guarantee the decision will ever turn into action. The decision-makers could move too slowly, or get sidetracked, or even [it happens] change their minds completely.

You can still influence that decision, however, if you go the extra mile and do proper follow-up.

DEADLY DANGER #12 - **POOR FOLLOW-UP**

AFTER WORDS

Think of your presentation as a proposal, and see your audience as people whose final decision will be made only *after* your talk--even after you leave the room and are on your way home. Ultimately, will your proposal be accepted or rejected?

If you'll learn to see each talk as the crux point in a larger, more complex total process, you'll understand better the power and importance of good follow-up. After the presentation itself is over, you must follow up to increase your chance for success. Here are some likely suggestions:

(1) *KEEP YOUR PROMISES.* Were questions raised that you couldn't answer?--where maybe you said, "I don't know but I'll find out." Be sure to find the answer, as promised, and report it back. Did you agree to look into something deeper, or to coordinate with someone else, or to refine some numbers and come back again? As a follow-up, then, do what you promised.

(2) *HONOR SPECIAL REQUESTS.* After the talk itself, were you asked for copies of your visuals or for extra handouts? Or did someone ask you to visit another organization or unit to make the same talk? Don't let such things slip through the cracks: follow up and act promptly.

(3) *DO A SELF-CRITIQUE.* To keep improving your ability to speak to groups, do an after-the-fact analysis of each pitch you give. Keep a written record of what went wrong (and right) and why. Especially note any questions raised that were relevant, yet totally unexpected, and be ready for these questions next time.

(4) *MONITOR THE OUTCOME.* Once a clear-cut decision has been made, track the results of that decision if you're directly concerned: Did they do what they agreed? Should you now do anything else (e.g., make a status-update report)? Know what happened afterwards.

(5) *PERSIST.* Do not simply wait, wonder, and worry alone in silent anxiety. Continue, politely but persistently, to show interest in the outcome of your proposal. Ask what's going on. If things seem to be bogged down, gently find a way to fan the flames to life again.

WATCH THAT LAST STEP

When you follow up, you "close the loop"; you take the process all the way to completion.

Follow-up is, therefore, your last safeguard against the Dozen Deadly Dangers, and the final one of the twelve RULES for effective oral presentations.

> **The essence of this book--its major lesson-- is to teach you how to build a solid, positive communication link between yourself and others while you control the entire situation (yourself, your presentation, and your audience) from start to finish.**

Follow these twelve rules and you will find yourself making presentations that are not only successful but truly enjoyable. (And don't lose the race at the finish line: Watch that last step, and follow up for success.)

ANDERSON'S RULES
FOR SPEAKING SUCCESS

1. FIND YOUR ACTION OBJECTIVE.

2. KNOW YOUR AUDIENCE.

3. BUILD FROM THE CLOSING.

4. HOOK YOUR AUDIENCE INSTANTLY.

5. CREATE A SCRIPT.

6. KEEP A SHARP FOCUS.

7. USE GOOD DELIVERY.

8. ADD IMPACT WITH VISUALS.

9. SELL THEM WITH PERSUASION.

10. KEEP A POSITIVE ATTITUDE.

11. BE TOTALLY PREPARED.

12. FOLLOW UP FOR SUCCESS.

Chapter 30

YOUR NEXT STEP

"Whatever you would make habitual, practice it."
-- Epictetus

BACK TO REALITY

By now, you have gained some realistic beliefs about speaking and about yourself, including an awareness that:

1. Good speakers are made, not born. Speaking to groups is a learnable skill.

2. Anyone (including yourself) can speak to groups successfully if you focus on the basic Keystones:

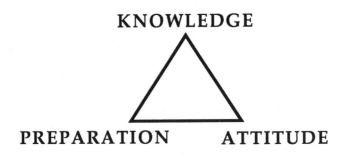

KNOWLEDGE

PREPARATION   ATTITUDE

In a nutshell:

    (a) know your subject thoroughly;
    (b) do your homework beforehand; and,
    (c) keep a positive, "can-do" attitude.

3. No single Keystone by itself (KNOWLEDGE, PREPARATION, ATTITUDE) can assure success. Like the three legs of a tripod, each Keystone is mutually essential to support the others.

4. The fourth Keystone (AUDIENCE) is often the most vital. Your real target--the mind of your audience--always exists outside yourself. So, above all: *Know your audience!*

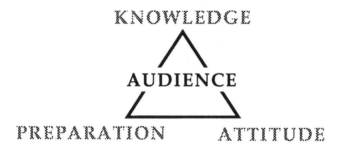

KNOWLEDGE

AUDIENCE

PREPARATION   ATTITUDE

5. Be pragmatic. Strive for excellence, not perfection. To master these skills, you need a sincere commitment to do so, plus a realistic flexibility. Things will seldom go exactly as planned (remember Murphy's Law). That's part of the adventure.

6. Ignore your fear or discomfort, and *go speak!* Almost everyone gets nervous at times--the sensation is common and normal. The feeling can best be conquered (and controlled) with direct action and successful practice.

7. Measure your success, *not* by your inner feelings, but where it counts--by the outer *results*. It's probably worth the grief, if you get what you want.

WHAT NOW? Learning to speak well before groups is not only worthwhile but--to accomplish many of your cherished personal goals--often essential and inescapable.

Your next step is to apply the skills you've learned, by gaining more experience and greater skill in speaking to groups. At this new moment of truth, I encourage you . . . I challenge you . . . to commit to *yourself* that you will:

 • **seek bold, new, interesting opportunities to speak** in a variety of settings;

 • **learn by doing well,** with positive critiques (by yourself or others) after each of your talks;

 • **nurture your positive attitude**--by clearly visualizing success and by highlighting what goes right as well as wrong;

 • **use the systematic approach** and get fully prepared, with the tools and techniques you've learned in this book.

FOR THE "INEXPERIENCED" SPEAKER

If you are an *inexperienced* speaker, here are a few special suggestions:

 * Don't try to master every skill at once. Start with your most critical need. The best skill to master first is probably basic message structure (Opening-Body-Closing).

 * Prepare each talk thoroughly and rehearse it. The time investment now will repay you for the rest of your life.

 * Participate with peers as a member of a regular group that is devoted to speaking improvement (Toastmasters International, Speakeasy, Speaker's Club, Speaker's Bureau, etc.).

 * Seek daily opportunities to practice your speaking skills everywhere: at on-the-job meetings, parties, social/community/political/religious gatherings, and elsewhere. This habit not only strengthens your skills, it also helps overcome shyness.

* Pick your top target of the twelve RULES and focus on improvement in that one area--where you need the most help--for the next 30 days. Then, once you've mastered that target, move on to the next (one per month).

* Listen, critically and appreciatively, to all others who speak to groups. Critique their performances in your own mind. What did they do well that you can apply? What "Deadly Dangers" did they commit?

FOR THE "VERY EXPERIENCED" SPEAKER

For the *very experienced* speaker, here are a few special suggestions, too:

* Don't assume you're a great speaker just because you've spent a lot of time talking to groups. Take stock, with candid feedback from a knowledgeable, objective source (such as a videotape recording, with critique by an experienced professional).

* Watch the tendency to ride on your laurels, making you lazy or careless. Even after you master your subject, keep doing your homework. For example, always slant your message for your audience's level (not yours).

* Continue to fine-tune your performances by making it a regular habit to do after-action assessments of each presentation--what went right/wrong, why, and how can you improve it next time?

* Share your own knowledge and encouragement with others who are just starting to risk speaking out more. Be a mentor, critic, or coach (as needed)--and volunteer your help; don't wait to be asked, and always beware of overly negative criticism: stay positive and helpful.

* Stay levelheaded about your own personal "foul-ups."
Your experience is no sure-fire protection against
Murphy's Law, either. Despite all your careful plans,
you, too, will still occasionally make mistakes. Look
forward, not backward, and do it better next time.

YOUR NEXT STEP . . . USE IT OR LOSE IT

By now you should know what it takes to speak to any
group with success. You should be able to recognize your
strengths and know where you need improvement. You
already have the professional tools to create and deliver top-
caliber talks with excellent results.

Your next step, then, is to convert your knowledge into
action. Those who speak well to groups--whether in a town
hall meeting, a Sunday sermon, or a briefing to the boss--are
this world's leaders.

Join them. Go find yourself a briefing or a speech or
some other reason to face a group and speak. Right away!
Today, if possible. Don't hesitate. Learn from your mistakes
and celebrate your victories.

You know the simple truth of the *Tao Te Ching*, in Lao
Tzu's well-known classical verse: "The journey of a thousand
miles begins with but a single step." If you feel reluctant, you
must act with courage in the spirit of the ancient samurai:
"The way to overcome a block to action is to act in spite of
it."[63] At times, you may have to follow Susan Jeffers' wise
advice: *Feel the fear . . . and do it anyway.*[64]

Now, beyond the horizon, out there over that hill, is . . .
whatever you want--if you speak up, and speak well.

The next step is yours.

---

[63]David J. Rogers, *Fighting to Win* (Garden City, N.Y.:
Doubleday, 1984), p. 47.
[64]See Bibilography (p. 358) or note 57, p. 280.

Appendix A

SELF-TEST SCORING

INSTRUCTIONS: For SELF-TEST from Chapter 2 (pages 23-27) . . . to total your **SELF-TEST SCORE:**

STEP #1: First, read the commentary on each question (below). As you do, add the number of points for each answer as your personal SCORE.

---

(1) A. Bad news. You're too uptight. Relax more, and you'll perform better. [0 points]

B. It's good to psych up. It's an edge. But don't forget to build a game plan. [+2 points]

C. The best answer! Do your homework. [+5 points]

D. Are you sure you're that ready? Beware of over-confidence. [+3 points]

(2) A. Excellent. You are fortunate. [+5 points]

B. Sounds good. [+3 points]

C. With practice, you'll improve. [+2 points]

D. You need to correct this problem--and you can. [+1 point]

E. Voice improvement is a high priority for you. [0 points]

(3) A. Congratulations. Either you are very
      experienced or just plain adventuresome.
      [+5 points]
     B. [+4 points]
     C. [+3 points]
     D. [+2 points]
     E. [0 points]

(4) A. Try making a better script. Game-plan it;
      rehearse it. Also, do mental relaxation. [0
      points]
     B. You need a better plan and more rehearsal.
      [+2 points]
     C. Glad to hear it. [+4 points]
     D. Great!--*if* you're not falsely *assuming* you are
      ready. Don't forget your script, too. [+5
      points]

(5) A. Maybe not. Think of all the truly brilliant
      experts you've heard who couldn't seem
      to explain their own private wisdom in
      clear, understandable English. [0 points]
     B. [+1 points]
     C. [+2 points]
     D. [+4 points]
     E. The danger signal in the statement is
      "automatically." [+5 points]

(6) A. Keep reading. Later, in this book, you'll learn
      a sure-fire way to break that logjam! [0
      points]
     B. With new habits, you can stop avoidable
      grief. Focus on systematic organization.
      [+1 point]
     C. Okay, better late than not at all--but you can
      do better. [+3 points]
     D. You need a better system--an efficient way to
      build your future talks, step by step. [+2
      points]
     E. Obviously the best answer, and not an
      impossible dream. [+5] points]

(7) A. You're either an accomplished pro or you get plenty of flattery. Either way, the confidence you gain is a plus. [+5 points]
  B. [+4 points]
  C. [+3 points]
  D. [+2 points]
  E. [0 points]

(8) A. Not good. You need to loosen up; let what comes, come. Mental paralysis is self-defeating. [0 points]
  B. At least you hang in there. [+2 points]
  C. The power of *usually*-positive thinking. [+4 points]
  D. The "gift of the gab" is yours, eh? [+5 points]

(9) The problem is: if your audience gets distracted by *how* you speak, they lose track of *what* you say:

  For every "YES" answer, add 0 points.
  For every "NO" answer, add +1 points.

(10) A. You need better preparation--including relaxation and mental imagery techniques. [0 points]
  B. Put more effort into planning and rehearsing your OPENING. [+3 points]
  C. This problem is worse than answer "B," because here you're heading towards an anticlimax ending. Have a well-planned CLOSING. [+2 points]
  D. This feeling is natural. In fact, you can actually convert your own anxiety into a positive energy source. [+5 points]
  E. Never? Self-confidence is great--but be sure you aren't fooling yourself. Are you smart enough to know when you *should* be nervous? [+4 points]

(11) A. The road to disaster. You must put the audience's level of understanding first-- speak *their* language, not only yours! [0 points]

B. Simplify, simplify. Brevity is strength. [+1 point]

C. Too little is as bad as too much. [+1 point]

D. You're on the right track. [+3 points]

E. Excellent. That's a *written* Audience Analysis, isn't it? [*YES* = +5 points; *NOT EXACTLY* = +3 points.]

(12) A. Danger! Good eye contact builds rapport and trust. You must learn to *really* look at people when you talk to them. [0 points]

B. [+1 point]

C. [+2 points]

D. [+3 points]

E. A good signal; a credibility-builder. [+5 points]

(13) A. You need help. Start by improving your *clarity* of expression. (Maybe they fail to act because they don't really understand what you want them to do.) [0 points]

B. Improve your persuasion and persist. [+1 point]

C. Sounds normal. [+2 points]

D. Sounds promising. [+4 points]

E. Sounds incredible! You must be good! [+5 points]

(14) These AV aids are basic for any versatile speaker. You must learn to use them well before you face an audience.

For each "*YES*" answer, add +1 point.
For each "*NO*" answer, add 0 points.

(15) A. A truthful answer here of "ALWAYS" can only indicate that you are already a highly experienced and (most likely) successful speaker. [+5 points]
B. [+4 points]
C. [+2 points]
D. [+1 point]
E. Please be assured, you can learn this skill with practice and motivation. [0 points]

(16) A. Understandable but ineffectual. [0 points]
B. A show of weakness, not of strength. [+1 point]
C. You're human. But to win the "big ones," you'll sometimes need to hold your tongue. [+3 points]
D. The best (and, at times, most difficult) approach. Stay adult, stay in control, even when your adversary tempts you to play the fool. [+5 points]
E. Feel better? It's fun to prove your superiority--but also self-destructive. The backlash will catch you every time. Learn to stay cool. [+2 points]

(17) A. You need more (successful) experience and better mental focus. [0 points]
B. You may need only reliable, objective feedback and more self-confidence. [+1 points]
C. Good. [+3 points]
D. Outstanding! [+5 points]

(18) A. Sorry to hear it--I hope to change your mind. [0 points]
B. Hopefully, as you improve your skills, you'll start to find speaking more enjoyable. [+2 points]
C. Good attitude. Do it more often! [+4 points]
D. To truly have this attitude, you must be a very good speaker. No one loves to do what he or she does badly. [+5 points]

(19) For genuine improvement, you need feedback that is meaningful, usable, and objective. These sources are among your best bets.

For each *"YES"* answer, add +1 point.
For each *"NO"* answer, add 0 points.

(20) A. You have much room for improvement, and (if you have the desire) you can definitely improve. [0 points]

B. You need to concentrate more on your preparations, before the actual talk. [+2 points]

C. Good. Why not be the best you can be? Keep working. [+3 points]

D. You sound like a gifted speaker. Talk on! [+5 points]

POSTSCRIPT: Anyone who is willing to work at it can learn to speak well to groups.

STEP #2: Now add up your **TOTAL SCORE** on the SELF-TEST:

If Your TOTAL SCORE is: Your COMPETENCE PROFILE is:
0 to 29 points .... LEVEL I
30 to 55 points .... LEVEL II
56 to 79 points .... LEVEL III
80 to 100 points .... LEVEL IV

Based on your **TOTAL SCORE** of _____
your personal **COMPETENCE PROFILE** is at LEVEL _____.

STEP #3: Now return to Chapter 2, page 27, for **HOW TO INTERPRET YOUR SCORE**.

◀█▉RETURN▁

Appendix B

DELIVERY TECHNIQUES: A QUICK CHECKLIST

A. **VOICE:**
- (1) QUALITY .... How pleasing is it?
- (2) PITCH .... How high or low?
- (3) RANGE .... How flexible?
- (4) LOUDNESS .... How loud or soft?
- (5) VARIETY .... How interesting?
- (6) RATE .... How fast or slow?
- (7) STRESS .... How intense?
- (8) ARTICULATION .... How clear and correct?

B. **PLATFORM SKILLS:**
- (1) EYE CONTACT ...is:
  - (a) Frequent?
  - (b) Person-to-person?
  - (c) Unpatterned?
  - (d) Genuine?
- (2) POSTURE ....is:
  - (a) Professional?
  - (b) Appropriate?
- (3) GESTURES ....are:
  - (a) Natural?
  - (b) Well-chosen?

C. **INTANGIBLES:**
- (1) ENTHUSIASM ....is:
  - (a) Genuine?
  - (b) Infectious?
- (2) IMAGE ....is:
  - (a) Appropriate?
  - (b) Neat and clean?
  - (c) Appealing?
- (3) POISE.......he/she is:
  - (a) Calm under pressure?
  - (b) Smooth?
  - (c) Decisive?

D. **STYLE** .... is:
- (1) Appropriate for topic?
- (2) Appropriate for audience?
- (3) Consistent throughout?

Appendix C

VOICE ANALYSIS

BACKGROUND:

The human voice can be evaluated on the basis of four primary vocal characteristics (see chapter 18, pp. 178-94):

- (1) **QUALITY,**
- (2) **PITCH,**
- (3) **LOUDNESS,** and
- (4) **VARIETY.**

To understand your own voice (and how *you* sound) better, you'll find it helpful to do a critical analysis of a real voice. This appendix will guide you in a step-by-step *Voice Analysis*, using each of the four primary vocal characteristics, plus the related aspects of RANGE, RATE, STRESS, and ARTICULATION.

INSTRUCTIONS:

To start, choose a good-quality audio tape of a speaker (preferably, not yourself) whom you would like to assess on the basis of his or her vocal characteristics.

In choosing your assessment tape, follow these guidelines:

- (1) Do *not* begin with a tape of yourself. It's much better to study someone else's voice first, to learn (more objectively) how to assess a voice before you apply it closer to home.

(2) At first, be sure to use an *audio* tape only--so you'll focus on voice, and screen out any positive or negative influences from the speaker's image, body language, etc.

(3) Consider this exercise to be private, for your own benefit exclusively. Your intention is to learn skills for future application to yourself, not (at least, now) to share your critiques with others.

(4) As a good choice for assessment tape, you might even pick a pre-recorded cassette featuring some popular, professional speaker, on a current business or self-improvement topic.

(5) Finally, for this exercise, you should set aside a block of quiet time (about one hour), so you can work alone and uninterrupted.

Voice Analysis: Step 1 - **QUALITY**

If you've now secured a tape, spend a few moments in the first step to learn about voice QUALITY. Play several minutes of the assessment tape and listen critically. Make notes to capture your general reaction to the *quality* (that is, the sound itself) of this person's voice.

When assessing a voice's QUALITY, you should consider such questions as these:

a. Does this voice strike you (in general) as positive, negative, or neutral?
b. Can you describe it more specifically--is it dull, pleasing, soothing, obnoxious? Can you tell why?
c. Does the voice sound "flat," or does it vibrate with deep resonance?
d. Do you hear any peculiar vocal characteristics-- for instance, is it nasal, breathy, whiney, gravelly?

e. Most importantly, would *how* this voice sounds tend to affect--in any way--your reaction to *what* the speaker is saying? If so, how?

Before leaving Step #1 in the Voice Analysis, you need to record your reactions to the sample voice in writing.

(*NOTE:* In all remaining steps, you should continue to use this same tape, as you examine each of the seven other vocal characteristics, also.)

Voice Analysis: Step 2 - **PITCH**

Return to your pre-recorded assessment tape to evaluate your chosen speaker on the basis of his or her vocal PITCH. Play several more minutes of the tape, again listening critically, with particular attention to the *pitch* of this voice.

When assessing a voice's PITCH, consider these questions:

a. Is this voice normally high-pitched, low-pitched, in-between, or does it shift?
b. Does it vary pitch enough to be interesting? (Any voice that talks on one note only is, by definition, a *mono*-tone).
c. Is INFLECTION well-used, raising and lowering pitch to add more meaning and emotion to the voice?
d. Does the pitch reveal the speaker's inner self: calm relaxation, quivering urgency, detached boredom, upbeat excitement, none of the above?
e. On balance, is this speaker using an appropriate and appealing tone of voice? Explain.

Before leaving Step #2, note your reactions to the sample voice in writing.

Voice Analysis: Step 3 - RANGE

This time, use your pre-recorded assessment tape to evaluate RANGE. Answer these questions about the speaker's *range*:

a. What is the speaker's apparent total vocal range: narrow, medium, or wide?
b. Does his/her PITCH hover within a small, restricted band of the total range, or is pitch varied over the entire range available?
c. Does this person ordinarily speak in the correct "middle" of his or her vocal range, or is the voice being strained above (towards "falsetto") or forced below its natural range?

As always, capture your reactions to the sample voice in writing.

Voice Analysis: Step 4 - LOUDNESS

Use your pre-recorded assessment tape to evaluate the speaker on the basis of LOUDNESS. Play several more minutes of the tape, listening critically, and consider these points about *loudness*:

a. What is the normal loudness level of this voice? Is it so loud you back off, so soft you strain, or just right?
b. Does this person's voice "reach out" to you with good projection, or does it taper off faintly before it ever arrives?
c. Do you think this speaker could adjust his or her loudness to the circumstances--to speak louder in a large auditorium, softer in a small meeting room?

Write down your new reactions to the sample voice, then continue.

Voice Analysis: Step 5 - **VARIETY**

Use your pre-recorded assessment tape, finally, to evaluate the speaker on the basis of his or her VARIETY. Play several more minutes of the tape, listening critically for variety, and ponder these questions:

a. How, overall, does this voice come across--does it have interesting variety, or monotonous sameness?

b. Does this person talk in repetitious patterns, or keep you attentive with occasional unpredictability?

c. In what ways, subjectively, would you describe this speaker's voice--for example, does it sparkle with vitality, or drone in a lifeless rote?

Write down your new reactions to the sample voice, then continue.

Voice Analysis: Step 6 - **RATE**

Use your pre-recorded assessment tape now to evaluate the speaker on the basis of his or her RATE. Consider these points about *rate*:

a. Is this person's rate of speaking easy to follow: not so fast that it provokes befuddled confusion, nor so slow that it generates hurry-up frustration?

b. Is the rate varied well--to add spice, and match the cadence to the verbal content?

c. Is the speaker compulsively filling every moment of "air time" with chatter; or does he/she seem able, once in a while, to comfortably insert a pause?

Before leaving this step, write down your new reactions to the sample voice.

Voice Analysis: Step 7 - **STRESS**

Use your pre-recorded assessment tape to evaluate the speaker on the basis of his or her STRESS. Consider these points about the voice's *stress*:

a. Does this speaker make you feel comfortable, uptight, in-between, or up-and-down? Why?
b. When you listen, do you experience a sensation of controlled excitement, of alert relaxation, or do you think the speaker just sounds like "blah-blah-blah"?
c. Does the speaker avoid unpleasant extremes: neither too loud nor too soft, too fast nor too slow, too high-pitched nor too low-pitched?

Before leaving Step #7, write down your new reactions to the sample voice, then continue.

Voice Analysis: Step 8 - **ARTICULATION**

Using your pre-recorded assessment tape, evaluate the speaker on the basis of his or her ARTICULATION. Play several more minutes of the tape, while listening critically for *articulation*, to consider questions like these:

a. Does the speaker have any obvious abnormality of speech (a lisp, stutter, hissing "s," etc.)? If so, does it impair your listening, to any degree?

　　b. Is there a prominent accent of any kind--national, regional, ethnic, or social? If so, what is the impact of this accent: a plus, a minus, or neutral?

　　c. Is the usage and pronunciation of words standard and correct, or are you distracted by glaring errors in grammar/syntax, or repeated mispronunciations?

　　d. Are the discrete articulated sounds (i.e., vowels, consonants, and diphthongs) pure and crisp, or muddy and slurred?

　　e. On balance, is this person's speech clear and easy to understand? Why, or why not?

To conclude your Voice Analysis, write down your new reactions to the sample voice.

At this point, you might also like to review your overall assessment of the target voice.

Voice Analysis: **PERSONAL APPLICATION**

Once you have performed a Voice Analysis of someone else's voice, you are ready to apply this same assessment to yourself. You can do a Voice Analysis on your own voice in two ways:

　　(1) alone - by conducting a personal Voice Analysis for yourself upon an audio tape of your own voice; or,

　　(2) with other people - by sharing helpful critiques of each other's voices, using audiotapes, videotapes, or simulated speeches.

Now, if you wish, return to Step 1 and perform a detailed Voice Analysis again for each of the vocal characteristics and aspects--this time using a tape of your own voice as the target sample.

Appendix D

**AUDIO-VISUAL AIDS &
TECHNOLOGY SELECTOR**

CHOOSING YOUR MEDIUM

Every audio-visual medium (simple or complex) has its own peculiar advantages and disadvantages. For your own situation, how can you be sure to choose the best one and use it skillfully?

To help you decide, here are some guidelines on the main kinds of AV media . . .

A. BOARD

For quite a while, the traditional *Chalkboard* (whether black or green) has been the speaker's basic tool. It is cheap, flexible, dynamic, and spontaneous. When you use a Board, the only accessories you need are chalk and an eraser.

A newer kind of Board is white porcelain, on which the user writes with special erasable color markers. As a visual aid, the *Porcelain Board* (also called an "erasable" or "write-and-wipe" board) eliminates the mess of chalk, adds the power of color, and is easier at a distance for the audience to read.

ADVANTAGES OF THE BOARD:

1. Since your visual is literally created before their eyes, the Board makes the process most spontaneous and immediate for your audience.

2. Unlike prefabricated visuals (like Slides or Charts), the Board can easily be altered: you can add, subtract, erase, re-write, and move things around. Of all visual aids, the Board is the most flexible.

3. When the economy is important, the Board is clearly superior in cost-effectiveness as an aid because it is the cheapest alternative.

4. The Board's excellent availability is obvious. Once it's there, it's there if you need it--to exemplify a key point or to create an instant visual in reply to a question.

5. The Board lets you respond to audience comments on the spot. You can adapt or modify a visual at once, since it isn't finalized in advance. The Board is ideal for interactive meetings and training.

LIMITATIONS OF THE BOARD:

1. Watch for legibility problems if you cannot draw clearly or write legibly (or even spell correctly) while under pressure. You'll be better off with a prepared visual (a Chart or Overhead).

2. With a Board, your visual is temporary ("one time only"). Once it's erased, you have to start all over to repeat the performance.

3. At a distance--even with huge lettering--the Board can be difficult to see and cannot be projected to a larger size. Its limited size normally makes it unsatisfactory for groups above 25 people (unless you write very large).

4. The Board permits no motion, sound, or (unless you have a Porcelain Board) color. With a Chalkboard, color is difficult to add because colored chalk is messy and doesn't show well: your visuals are thus limited or over-simplified.

5. Although the Board can create visuals quickly, it consumes extra time while you write and draw. If your agenda is tight, you may prefer to save time with a prepared visual and forget spontaneity.

6. The Board projects a more informal, <u>less polished image</u> to your talk. For some talks, you may feel that this "schoolroom" or "chalk talk" atmosphere is too casual.

TIPS ON USING THE BOARD:

- Draw simply and boldly. Make all drawings clear and direct, showing only the main details.
- Write legibly and big. Use "bullet" phrases with short key words and highlights only.
- Keep the talk flowing. Don't make your audience sit and watch you silently write for too long.
- Before you create a new visual, erase any that you've already done.
- Avoid glancing at the board too often: keep eye contact with your audience.
- Know in advance what you'll put on the board. When you rehearse, practice drawing your visuals, too.

B. CHART

A Chart is basically a visual aid created in large format on paper or card stock. Charts may be either Card Charts, Flipcharts, or Lap Charts.

Card Charts are individual charts on heavy paper stock, varying in size from regular document size (8 1/2 x 11 inches), upward. Smaller ones are hand-held by the speaker or assistant; larger ones are placed upon an easel.

A *Flipchart* is a tablet pad of paper attached at the top to a chart stand. Its pages are turned during the talk to reveal each chart in sequence. The standard size for Flipcharts is around 27 x 34 inches.

A *Lap Chart* is usually a follow-along summary of the presentation, given to a listener before the talk starts. A Lap Chart offers many of the advantages of Charts and Handouts (being a hybrid of both), but also has all the dangers and disadvantages of a Handout.[*]

---

[*]See the discussion of Handouts in Section C, pp. 333-336.

ADVANTAGES OF A CHART:

1. Since CHARTS are made in advance, they let you present information with a prepared, polished look. The lettering can be more exact and the drawing more artistic.

2. Once created, CHARTS will remain the same, and can have repeat uses in future presentations, over and over. With thick paper and proper care, they can last for years.

3. Unless you incur high labor costs (such as for a professional artist), using Charts is economical, costing only slightly more than using the Board. Compared to the benefits, the cost is extremely low.

4. Charts make it possible for you to add color to the visual aid, which gives stronger impact and allows you to present more detail and more complex ideas in a visual form.

5. A Flipchart is an ideal tool for making a visible historical record of a dynamic event in process (say, an interactive meeting). You capture ideas or decisions as they occur, on the blank Flipchart, then afterwards can give everyone a transcribed copy.

LIMITATIONS OF A CHART:

1. Because they are somewhat large (and usually require a stand), Charts are less portable, and can be cumbersome and inconvenient to carry from place to place.

2. Card Charts or Flipcharts of standard size can pose visibility problems. They are usually too small to be seen well by large groups. (A reasonable cut-off point is to avoid using charts if you expect over 20 people.)

3. Charts made of thin paper (especially Flipcharts) are fragile, not sturdy. Their pages show wear-and-tear quickly and may even rip while you are turning them in front of your audience.

4. Some chart paper is so thin it causes "see-through" distractions for people who notice the page underneath. Also, some speakers carelessly cover their own words with noise by turning pages in a rustling sweep while they talk.

5. Charts cost you extra preparation time beforehand to create. During the presentation, however, they save you time because (unlike the Board) they are already made and ready to use.

TIPS ON USING CHARTS:

- Use only a few, well-done charts (say, from one to five), not an overwhelming parade of chart after chart.
- Make your charts simple and bold. Keep all drawings basic and use key words, not complete sentences.
- Add color to complex visuals so the main features stand out and are easier to find.
- Don't write on a Chart while talking (as if it were a Board) unless: (a) you want to make a static chart more dynamic by progressively adding to it; (b) you seek to stimulate back-and-forth interplay with the audience; or, (c) you need a written record of the outcome for later.
- If you plan to write on the Chart, put the chart-stand to your left (as you face the audience) if you are right-handed, to your right if you are left-handed. (This arrangement helps you maintain eye contact with the audience when you write.)
- If you do write on the Chart, avoid squeaky markers: they are annoying and unprofessional.

C. HANDOUT

A *Handout* can be virtually anything you "hand out" to your audience. Sometimes, you'll expect it to be passed around and returned, but more commonly you'll intend audience members to keep their Handouts for future reference.

The Handout gives people a way to review your overall talk afterwards, to refresh their lost memories on fuzzy spots, to explore specific ideas in deeper detail, or to apply the lessons in an immediate, practical way.

Typical Handout materials are:

(1) the "real thing" (if small enough);

(2) a summary roadmap of the whole talk (in Lap Chart or outline form);

(3) a "hard" (paper) copy of some or all of the visuals;

(4) the complete documentation (statistics, derivations, etc.) upon which your presentation, in capsule, is based;

(5) an actual copy of a form, document, brochure, etc., being discussed;

(6) a copy of a photograph or drawing;

(7) a sample of something from the talk (printout, model, wine, cake, perfume, or you-name-it);

(8) a list of resources (key-contact addresses, phone numbers, order numbers, etc.).

Handouts can be as varied, unique, or worthwhile as the topics and speakers they represent.

ADVANTAGES OF HANDOUTS:

1. Handouts (if well done) give speakers an effective aid for group coverage, no matter what size audience, small or large. When you expect to speak to more than 35 people at once, the first visual aid considered should be a Handout.

2. Unlike Slides, Viewgraphs, or Charts (which may flash past a distracted viewer too fast to be comprehended fully), the Handout is ideal for later reference since the audience can take it along for study elsewhere at their own pace.

3. When your listeners must use the actual item later (for example, a printed document to be completed on-the-job), your best aid for "how-to" presentations is probably a handout copy of the real thing, for hands-on learning.

4. Handouts are very economical. For an informal talk, a Handout is one of the cheapest and quickest aids possible, since it can be no more than a photocopy ("Xerox") of a target document. On the other hand, as you resort to graphics support for artwork, the required time and costs will increase steadily.

5. A good Handout offers you a way to get interaction and feedback from your audience with "do-as-we-go" exercises. For example, you can demonstrate how to use a form, then give participants each a copy and let them try it.

6. In a sales situation, a good Handout provides positive reinforcement of your product/service, organization, or self. The Handout works as a reminder of your message when you're not around.

LIMITATIONS OF HANDOUTS:

1. A Handout--if given out before or during the talk--can be a serious distraction, since it's impossible for a listener to pay total attention both to the Handout and to you. Sometimes, people get more engrossed in the Handout than in your spoken words, or they make noise handling it and thus distract others.

2. If your audience has the whole story in-hand already, there's a danger they'll impatiently skip ahead to the "bottom line," without waiting for your full argument. If so, you have a loss of control of the sequence of ideas, and may therefore fail to persuade them.

3. Color is seldom found in Handouts because it's usually costly or time-consuming. For cheap color Handouts, your best bet is to get copies of some color brochure, pamphlet, etc., already printed elsewhere (a manufacturer's flier, for example).

4. If your Handout is more than just photocopied paper (for example, a model, videotape, sample, or book), the quantity expense of giving out large numbers can add up quickly. (Remember that typically, if you provide a Handout, everyone in your audience will want one.)

5. When the size of your audience is expected to be large (but impossible to really calculate), it's difficult to estimate exactly how many Handout copies to reproduce. Should you intentionally print too many (and waste money), or try to guess precisely (and risk not having enough handouts)?

TIPS ON USING HANDOUTS:

• Handouts are unlike other visual aids. A Handout needs more explanatory detail than a Chart or Overhead. Think carefully before you simply run off copies of other visuals and call them "handouts."

- Check the clarity, accuracy, and professional quality of all your handouts. Can they stand alone to make full sense days or weeks later?
- Follow the same basic rules of good graphic display for Handouts as for all other visuals. (Avoid using amateur-looking Handouts.)
- The best time to give people a Handout is usually at the end of your talk (to avoid potential distractions).
- Giving Handouts at the beginning shows an overview, forestalls premature questions, and gives your audience a place to write. Still, avoid giving anyone a Handout before or while you talk unless your justification is overwhelming.
- With interactive handouts (such as documents that people fill in by following "do-as-we-go" instructions), the best approach is usually two-step: *first,* show your audience how to use the document in a magnified version (by Viewgraph, Slide, Chart); *then,* give each person a copy of the real thing for practice.
- Have enough Handouts for everyone. (If you come up short, get business cards from all attendees left out and send copies to them promptly afterwards.)

D. OVERHEAD (Viewgraph)

The *Overhead* (or "viewgraph") projector uses a system of light, prism, and lens to project enlarged images (via transparencies) onto a screen. Each viewgraph slide is normally 10" x 12" or 11" x 12" in size. The projected image becomes larger depending on the size of the screen, room lighting, and the "throw" power of the projector itself.

Modern technology now offers more sophisticated options (such as Videotape or 35mm Slides generated by computer graphics). The traditional Overhead (viewgraph) projector is still commonly used, however, in many organizational briefings today.

ADVANTAGES OF THE OVERHEAD:

1. One obvious advantage of the Overhead is that--unlike the Board, Chart, or Handout--its image size is not fixed but can be enlarged much bigger through projection. By viewing a larger picture, an audience of 15 or more people can see more detail.

2. Overheads (like Charts) allow for many repeat uses, let you add color effectively, and reinforce your message with extra professional polish.

3. Overheads give you excellent flexibility and control over your presentation. Since each frame is a separate item, you can easily make future changes--to update data tables; to have different versions of the same talk (short, medium, or long); and to rearrange the sequence of visuals on quick notice.

4. Depending on the quality demanded, an Overhead has the virtue of speed. Overheads often give you the finest visual aid in the shortest amount of time. [A so-called "quick-and-dirty" Overhead can be made in minutes by writing on a blank transparency with a grease pencil or special color marking pen. Higher quality viewgraphs, of course, require more time and higher cost.]

5. Overhead projectors are widely available and Viewgraphs themselves are very portable. Since they are light and easy to carry, they are especially good for a stand-up pitch given over and over at many different locations in much the same form.

LIMITATIONS OF THE OVERHEAD:

1. The act of changing from one Overhead to another during a presentation can cause distractions for both the audience (who is aware of every slip-up) and the presenter (who may talk to the visual instead of to people, or lose Authority Posture by leaning over to shuffle noisy transparencies).

2. The Overhead machine itself is always hard to position in a room without being an obstacle that blocks someone's view. It's also difficult for a speaker to stand up front, stage-center, without being a barrier between the screen and the audience.

3. Overheads create a definite "show and tell" atmosphere that for your situation may not be desirable or appropriate. If you are selling a product or service to the public, another AV tool (Handouts, Videotape, Slides, Demonstration) may work better.

4. Because Overhead projectors get a lot of use (and abuse), they are often temperamental and cause snafus. Be sure to check the machine's operation beforehand. (The most common problems are: difficult focus, no power, or a burnt-out bulb. Also beware of rooms that prohibit a good setup because of no projection screen, a lectern that's poorly located, or bad placement of electrical outlets.)

5. Some people hate viewgraphs--because they've seen so many poor presentations using bad viewgraphs in the past. So as soon as they see a viewgraph machine, they get negative expectations. (Your best bet, if you're considering an Overhead, is to check your audience's preferences beforehand.)

TIPS ON USING THE OVERHEAD:

- Before you face an audience, do plenty of practice including a hands-on rehearsal, on-site. Be sure the projector is working properly and know who/how/where to call for help.
- Reduce ambient light in the room: close drapes; lower blinds. If overhead light banks can be cut off separately, start closest to the screen and experiment, moving back. If available, use a rheostat (dimmer)
- Don't project off a wall: the image will blur and be tinged by the paint color. Always be sure you'll have a projection screen.
- Put all your slides in frames--preferably cardboard ones, which are easier to write on and handle. Loose transparencies wrinkle, make noise, stick together, and may slip onto the floor at the worst possible moment.
- Number all your viewgraphs in proper sequence-- on the frame, not the transparency.

- Write your notes directly onto "hard" (paper) copies of the visuals as they'll appear on the screen. (You will be less likely during your talk to keep glancing over your shoulder, turning your back to the audience.)
- An economical method for adding color to overhead transparencies is to draw onto them directly with multi-color felt-tip pens especially designed for this purpose (which can be purchased in office-supply or graphic-arts stores).
- Make static visuals more dynamic by using overlays, write-on's, or reveal techniques.*
- Don't just stand at the lectern, immobile. Instead, move back beside the screen and get involved. Be the pathway of communication between the visual and your audience.
- Explain every visual: Why are you showing it? What should the audience learn?
- To focus people's attention on specific parts of a complex visual, use a pointer. (For a large screen, obtain a red laser pointer.)
- If you can't walk to the screen, point to key items with a small pointer or pen directly onto the viewgraph itself at the projector.
- Keep eye contact and involvement with the audience. Avoid looking continuously back over your shoulder at your viewgraphs.
- Never show your audience a blank screen with nothing on it but projected light. Have the first slide set up before you turn the projector on. When you change slides, use a DISSOLVE technique--that is: before you pull the old slide off, cover it for a brief moment with the new one.

---

*An *overlay* is a separate piece of transparency, attached to the same visual, and flipped into place to add more information. The *write-on* technique is to write or draw additional information, by hand, upon a prepared viewgraph. The *reveal* technique is the opposite of an overlay--portions of a visual are hidden by strips of cardboard, then uncovered during the presentation.

- For an interim--with *nothing* on the screen--don't turn off the projector. Instead, put a *solid* (all-cardboard) viewgraph on the projector like a normal slide, so no light shines through.
- For a written list, cover it with a piece of paper and gradually reveal each item one at a time. Simultaneously push the viewgraph up so you're always using only the top-half of the screen. (The projector or lectern often blocks people's views of the bottom half.)
- Never touch a projector bulb with your fingers. If it's burnt-out, the residual heat can blister your skin. If it's brand new and right out of the box, still don't touch it: the oils in your hand will shorten the bulb's life. (Insert a new bulb by holding it with a soft, clean cloth.)
- If possible, use the kind of projector that contains two bulbs inside, which are changed quickly and easily by a tandem switch.
- Coordinate the sequence of all events beforehand--when lights get turned on and off, which slides are intentionally solid, who does what.

E. PHOTOGRAPH

A *Photograph* can be either black-&-white or color, in slide or print form. The standard size for a print is 8" x 10"--although with enlargement and cropping, a photograph can be virtually any size, smaller or larger.

Very large color photos ("poster" size) are possible but sometimes costly.

ADVANTAGES OF PHOTOGRAPHS:

1. A Photograph allows you to represent a place or object in full detail with accurate <u>realism</u> (even in life-like color).

2. Photos are relatively small and <u>easily portable</u>. Unlike Overheads or Slides, showing them does not require a projector or other equipment.

3. A realistic photograph of a thing can have more impact (and thus be more memorable and persuasive) than a drawing or verbal description. The cliche is true: Seeing is believing.

4. Once a master negative is made, hundreds of prints of a single Photo can be reproduced in quantity from it. (The more copies you make, the lower will be your per-unit cost.)

LIMITATIONS OF PHOTOGRAPHS:

1. Unless you make large, costly blow-ups, the small size of hand-held Photos makes them hard to see except in small groups. (If you pass around Photos while you talk, they become a distraction.)

2. To plan, shoot, process, and print one or more rolls of film correctly takes extra time. Normally, even on an absolute "rush" basis, allow at least three working days to obtain a new Photo (preferably, more).

3. Getting good Photographs involves complexity. You need the proper equipment, plus an experienced person who knows how to use it. If you or your staff cannot do the job right, you must hire professional help.

4. A Photo captures one frozen moment in time; it allows no motion. If your subject is not static but in reality changes, no still Photo tells the whole story. (You'll need a Movie or Videotape, instead.)

TIPS ON USING PHOTOGRAPHS:

- Be certain that the technical quality of any Photograph you show is superior--that it has correct exposure, focus, and framing. (If not, leave it out.)
- If your audience contains more than 15 people, do not show them a hand-held Photo. (It is too small for them to see fine details at a distance.)
- If you must show one or more photographs to a large group, convert them into a 35mm Slides, which can be projected (and thus enlarged).

• Clean all cameras often using a can of compressed air. Screw a UV (ultraviolet) filter onto each lens for extra protection. Transport all equipment in strong, sturdy cases. (Also, with photo and other AV equipment, always get adequate insurance against theft.)

F. SLIDE

Since a *Slide* is a transparency, it allows you to project an enlarged image of a photograph onto a screen. Slides are normally in 35mm color format. (The same camera can shoot either Photos or Slides, depending only upon the film used.) As viewed by an audience, the practical difference between a Slide and a Photo is its image size.

To show Slides also requires a screen and slide projector. There are different kinds of slide projectors but the one used most commonly is the Carousel type, which holds slides in a revolving tray on top.

ADVANTAGES OF SLIDES:

1. By enlargement (when projected), Slides allow an audience to see much greater detail than Photos.

2. Slides are easily transported from place to place without burden. [Before travelling, however, be sure each Slide is numbered, and (for Carousel-style projectors) that the locking ring in the center of each slide tray is correctly seated to hold the slides.]

3. Slides offer great flexibility: the sequence or content of a program can be changed easily and quickly. Also, the same Slides can be re-used often--such as in a canned pitch that is given repeatedly.

4. By using a hand-held remote control, a lone speaker can control an entire presentation, from a distance, making the visuals advance, stop, or reverse at will. (No assistant is necessary.)

5. For realism--to capture an authentic view of something in detail and in color, but without motion--your best AV choice is usually Slides.

LIMITATIONS OF SLIDES:

1. Like a Photograph, a Slide shows <u>no motion</u>, but only a static, frozen picture.

2. Slides are usually best for showing pictures, not <u>words</u>. Titles, captions, and labels can be added to Slides, but they require special techniques that the average office (which lacks professional photographic or graphic capabilities) does not have.

3. Being <u>mechanical</u>, a Slide projector requires time to prepare and set up. Moreover, if the equipment is not well-maintained nor properly checked, it can cause major problems (such as slide jamming).

4. A talk with too many Slides (unless they are extremely interesting) can quickly drug most audiences by <u>overkill</u> into sleep. A Slide show seems to trigger old memories of boring baby pictures or a brother-in-law's European vacation.

TIPS ON USING SLIDES:

• Number all slides (on the frame) and keep them in proper sequence. (If you change the order, of course, remember to change the numbers, too.)

• Keep consistency. Don't mix poorly-shot slides in with professional, high-quality ones if you can avoid it.

• With 35mm slides, you do not need an assistant: you can easily operate the projector by yourself, using a remote control hand switch.

• Consider speaking from the back of the room, changing slides by remote--so while you talk, you see the show the same as your audience sees it.

• On each Slide frame, draw a color bar (with a felt-tip pen) to help you orient the slide in the tray the correct way. (When all Slides are in the tray correctly, all color bars should show at the top.)

- If you use a Kodak Carousel projector (with slide trays that rotate on top), be sure all slides are secured in their trays by the smaller circular locking rings that fit onto the trays. (Then if a tray gets dropped, your whole array won't spill onto the floor.)
- If more than one slide projector will be used at once (sometimes called a "multimedia" presentation), put a different color bar on each projector's slides (red for one, green for the other).
- Use a zoom lens--which allows you to make the image bigger or smaller on the screen without having to move the projector.
- Don't forget the accessories: extension cord, adapter plug, projection screen, remote control, and pointer.

G. MOVIE

A *Movie* can be in color or black-&-white, with or without sound. Movies are made in formats ranging from 8mm to 70mm. For business and educational use, however, the common format is 16mm. (To work together, the projector and film must be in the same format.)

The primary differences between a Movie and Videotape are that: (a) the image quality of a Movie is (currently) sharper than Videotape, and (b) Videotape can be replayed instantly while Movie film must be processed and printed before it is viewed.

ADVANTAGES OF A MOVIE:

1. Motion and Sound. To capture an action or event, as close as possible to reality with motion and sound, one of your main options will be a Movie. (The other options are Videotape, Demonstration, Videodisk, or Computer).

2. A color Movie with sound engages people's senses and attention with greater dramatic impact than silent, static aids like an Overhead, Photo, or Chart.

3. A Movie (if properly cared for) can be durable enough for <u>re-use</u> a hundred times or more (or until it grows out-of-date).

4. The Movie itself is <u>easy to carry</u> and in most organizations a 16mm projector is either already available or can easily be rented.

LIMITATIONS OF A MOVIE:

1. An original Movie is one of the most <u>expensive</u> kinds of AV aid you can produce. For even just a few minutes of professionally-produced film, be prepared to spend thousands of dollars.

2. Once printed in final form, a Movie is <u>inflexible</u>: it is impossible to change without a slow, expensive job of re-shooting, re-editing, and re-printing.

3. Movie projectors look deceptively simple to operate but they often develop <u>mechanical problems</u>, acting ornery and frustrating. (Be sure to get a "self-threading" type of projector, and become intimately familiar with it before you ever use it in front of an audience.)

4. Movie-making is complex and consumes a long span of <u>time</u>. If it can take Hollywood a year or more to make a film, you can't expect to make your own overnight. (In planning your Movie, allow a minimum of three months from start of production to final print.)

TIPS ON USING MOVIES:

• Never show any Movie you haven't viewed completely yourself in advance. It might be inaccurate or out-of-date, contradict your message, or be inappropriate or embarrassing for the audience.

• Whenever possible, have an assistant to run the projector for you.

• Choose a projectionist who is experienced. If you must do it yourself, do plenty of hands-on practice beforehand, and learn how to troubleshoot common problems such as broken film, a lost loop, or a burnt-out bulb.

- Be sure you always have a take-up reel (the second, empty reel at the back of the projector) to collect the film. Also, be sure it's not smaller than the reel of film.
- Before the presentation, have the projector completely set up, ready to start at exactly the film's first frame of picture. (Don't make your audience watch the film-leader countdown: "4-3-2-1".)
- Pay particular attention to screening conditions (ambient room light, external noise, climate control, sound playback, noisy projectors, positioning of image on the screen).
- Instead of just starting a Movie, first introduce it. Tell your audience why you are showing this film and what you expect them to gain from it.
- After the Movie, close the communication loop: Invite comments by the audience; stimulate discussion of what they've seen.

H. AUDIO

An AV aid can also be merely *Audio*--providing sound by means of vinyl record, compact disk, or (most commonly) audiocassette. Each requires its own, separate kind of playback device.

Normally, any records or compact disks you use will be pre-recorded from other sources. If you must record and playback sounds, on-the-spot, you'll prefer Audiocassette tapes (although they, too, may be prerecorded.

ADVANTAGES OF AUDIO:

1. When all you need is sound, an Audio aid helps you focus your audience's attention on that sense only, without dilution by seeing.

2. Audio aids are relatively economical compared to the cost of aids that are visual (Slides, Photos) or audio *and* visual (Movies, Videotape).

3. An Audio aid can enable you to <u>record and replay</u> a sound yourself--either beforehand or as part of your presentation.

LIMITATIONS OF AUDIO:

1. An Audio aid gives <u>no picture</u> so it is clearly the wrong choice if you need more than sound.
2. Unless you have a full, high-fidelity system available, the average <u>quality</u> of audiocassette players is not good for playback in a large presentation.
3. Since an Audio aid does use sound only, listeners are more susceptible to <u>distractions</u> by random things that occur in the audience (people walking by, coughing, talking).

TIPS ON USING AUDIO:

- Get the best-quality playback system you can manage and test the equipment before using it.
- Have the tape ready in advance, at the exact spot your audience should hear, so all you have to do is hit the "PLAY" button.
- Treat your records and tapes with care. Records can be scratched; tapes can break, stretch, or come loose.
- For best clarity, periodically clean and demagnetize the recording-playback heads of audiocassette recorders (with a head-cleaning tape or alcohol, swab, and demagnetizer) after every 18 hours of playing time.

I. VIDEOTAPE (VCR)

Videotape is overall the most versatile AV aid in use today. It provides sight, sound, color, the ability to record and replay instantly, plus additional special effects.

Earlier, the standard Videotape format for government, education, and business was 3/4-inch. Now, the videocassette recorder (VCR) chosen more often is in a 1/2-inch format (in two versions: Beta or VHS).

A 1/2-inch machine is cheaper, easier to transport and set up, and more likely to have special effects (such as freeze-frame, slow motion, and search).

The Beta format has lost ground and VHS has become the primary, standard format. In addition, a new economy 8mm tape format is available.

The ease of popping in a cassette (versus the hassles a film projector can bring) makes the continued widespread use of videotape a certainty in the future.

ADVANTAGES OF VIDEOTAPE:

1. Like a Movie, a Videotape allows you to capture an actual event in realistic detail with <u>motion</u> and <u>sound</u> in living <u>color</u>.

2. The ability to <u>record and replay</u> instantly makes Videotape a great tool for learning situation, to help people improve their skills in activities like golf, tennis, bowling, and public speaking.

3. Besides showing an action or event realistically, Videotape can alter reality with <u>special effects</u>: to freeze motion, slow down motion in time, move forward/backward faster than normal, and more. If used well (not as gimmicks), these capabilities can be invaluable.

4. As an aid, Videotape can generate maximum <u>interaction</u> between speaker and audience. For example, Videotape is excellent for a series of interrupted vignettes-- where you might show one, stop to discuss it, then show and discuss the next one, and so on.

5. Videotape production often gives an organization more direct <u>control</u> than making a Movie. Video technology is now so automatic that it allows a person almost to just point and shoot, then check the results.

LIMITATIONS OF VIDEOTAPE:

1. Some people are adept at handling photo and electronic equipment; others are not. For people without the knack, the <u>complexity</u> and intricacies of Videotape can be difficult until they gain practical experience.

2. A single videocassette is not expensive, but to install Videotape as a medium can be costly because of all the equipment required: a VCR unit and monitor, plus (for record/playback) a camera and tripod. (One alternative has been the *camcorder*, which combines both camera and VCR in a single, compact unit.)

3. The viewing size of most TV monitors is comparatively small (typically 19" diagonally or less), so unless you have large-screen projection, you'll find Videotape hard to use with an audience of more than 15 people.

4. Despite the even-smaller, ever-better VCR's that appear, Videotape equipment can still be hard to transport off-site (unless you carry only a cassette and have the equipment taken and set up by someone else).

5. Perhaps because the equipment is complex and more sophisticated, a VCR--especially one that is used often, by many different people--can find innumerable snafus and quirky ways to annoy you. (Murphy strikes again!) So, be prepared with a "Plan B," just in case.

TIPS ON USING VIDEOTAPE:

- Be sure your VCR and videocassette are both in the same format (e.g., 1/2" Beta or VHS).
- Allow plenty of time beforehand. For proper set-up, a VCR requires more than simply plugging in a few cables.
- Know your equipment; not all VCR's are identical. For example, some older machines require you to push two buttons together (PLAY and RECORD) to record; others have one-button RECORD.
- Check all connector cables: Are there correct plugs (phone plug, pin plug, etc.) at each end? It's very unsettling to find that your camera or monitor can't be connected to the VCR because the plugs don't match.
- Remember to have a good, long extension cord (for safety: 3-prong grounded or 2-prong polarized) with at least three plug-in outlets, plus a separate 3-to-2 adapter plug.

- Position the monitor high (such as on a TV stand) so everyone in the audience can see it easily. Consider extra monitors so all can see easily.
- If your VCR has a built-in digital clock, set the time accurately so its readout doesn't constantly blink, distracting the audience.
- Never point the camera at a light source (it can damage the tube inside) and always keep the lens cap on when the camera is not in use.
- If you plan to record anything, be sure to get a camera tripod that moves easily both sideways (a "pan") and up-and-down (a "tilt"). Also be sure you have a zoom lens (to "zoom" the picture closer in or farther out).
- Before recording in color, set the *"color balance"* on the camera so the color attained is natural and true. Also check audio levels to be sure you're recording sound and not just picture.
- As periodic maintenance, have a trained technician clean the heads and check all adjustments on the VCR.
- To do a rapid series of recording and playback smoothly requires careful coordination. Practice, practice, practice, until it's all natural for you.

J. DEMONSTRATION

Sometimes, the best way to explain something is to show how it really happens--using simulation, reenactment, or actual performance. Instead of talking about it, you *do* it.

A *Demonstration* can involve the real thing or a proxy (such as scale models, movable props, or people acting in role-play).

Examples of a demonstration include:

(a) the test-firing of a missile;

(b) the reenactment of a Civil War event; or,

(c) a step-by-step presentation in a kitchen, showing how to use a food processor.

In some ways, demonstrations are like skits or plays and, like these, should be carefully planned, orchestrated, and rehearsed beforehand. Since the demonstration is "live," there is little room for error: if it fails, credibility is damaged, seriously and immediately. (If it works, on the other hand, this risk of failure can enhance credibility.)

ADVANTAGES OF A DEMONSTRATION:

1. A live Demonstration has immediacy: the possibility that something could go wrong helps to generate more intensity, excitement, and audience involvement,

2. A Demonstration (unlike other methods) has the potential sensory range to invoke all five of your audience's senses. Beyond what they see or hear, you can have them taste, smell, or touch objects firsthand.

3. Since the total impact of a Demonstration is more high-powered, audience retention is likely to be better: they'll remember your message longer and stronger.

LIMITATIONS OF A DEMONSTRATION:

1. Unlike other AV aids (which can be edited and redone over and over until they are right), a live Demonstration introduces more unpredictability: it occurs in real time, so "what's done is done." Things seldom go exactly as planned and failures may be irreversible.

2. Doing a Demonstration of something might look simple--just stand up and do it. With so much at stake, however, demonstrations require better planning and more preparation than most other approaches.

3. Demonstrations that involve other people (such as role-play enactments) demand the most careful preparation of all because you have the most likely loss of control of events. Unlike a Movie or Videotape, the outcome is uncontrollable in advance.

TIPS ON USING A DEMONSTRATION:

• Leave nothing to chance. Plan thoroughly and
   rehearse meticulously.

- You can add more suspense and excitement by *emphasizing* to your audience the danger of potential failure (like an escape artist who plays up the risks before being bound in chains and tossed into a river).
- If a Demonstration requires other people, never assume they understand exactly what you want. Always do a complete run-through as a test and for fine-tuning. If necessary, make a written script.

K. COMPUTER

The *Computer* offers you potentially the most powerful audio-visual technology imaginable. Although a larger mainframe or mini computer can be used for AV applications, the smaller micro ("personal" or "desktop") computer is often more available and sometimes more advanced for many people's AV needs.

In general, your best tool today for making color visuals quickly and easily (after you've assembled the system and learned how to use it) is probably on a desktop computer using *presentation graphics* software with a plotter or color printer.

Unlike other output devices (like matrix or letter-quality printers), a plotter allows you to print graphic designs, symbols, words, or pictures onto paper or transparency in one or more *colors*. As computer technology continues to advance, the plotter itself will eventually give way to other tools such as the color laser printer.

With a Computer and a presentation graphics program, you can manipulate images on-screen until you're satisfied, then output a professional-quality visual either: (a) as a HANDOUT or OVERHEAD (via plotter or printer), or (b) as a color SLIDE (via special camera or photo system).

Thus, using a computer system with the proper hardware, software, and peripherals, one artistic individual can imagine, design, and produce an entire set of presentation aids, in-house, at a single sitting.

A program that is "menu-driven" (and thus easier to learn) will also usually give you less options, less control. On the other hand, a more sophisticated program that gives you more flexibility will often be harder to learn.

In its most advanced application, the Computer can become a tool for *animation* and *simulation*, producing sight, sound, color, special effects and, most dramatically, the instantaneous impact of various "what-if" changes in a simulated complex reality (for example, the simulation of flying a 747 airplane in a computer-based learning exercise).

For animated or dynamic computer displays, Computer Projectors are available (for purchase or rental), which can project whatever is on the computer screen onto a projection screen at a much larger viewing size for larger audiences.

Computer graphics are now being explored as an exciting AV tool. Though they are not readily available to all presenters, their use is growing fast. You should be aware of their capabilities and learn to exploit them for yourself.

ADVANTAGES OF A COMPUTER:

1. A complete "presentation graphics" set-up gives an individual or organization greater direct control over the final output. Everything can be done at one time in one place by one person or group.

2. Likewise, because all work can now be done in-house, the computer allows you to create top-quality graphics faster and cheaper. Your deadlines and budgets are no longer totally reliant upon outside sources of supply.

3. The computer gives you new AV capabilities--such as animation, simulation, color effects, and the ability to convert spreadsheet or database numbers instantly into a graphic display.

4. For even the simplest applications, the computer provides the individual user with tools for better quality control (such as built-in spelling checkers and computer-formed lettering).

5. By using a computer (as opposed to more conventional AV tools), you add a greater variety of AV choices, so your resulting visuals are usually more interesting.

LIMITATIONS OF A COMPUTER:

1. Almost any computer or software program will require a <u>significant time investment</u> for learning to use it before you can apply it.

2. Normally, using a computer for making AV aids is an "add-on" capability. If bought for this purpose only, the <u>high initial cost</u> of hardware and software would usually be prohibitive.

3. If the computer itself is used as the AV tool (such as with a Computer Projector), you may encounter some <u>difficulty in transporting</u> and setting up the equipment.

4. Like all sophisticated equipment--if not more so--computers and computer programs are often infuriatingly vulnerable to potential <u>bugs, quirks, and gremlins</u>. (Murphy, aided by human error, strikes again.) Be ready for strange surprises at inconvenient times.

5. The variety and control offered by "presentation graphics" packages is deceptive. By allowing so many choices--of typeface, line width, box design, and so forth--computers invite everyday people (who may lack artistic/graphic skills and training) to create bad, ugly visuals with <u>poor, amateur designs</u>.

TIPS ON USING A COMPUTER

- Be sure the software and hardware are compatible. For instance, will your printer/plotter work with the graphics package? Can you interface with your other programs, such as to convert data from an existing data base or spreadsheet into the new package's graphic form?

- Start planning your computer application by deciding on the end-product you'll need--a hard copy, overhead, slide, or simulation?

- Always have a Plan B, just in case chaos strikes and your computer program is suddenly crashing. (And during preparation, make frequent backup disk copies of all your work.)

- Don't try to learn "on the run." Invest the time to master all hardware/software *before* you must try making your own presentation graphics while facing a tough deadline.

- Anticipate future as well as current needs. If you expect to do graphic design on a personal computer, a *hard disk* for storage is essential.

- Keep designs simple and elegant. Avoid the temptation to get extravagantly fancy. Stay with one major type font and style.

L. OTHER AIDS

Anything is a good "aid" if it helps get your point across more quickly, clearly, memorably, or persuasively. Here are a few other AV aids that are sometimes used:

(1) **FILMSTRIP** - A Filmstrip is like a set of Slides that are not separate but in sequence on a single strip of film. To show a Filmstrip, you insert it into a special filmstrip projector.

   Filmstrips are not used frequently--perhaps because more people already own equipment for creating and projecting Slides. They are not so versatile, since they cannot be re-edited, once produced. Also, some commercially-prepared Filmstrip programs tend to be simplistic and unsophisticated.

(2) **OPAQUE PROJECTOR** - An Opaque Projector (unlike an Overhead or Slide projector) allows you to project and enlarge a paper document, as is, without having to convert it into a transparency.

   As a production tool, Opaque Projectors are also good for making flip charts (by projecting and then tracing the image directly on the paper).

Opaque Projectors have obvious advantages but, compared to other projectors, they have practical problems, too. Typically, they are larger, louder, and more expensive, plus they require more darkness. Worse, few organizations have them on hand.

(3) **VIDEODISK** - The Videodisk is an optical disk system that can store immense amounts of information--in both pictorial or digital form. A Videodisk player is required for viewing the disk.

With Videodisk, pictures can be played back either as single, still frames (like a Slide) or dynamic, moving sequences (like a Movie). Moreover, because the mechanism is laser-driven, any address on the disk can be accessed almost instantly.

For general use, the Videodisk today has drawbacks: Of all aids, it will usually take the most time and have the highest costs. Also, it has been essentially "playback only," without a record-and-playback feature like Videotape. (Mass Videodisk production must be done by a professional videodisk house.)

Nevertheless, the Videodisk has immense potential. Related to the Videodisk is the CD ROM (i.e., "Compact Disk Read-Only Memory")--a data-storage device for computers that writes the information onto high-capacity compact disks.

The Videodisk and CD ROM are likely to revolutionize the ways that people communicate information (visual or otherwise) in business and education worldwide.

Bibliography

Ailes, Roger, with Jon Kraushar. *You Are the Message*. Homewood, Ill.: Dow Jones-Irwin, 1988.

Aristotle. *Rhetoric*, trans. W. Rhys Roberts. New York: Random House, 1954.

Bennis, Warren, and Burt Nanus. *Leaders*. New York: Harper & Row, 1985.

Benson, Herbert. *The Relaxation Response*. New York: Avon Books, 1975.

_____, with William Proctor. *Beyond the Relaxation Response*. New York: Times Books, 1984.

Bliss, Edwin C. *Getting Things Done*. New York: Charles Scribner's Sons, 1975.

Blotnick, Srully. "Loosen That Tie." *Forbes* (December 29, 1986): 124.

Campbell, David. *Take the road to creativity and get off your dead end*. Niles, Ill.: Argus, 1977.

Cathcart, Jim. *Relationship Selling*. Costa Mesa, Ca.: HDL Publishing, 1988.

Cooper, Morton. *Change Your Voice Change Your Life*. New York: Macmillan, 1984.

De Bono, Edward. *New Think*. New York: Basic Books, 1968.

_____. *Lateral Thinking*. New York: Harper & Row, 1970.

Deal, Terrence E., and Allen A. Kennedy. *Corporate Cultures*. Reading, Mass.: Addison-Wesley, 1982.

Dodgson, Charles Lutwidge ("Lewis Carroll"). *Alice's Adventures in Wonderland*. Oxford, 1865.

Drucker, Peter. *Managing for Results*. New York: Harper & Row, 1964.

Durant, Will. *The Life of Greece*. The Story of Civilization, Volume II. New York: Simon and Schuster, 1939.

Edwards, Betty. *Drawing on the Right Side of the Brain*. Los Angeles: J.P. Tarcher, 1979.

Ellis, Alfred, and Robert A. Harper. *A New Guide to Rational Living*. North Hollywood, Ca.: Wilshire Book Co., 1975.

Elsea, Janet G. *The Four-Minute Sell*. New York: Simon and Schuster, 1984.

Fast, Julius. *Body Language*. New York: Pocket Books, 1970.

Frankl, Viktor. *Man's Search for Meaning*. New York: Pocket Books, 1939/1963.

Gamow, George. *One Two Three ... Infinity*. New York: Bantam, 1961.

Garfield, Charles. *Peak Performance* (audiocassette program). Chicago: Nightingale-Conant, 1983.

_____. *Peak Performance*. Los Angeles: Jeremy P. Tarcher, 1984.

_____. *Peak Performance: The New Heroes of American Business*. New York: William Morrow, 1986.

Geneen, Harold, with Alvin Moscow. *Managing*. Garden City, N.Y.: Doubleday & Co., 1984.

Girard, Joe. *How to Sell Anything to Anybody*. New York: Warner Books, 1977.

_____. *How to Sell Yourself*. New York: Warner Books, 1979.

Gregory, Richard L., ed. *Oxford Companion to the Mind*. Oxford: Oxford University Press, 1987.

Helmstetter, Shad. *What to Say When You Talk to Your Self*. New York: Pocket Books, 1986.

_____. *The Self-Talk Solution*. New York: William Morrow, 1987.

Hitler, Adolf. *Mein Kampf*, trans. Ralph Manheim. Boston: Houghton Mifflin Co., 1962.

Hittleman, Richard. *Yoga: 28 Day Exercise Plan*. Toronto: Bantam Books, 1969.

Iacocca, Lee, with William Novak. *Iacocca: An Autobiography*. New York: Bantam Books, 1984.

Jackson, Carole. *Color Me Beautiful*. New York: Ballantine Books, 1984.

_____, with Kalia Lulow. *Color for Men*. New York: Ballantine Books, 1984.

Jacobson, Edmund. *You Must Relax*. New York: McGraw-Hill, 1957.

Jeffers, Susan. *Feel the Fear and Do It Anyway*. New York: Fawcett Columbine, 1987.

Kriegel, Robert, and Marilyn Harris Kriegel. *The C Zone: Peak Performance Under Pressure*. Garden City, N.Y.: Anchor,1984.

Lakein, Alan. *How to Get Control of Your Time and Your Life*. New York: Signet, 1973.

Lang, Doe. *The Secret of Charisma*. New Choices Press, 1980.

Livingston, J. Sterling. "Pygmalion in Management." *Harvard Business Review* (July-August 1969).

Loehr, James, and Peter McLaughlin. *Mentally Tough*. New York: M. Evans, 1986.

Mackenzie, R. Alec. *The Time Trap*. New York: McGraw-Hill, 1975.

Masello, Robert. "Mr. Dress for Success Fights Back." *Success* (April 1984): 18-22.

Miller, Robert E., and Stephen E. Heiman, with Tad Tuleja. *Strategic Selling*. New York: William Morrow, 1985.

Molloy, John T. *Dress for Success*. New York: Warner Books, 1975.

_____. *Live for Success*. New York: William Morrow, 1981.

Nierenberg, Gerard I., and Henry H. Calero. *How to Read a Person Like a Book*. New York: Pocket Books, 1971.

_____, and Henry H. Calero. *Meta-Talk*. New York: Cornerstone Library, 1973.

Osborne, Alex. *Applied Imagination*. New York: Charles Scribner's Sons, 1953.

Peale, Norman Vincent. *The Power of Positive Thinking*. Greenwich, Conn.: Fawcett Crest, 1952.

Pease, Allen. *Signals*. Toronto: Bantam Books, 1984.

Peters, Thomas J., and Robert H. Waterman. *In Search of Excellence*. New York: Harper & Row, 1982.

_____ , and Nancy Austin. *A Passion for Excellence*. New York: Random House, 1985.

_____. *Thriving on Chaos*. New York: Alfred A. Knopf, 1987.

Plutarch. *Lives of the Noble Greeks*, ed. Edmund Fuller. New York: Dell, 1959.

Reynolds, David K. *Playing Ball on Running Water*. New York: Quill, 1984.

_____. *Even in Summer the Ice Doesn't Melt*. New York: Quill, 1986.

_____. *Water Bears No Scars*. New York: Quill, 1987.

Rico, Gabriele Lusser. *Writing the Natural Way*. Los Angeles: J.P. Tarcher, 1983.

Riggio, Ronald E. *The Charisma Quotient*. New York: Dodd, Mead & Co., 1987.

Rogers, David J. *Fighting to Win*. Garden City, N.Y.: Doubleday, 1984.

Rosenthal, Robert. "The Pygmalion Effect Lives." *Psychology Today* (September 1973): 56-63.

Russell, Bertrand. *The ABC of Relativity*, rev. ed., ed. Felix Pirani. London: George Allen & Unwin, 1958.

Salinger, Pierre. *With Kennedy*. Garden City, N.Y.: Doubleday, 1966.

Sampson, Anthony. *The Sovereign State of ITT*. New York: W.W. Norton, 1985.

Sandburg, Carl. *Abraham Lincoln: The Prairie Years and The War Years*. New York: Harcourt, Brace & World, 1954.

Sarnoff, Dorothy. *Speech Can Change Your Life*. New York: Dell, 1970.

Schuller, Robert H. *Discover Your Possibilities*. New York: Ballantine Books, 1978.

Selye, Hans. *Stress without Distress*. New York: Signet, 1974.

Shakespeare, William. *The Living Shakespeare*, ed. Oscar J. Campbell. New York: Macmillan, 1958.

Sorensen, Theodore C. *Kennedy*. New York: Harper & Row, 1965.

Sybervision Systems, Inc. *The Neuropsychology of Achievement* (audiocassette program). San Leandro, Ca.: Sybervision, 1982.

Wallechinsky, David; Irving Wallace; and Amy Wallace. *The Book of Lists*. New York: Bantam Books, 1978.

Waterman, Robert H., Jr. *The Renewal Factor*. Toronto: Bantam Books, 1987.

Wilder, Lilyan. *Professionally Speaking*. New York: Simon & Schuster, 1986.

Willingham, Ron. *Integrity Selling*. Garden City, N.Y.: Doubleday, 1987.

Wonder, Jacquelyn, and Priscilla Donovan. *Whole-Brain Thinking*. New York: William Morrow, 1984.

Zi, Nancy. *The Art of Breathing*. Toronto: Bantam Books, 1986.

Zilbergeld, Bernie, and Arnold A. Lazarus. *Mind Power*. Boston: Little, Brown & Co., 1987.

Zunin, Leonard, and Natalie Zunin. *Contact: The First Four Minutes*. New York: Ballantine Books, 1973.

Colophon

TEXT: This book was begun in 1982 on an IBM PC using MicroPro *WordStar* 3.2 and, later, *WordStar Professional* 4.0. Drafts were output via a NEC 3550 *Spinwriter* letter-quality printer. In 1988, the completed draft was transported into an Apple Macintosh II system via DataViz *MacLink Plus*. Additional editing was then done using Microsoft *Word* on the Mac II (with a DataFrame XP60 hard disk, an AppleColor High-Resolution RGB monitor, and a Radius Full Page Display). The main text type style is Palatino 11/12.

GRAPHICS: The visual concepts were first developed on the IBM PC using Broderbund's *Print Shop* and Lotus *1-2-3*. The graphics were refined on the Mac II using Claris *MacPaint* and Microsoft *Excel*. Most final illustrations were created using Adobe *Illustrator* 88 (in Encapsulated PostScript format). Also, the picture tools of Quark *Express* 1.1 and Quark *XPress* 2.0 were relied upon throughout the final formatting of the book.

LAYOUT: Page layout was done on the Mac II using Quark *Express* 1.1 and Quark *XPress* 2.0. The book was completed in 1989 and camera-ready output was produced via an Apple LaserWriter II NTX printer at 300 dpi.

COVER: The cover design and artwork were done by Tim Girvin Design, Inc. (Seattle, Wa.). Cover type was created on the Mac II in Quark *XPress* 2.0 and output at 1270 dpi via a Linotronic 300 phototypesetter at Darby Graphics, Inc. (Reston, Va.). Cover mechanicals were done at Darby Graphics, Inc. (Alexandria, Va.). Color separations were produced by Lanman-Progressive, Inc. (Washington, D.C.). ISBN Bookland EAN Film Masters were provided by GGX Associates, Inc. (Great Neck, N.Y.). The author photo was shot by Nina N. Deuel.

PRINTING: Printing was done via offset lithography by Thomson-Shore, Inc. (Dexter, Mi.). The paper is 60# Glatfelter Spring Forge white (acid free). The first edition press run was 5,000 copies (1,000 of these hardbound).

Index

Follow-Up

If you would like to write Jim Anderson about your
reactions to his book, write to . . .

> Dr. Jim Anderson
> c/o *Wyndmoor Press*
> P.O. Box 2105 (Attn: JBA)
> Vienna, VA 22183

If you enjoyed *Speaking to Groups: Eyeball to Eyeball*
and wish **to order more copies** . . .

see the ORDER FORM on the next page ⟶

Please address all inquiries about Dr. Anderson's
**consulting services, workshops, or private
coaching** to . . .

> Client Programs
> *Anderson Management Group, Inc.*
> P.O. Box 1745 (Attn: VIP)
> Vienna, VA 22183
> Telephone: (703) 938-9672

Order Form

TO: WYNDMOOR PRESS
Attn: **Order Desk**
P.O. Box 2105 (STG)
Vienna, VA 22183

Please rush me the book, *Speaking to Groups: Eyeball to Eyeball*, by Dr. James B. Anderson:

_____copies, Hardbound (@ $29.95 each) = _____
_____copies, Softbound (@ $19.95 each) = _____
       SUB-TOTAL .... _____
Virginia residents, add 4.5% sales tax: _____

Shipping Costs: *Regular* (3-4 weeks):
$2.00 for first book; 1.00 each additional
book. *UPS or Air Mail*: $3.00 per book. ....

TOTAL ENCLOSED ....

Enclose check or money order payable to "*WYNDMOOR PRESS.*"

_____
NAME (Please Type or Print)

_____
ORGANIZATION (If Applicable)

_____
ADDRESS

_____
CITY   STATE   ZIP

SATISFACTION GUARANTEED: I understand that if I am not completely satisfied with any Wyndmoor Press book, I may return it immediately for a full refund.

ANY QUESTIONS about ordering your books? . . .
Call the WYNDMOOR *Order Desk*, at **(703) 242-8300**.